A look into Maggie Milo's jewemond rings, gold bracelets, a1
"If our man came here to rob
"he did a piss-poor job."

Walking to the window, he noticed that the blind was raised and the curtains slightly parted. From the upstairs vantage point the investigator had a clear view of the cul-de-sac and most of the driveway, but a five-foot ledge obscured his view of the front porch, almost directly below. Milo, he thought, would have been unable to see the killer if he had, in fact, been at the front door.

Turning his attention back to the bedroom, he noted that the satin sheets on one side of the king-sized bed were wrinkled and pushed away to the opposite side. The clothes Milo had evidently worn before his death were scattered on the floor. It seemed apparent that the victim had been in bed before something had summoned him downstairs to his death.

On the floor near the unmade side of the bed, Momchilov noticed a wadded piece of tissue. As he placed it carefully into one of the clear plastic evidence bags he carried in his coat pocket, he was ready to bet the laboratory would find that the tissue contained traces of semen.

Before his search of the room was complete, he found himself wondering about the sexual habits of Dean Milo. On the nightstand nearest what was likely his side of the bed was a stack of *Playboy* and *Penthouse* magazines, contrasting starkly with the religious reading material on the table near his wife's side.

Copyright ©1989 by William C. Dear & Carlton Stowers
ISBN 978-1-949914-22-1
All rights reserved. No part of this book may be used or reproduced in any manner
whatsoever without written permission except in the case of
brief quotations embodied in critical articles and reviews
For information address Crossroad Press at 141 Brayden Dr., Hertford, NC 27944
www.crossroadpress.com

Crossroad Press Trade Edition

"PLEASE DON'T KILL ME"

THE TRUE STORY OF THE MILO MURDER

BY WILLIAM C. DEAR
& CARLTON STOWERS

I dedicate this book to my son Michael, who has made my life so worthwhile.

To my son Adam and to Gini I owe so much. Thanks for the fresh air that has been brought into my life.

To my parents, James and Lucille Dear; I love you.

To my young friend Mark Courson, who has gone to be with God.

—Bill Dear

For Pat, whose courage is a great inspiration.

—Carlton Stowers

NOTE TO THE READER

The events and conversations in this book are based on a number of sources, from the voluminous written files and tape recordings kept by Bill Dear during the course of his investigation to official police and court records. The recollections of those involved in the case, the hunters and the hunted, were sought in the interest of accuracy. The dialogue, though often re-created, is as close to what was actually said as the memories of those involved in the conversations can provide.

It was the decision of the authors to make a number of name changes, some for legal considerations, others to protect the privacy of people who played important roles in the solution of the case but were in no way involved in the crime. Jake Solazo, Glen Gosdin, Patsy Caldwell, Ray Lemon, Darlene Drake, Sally Reeves, Cal Loomis, Tom Mandy, Joy Stephens, Bill Cousins, John Ritchie, and Bennie Railey are fictitious names given to real people.

ACKNOWLEDGMENTS

"*Please ... Don't Kill Me*" is not just a murder case. It is a true story of devotion, dedication, danger, intrigue, suspense, and sadness. Sadness not just for Dean Milo and his family but for all the lives touched and damaged along the way. I would like to thank the many people involved in the investigation and those who helped me make it through some very difficult times.

To my special friend Lieutenant Larry Momchilov, Summit County sheriff's office, I say thanks not only to a true friend but to a dedicated law enforcement officer *who cares*.

To all law enforcement officers around the world who never receive but deserve recognition—to them, I say thank you.

Special gratitude goes to Michael Wolff, formerly Summit County prosecutor, whose help and friendship meant so much, and still does.

To the devoted friends of Dean Milo and to the staff of Milo Corporation who held on through the tough times and whose dedication cost them dearly. No words can convey that type of loyalty: Gary Winterhalter, Bud and Judy Eisenhart, Paul Vaughn, Terry Smith, Rick Briggs, Cathy Donze, Linda Snyder, Ben Lowery, Kevin Van Nest, Tim Morrissey, Chuck Innis, Louis Fisi, Al Dejordy, and Jerry Pappas.

Special thanks also go to Summit County law enforcement officers Lieutenant Bill Lewis, Lieutenant David Bailey, Captain Tom Bostick, Chief Ed Duvall, Sergeant Mark Martin, Lieutenant Charles Pongracz, Lieutenant Bob Scalise, Bill Evans, and Sergeant Doug Jennings.

My gratitude as well to William E. White of the FBI; Fred Zuch, Summit County Prosecutor's Office; Detective John Bailey,

Akron Police Department; George Graham, Drug Enforcement Administration, Phoenix; Detective Richard Craven and Detective Paul Arnold, Scottsdale (Arizona) Police Department; and Lieutenant Richard Munsey and Sergeant Kirk Shively, Bath (Ohio) Police Department.

I am also grateful for the support of my staff investigators: Richard Riddle, Frank Lambert, Terry Hurley, Carl Lilly, and Joe Villanueva.

Others who helped me were Jerry and Sandy Forrester; Sidney and Addie Banz; Dr. C. Miller Ballem; Dr. Joe Phipps; Gregg Happ; Tony and Kay Bauer; Harry, Joan, Brenda, Jody, Bo, and Ron Eubanks; Mike and Donna Phipps; Preson DeShazo; Alfred Ellis; Thomas Hight; John, Jo, and Julie Ann Ritchie; Donna, Danny, Barbara, Mark, and Julie Cockerham; Stu Bonnett; Doris Hagerman; Dottie and Curt Rice; Fred Cochran; Richard and Diane Eubanks; Dr. Marilyn Cebelin; Marianne and Carey Courson; Bob Living; Gary Richardson; Vic and Berni Feazell; Dale Constancio; Diane and Chad Beckon; Judy and Ron Taylor; Myrna Bartle; Fred and Helena Drechtsel; Kay and Floyd Fisher; Mike and Nancy Furlich; Tommy and Patricia Fallin; Jimmy Furr; Larry and Tommy Price; Lynn and Lara Ferguson; Sally Foster; Kim, Stacy, and Bobby Rourk; Avon Franks; Sandy Goroff; Martyn and Marcella Burke; Wendy Jackson; Andrea Kurachia; Debbie Lockhurst; Ron Woods; John McCready; Dr. Charles, Claude, and Sophie Hirsch; Clo Holford; Brian, Bud, and Eloise Jones; Jill McCormick; Betty Sue May; Marla Messersmith; Dan and Jerry McBride; C. Al Miller; John Pictou; Jerry Hall; Jim Proudfoot; Billie Jo Mills; Doug Nichols; Tom Neylon; Chris Hykel; Mrs. Eli Momchilov; Allie Martin, Jr.; Bruce McNabb; Mr. and Mrs. Doyle McDonald; Dennis McEaneney; Marge and Mark McGill; Joan McFall; Doris Maillous; Tim and Becky McDonald; Tom Styer; Jerry and Janet Zucker; Arnold and Marie Shapiro; David Nerman and Guy Laine St. Onge; Nita Coe Wilson; Karon Hendricks; Pat and Lee Pulling; Pat Parks; Ruth and Elijah Pitts; Kim Palm; Richard Russell; Robert and Fran Russell, Jr.; Gracie Banks; Stephanee Camp; Teresa Whitaker; Renee Lennard; Debra Ramsey; Pat Stowers; Dave and Sandra Salyers; Wanda Sullivan; Peggy Smith; Richard and

Kathleen Stallings; Barbara and Jenifer Sollberger; Kristi Lynn Wester; Jean Witenhafer; Steve, Andy, and Nancy Dixon; Betty Kisor; Bill Courson; Mark Courson; Willard Green; Blue and Helen Clark; Cheri Anne Kennedy; Bill and Judy Hoffman; Lea, Ethan, and Micah Llewis; Don and Marie Tucker; Sal and Patty Gambino; Johnny Webb; John Porter; Ray Jiles; Deborah Calvert; George and Betty Hughes; Lou Acker; Brad and Jan Angers; Tom Apple; Jack Barnett; Fred Conover; Gini Cozart; Debbie Rathmell; Lisa Garcia; Lisa Medlin; Bob France; Donna Yates; Aubrey land Judith Golden; Randy Roberts; Kathy Schmaltz; Vernon Scott; Shelley and Ya El Elnekave; Manny and Renee Better; Richard and Gloria Leonard; Val Benitez; Gini and Keith Krueger; John Murray; Eric and Helen Murray; Rita Wong; Tom O'Carroll and Alfonse Altman.

—Bill Dear

1

The sudden arrival of boiling black clouds, threatening another of the violent thunderstorms that visit the Akron, Ohio, area in late summer, had brought a cool break in the tedious August heat. It was Monday afternoon, August 11, 1980, and Detective Lieutenant Larry Momchilov was hurrying from the Summit County sheriff's office toward the parking garage in the courthouse basement, his thoughts far removed from the weather. Stepping his pace up to a jog, he dug in his pocket for car keys even before reaching his car. A few steps behind, his new partner hurried to catch up.

Minutes earlier Momchilov had been upstairs, sitting at a desk in the office of the county prosecutor, completing paperwork on a series of blue-collar crime cases he had been working, when the sheriff summoned him with an urgency in his voice that hinted to Momchilov that his reports might have to wait for some time.

A detective with the police department in Bath Township, a nearby Akron suburb, had called to request help in the investigation of a homicide. In the sheriff's office, Momchilov had listened to the sketchy details his superior provided, sighed, shook his head, and said nothing until he was out in the hallway. As he impatiently watched the blinking lights signal the course of the antiquated, slow-moving elevator and waited for the appearance of his partner, the detective stuffed his hands deep into the pockets of his trousers and said, "Shit."

Back at work only a week following his honeymoon, he was not ready for the grinding demands a murder investigation always seemed to make. A few days earlier, he had told his new wife, Joan, a reporter for the *Akron Beacon Journal,* that he had planned to ease back into his work routine and clear away the backlog. He hoped for a quiet spell before getting involved in any new cases.

Momchilov had been a member of the department since 1967, and in that time a violent crime in an affluent suburb had been a rarity. He had a gut feeling that the case he was about to enter would be a great deal more complicated than the Saturday night shootings which had long been part of his routine. He had, in fact, never even been in the residential areas of Bath Township, though he was a lifelong resident of the Akron area. His first visit would, no doubt, be unpleasant.

For Momchilov, it was always the same. Though he had long ago ceased keeping track of the number of murders he had investigated, he privately admitted that no phase of law enforcement excited him like working a questionable death. The mystery of man's ultimate inhumanity to man held an inexplicable fascination for him, as it does for most good homicide investigators. That, many of his peers would point out, was why Larry Momchilov, at age forty-two, was the senior officer in the Summit County detective bureau. Though his methods were sometimes viewed as unorthodox and his country boy manner didn't go with his FBI training, he generally solved the cases he worked. He did so with around-the-clock work habits many of his colleagues felt bordered on the obsessive. On more than one case, he had returned to the scene of a crime time and time again, spending hours trying to reconstruct the event until he felt he knew exactly what had taken place. "When Larry gets on a murder case," said one fellow officer, "he's like a bulldog. He grabs hold of whatever he can and growls and raises hell and just won't let go until he's done what he set out to do—which is to put the bad guy behind bars."

With the first step of the investigation still a twenty-minute drive away, he could already feel the familiar knot of anticipation in the pit of his stomach. But beyond that, Larry Momchilov had, for reasons he could not explain, begun to sense that something out of the ordinary awaited in Bath Township.

His newly assigned partner, thirty-seven-year-old Bill Lewis, easygoing and a practical joker, did not share Momchilov's low-key intensity. He had just recently been promoted from the traffic division to detective status, and as they reached the car and he climbed into the passenger seat, he made no attempt to hide his enthusiasm over his first homicide investigation. Working the case with Momchilov, he thought, would give him the chance to learn something. Even as they pulled out of the garage, he was beginning to feel the almost electric tension that grows as an officer speeds toward a murder scene.

That tension built even more when, after leaving the downtown area and entering the expressway leading to Bath, they were forced to pull off to the side of the road. The thunderstorm had erupted in full force; its driving, windswept rain reduced the visibility to zero.

Waiting impatiently for the rain to stop, Momchilov drummed his fingers on the steering wheel as Lewis sat in silence. Several times Momchilov thought of attempting to move back onto the expressway, but each time he started the motor the roar of the storm seemed to increase, as if issuing a renewed warning. "Whoever it is," he said, "is already dead. I guess he'll wait."

Lewis grinned with relief. "What do you think we're looking at on this thing?" he asked.

"You never know," Momchilov replied, "but chances are it will be hard to get much of a handle on. Suburban killings aren't like those in some apartment complex or the parking lot of a go-go joint. Things are much more isolated. Houses are on big lots, too far apart for there to be many witnesses. People in the suburbs, especially one like Bath, aren't expecting violent crime in their quiet little neighborhoods.

"From what the sheriff told me, this guy might have been dead for several days. Whoever did him in is probably long gone. Trails get cold in a hurry in cases like this. If that's true about this one, it damn sure ain't gonna be any fun, believe me."

Lewis nodded and turned his attention to the sheets of rain that continued to pelt the windshield. He was beginning to share his partner's impatience.

It had been just after two in the afternoon when Georgia Tsarnas, her three children in the back seat, turned her station wagon into the cul-de-sac and parked in the driveway of the home of Dean and Maggie Milo.

She was no stranger to the $300,000 brick colonial house that sat on a small hill, the showplace of Everest Circle. Her husband, George, had long served as Dean Milo's attorney. Over the years a strong friendship had developed between the two couples. The Milo home, with its carefully manicured lawn, its colorful splash of flowers and expertly trimmed shrubs, was a place Georgia always looked forward to visiting. Her children, in fact, had in recent years begun to refer to the Milos as Aunt Maggie and Uncle Dean.

George Tsarnas had called her earlier, asking that she drive over to the Milo house and see if everything was okay. He had expressed mild concern the previous evening when Dean failed to keep a dinner date, but had decided that Milo must have been delayed on an out-of-town trip he had been scheduled to make. On Monday, when several calls to the Milo house went unanswered, he became apprehensive. It was not like Dean to stay out of touch for so long, even if he was out of town on business.

"Take the key Maggie gave you," Tsarnas told his wife. "If no one answers at the door, go in and check the house. Then give me a call at the office, okay?"

"You think maybe he's sick?" his wife asked.

"I don't know. But it isn't like him not to call."

Instructing her children to remain in the station wagon, she walked first to the garage where, cupping her hands around her eyes, she peered inside to find that Dean Milo's red-and-white Cadillac Eldorado and blue Mercedes were there. Moving along the brick walkway to the front porch, she rang the doorbell several times, then knocked softly. As she waited, hoping to hear Dean's voice, perhaps coming from the upstairs bedroom window, or to see him open the door, an uneasiness swept over her. As she reached in her purse for the house key, she suddenly felt that she was intruding and wished her husband hadn't suggested she enter the house.

Placing the key in the lock, she was surprised when the slight pressure eased the large wooden door open. The urge to scream froze in her throat as she immediately saw the figure of a man lying spread-eagled on the floor of the foyer. Fearing that her children might be alerted to her horror and leave the station wagon, she quickly stepped inside.

The man, dressed only in boxer shorts, was face down in a pool of dried blood. His head was covered with a yellow foam-filled cushion that she had often seen on one of the chairs in the adjacent living room.

Georgia Tsarnas's entire body began to shake and she felt a wave of nausea overcoming her. She was suddenly aware of an oppressive heat inside the house, one even more discomforting than the prestorm humidity outside, and she feared she might faint.

Cautiously she moved to the body and lifted the cushion slightly. She began to cry hysterically when she saw that the dead man was, in fact, Dean Milo.

There is nothing in the human experience to prepare one for what she would view in those split seconds. Milo's swollen head was turned slightly to the right, his face drained of any color. His eyes had swelled tightly shut and his mouth hung partially open, covered by what appeared to be small wads of cotton. His right wrist, with its gold bracelet, rested in a black pool of dried blood.

Gently putting the cushion back in place, Georgia walked unsteadily through the living room and out into the kitchen, where she knew a telephone was located. Only after several shaky starts was she finally able to dial the number of her husband's office.

"Dean's dead," she said immediately after George Tsarnas answered. "There's blood everywhere. God, it's horrible."

Her voice was a monotone. Tsarnas was both stunned by what she had said and gripped with fear that she was in shock. "Can you call the police?" he asked.

"Yes."

"Call them and then get out of the house," he instructed. "I'll be right there."

By the time the storm subsided enough for Lieutenant Momchilov to complete the drive to 2694 Everest Circle, officers from the Bath Police Department had arrived and the investigation had begun.

The fifteen-mile trip from the sheriff's office to the Milo house had taken forty-five minutes and the delay had resulted in exactly what Momchilov feared most. As he pulled into the cul-de-sac he saw several people milling around. In addition to officers from the Bath Police Department, he recognized a couple of investigators from the county coroner's office. The others, standing in the front yard, he assumed, were curious neighbors and passersby. Momchilov shook his head. Too many people at a crime scene is an investigator's worst nightmare.

As he hurried up the walk to the front door he was met by Detective Sergeant Richard Munsey of the Bath Police Department. It was Munsey who had called the sheriff's department and specifically asked that Momchilov be dispatched to the scene. The twenty-six-year-old Munsey, who was gaining a reputation as a promising investigator after beginning his career as a teenage dispatcher, had attended several law enforcement courses taught by Momchilov at the University of Akron and considered him both his mentor and far and away the best homicide investigator he'd met.

"Glad you're here," Munsey said, reaching out to shake Momchilov's hand. "Looks like we've got a nasty one."

Momchilov nodded and looked inside the open door. "The first thing we need to do do is get everybody out of that damn house—right now." Clearly it was an order, not a suggestion.

Taking charge of the investigation, he spoke first with Bath patrolman Kirk Shively, a young officer who had been the first to arrive at the scene. He had, he said, spoken with Mrs. Tsarnas, who had told him of finding the body.

Though he had never before investigated a homicide, Shively had responded to the occasion professionally. Thinking that the killer might still be in the house, he had ordered Mrs. Tsarnas to remain outside, then called for back-up before he searched the rest of the rooms.

"Everything's neat as a pin," Shively said. "No sign of a struggle, no indication that anybody tossed the place looking for things to steal.

"And there was no weapon on or near the body. Just a couple of spent shell casings."

From Mrs. Tsarnas he had learned that Dean Milo was the president of family-owned Milo Barber and Beauty Supply Corporation, a national wholesale distribution firm. "Big bucks," the officer added.

He had also learned that Milo's wife, Magdaline, and the couple's three children were supposed to be in Clearwater, Florida, visiting friends.

As Shively continued filling him in on the sketchy details he had been able to gather, Momchilov stared down at the body. For the first time he noticed the house was in darkness and asked that someone turn on some lights.

"Can't," said Munsey. "The storm evidently knocked out the power. They're working on it. We've already taken a lot of pictures."

"We're gonna take more," Momchilov said. "I want pictures of everything in this house, top to bottom, inside and out." With that he knelt next to the body, saying nothing as he attempted to form a mental picture of what had occurred. He saw little that made sense. Though there was obviously a bullet hole through the cushion that had covered Milo's head, the victim had clearly been shot twice, once in the head, once in the back of the neck. The cotton in Milo's mouth was a puzzle. But not so much as the fact that his undershorts, now stained with blood and urine, were on backwards.

"Weird, huh?" offered Munsey.

Momchilov nodded in agreement.

Under Ohio law, the Summit County coroner, Dr. A. H. Kyriakides, would have been the officer in charge of any homicide investigation, but he was out of town and not expected to return until the following day. In his place, two investigators from his office, James Crano and Richard Scott, had come to the Milo house.

Momchilov was first aware of their presence when he saw

Scott pick up a wadded-up piece of yellow paper. "What's that?" the lieutenant asked.

"Looks like a blank telegram," Scott shrugged as he unfolded it.

For the first time since their arrival, Lewis spoke up. "Dammit, man, that just might be evidence. For all we know that might be the way the killer got into the house."

Momchilov, pleased that his partner had flared up at the casual attitude of the coroner's investigators, ordered the paper placed in an evidence bag.

Once the forensic work was completed—photographs taken, fingerprinting done, diagrams made, and evidence bagged—Momchilov called all of the investigators into the family room and began making assignments. He wanted to know the whereabouts of Milo's family members during the last seventy-two hours. He wanted to know what Milo's movements had been in recent days; whom he had talked with, where he had been. He wanted everyone in the neighborhood interviewed to see if anyone had heard or seen anything. And he wanted to know a great deal more about Dean Milo's business.

With that, he dismissed the meeting and, with Captain Thomas Bostick, chief of the sheriff's detective bureau, who had just arrived, began a walk-through of the Milo house. He quickly realized there were no signs of forcible entry or struggle anywhere but the hallway where the victim was found; Milo might well have let the killer into the house himself.

It was the master bedroom that most interested Momchilov. Since Dean Milo had been dressed only in his shorts, he had most likely been in bed when the assailant arrived.

When the electricity came back on, so did a small clock radio and a lamp on the nightstand near the bed. A wallet containing thirty-three dollars and several credit cards lay on top of a nearby dresser. Atop the television set was another forty dollars in cash, along with a watch and a gold wedding ring. Milo's briefcase, filled with a variety of business papers and a check in the amount of twenty-four thousand dollars made out to him from the U.S. Internal Revenue Service, sat open but undisturbed.

A look into Maggie Milo's jewelry box revealed several diamond rings, gold bracelets, an emerald brooch, and pearls.

"If our man came here to rob the place," Momchilov said, "he did a piss-poor job."

Walking to the window, he noticed that the blind was raised and the curtains slightly parted. From the upstairs vantage point the investigator had a clear view of the cul-de-sac and most of the driveway, but a five-foot ledge obscured his view of the front porch, almost directly below. Milo, he thought, would have been unable to see the killer if he had, in fact, been at the front door.

Turning his attention back to the bedroom, he noted that the satin sheets on one side of the king-sized bed were wrinkled and pushed away to the opposite side. The clothes Milo had evidently worn before his death were scattered on the floor. It seemed apparent that the victim had been in bed before something had summoned him downstairs to his death.

On the floor near the unmade side of the bed, Momchilov noticed a wadded piece of tissue. As he placed it carefully into one of the clear plastic evidence bags he carried in his coat pocket, he was ready to bet the laboratory would find that the tissue contained traces of semen.

Before his search of the room was complete, he found himself wondering about the sexual habits of Dean Milo. On the nightstand nearest what was likely his side of the bed was a stack of *Playboy* and *Penthouse* magazines, contrasting starkly with the religious reading material on the table near his wife's side.

And in the closet where Bostick had been searching there was a brown paper bag containing four pornographic films, each packaged in a colorful, highly graphic box. Three of the films dealt with explicit male-female sex—*Wild Beauty, Deep Throat,* and *Super Cock*—while the fourth, *The Crisco Kid,* starred gay males.

Momchilov's thoughts returned to the fact that Dean Milo's body had been found with his underwear on backwards. "We've got some kind of kinky sex thing here," he said to Captain Bostick. "This whole damn thing is crazy."

"So, what do you think?"

"I hate to say it, but right now I'm thinking this sonuvabitch just might not get solved," Momchilov answered.

Bostick smiled and placed a reassuring hand on his lieutenant's shoulder. "It'll get solved," he said. "Somehow. But I have to say this …"

"What's that?"

"Looks to me like you picked yourself a helluva time to get married."

For the next three weeks, the Summit County Sheriff's Department and Bath Township police worked the case around the clock. Momchilov, heading the investigation, regularly arrived at home in the early morning hours, long after his wife, Joan, had gone to bed. And, more often than not, he was up and back at work before she woke the next day.

He was relieved to hear her reassure him on each occasion he managed time for a quick phone call that she understood how important the case was. "Hey, we went over all this before we got married," she would say. "I told you I could handle being a cop's wife, so don't worry about it, okay?"

In truth, Momchilov's marriage was going much better than the investigation. The maze of questions that swirled in his head had few answers. Interviews with family members, neighbors, business associates, even several underworld contacts he had made while investigating corporate crimes provided no solid lead.

The only thing that was clear after three weeks of long hours and blind alleys was that Dean Milo wouldn't have scratched in a popularity contest. Along with his brilliant business success had come a lengthy list of enemies that began in his immediate family and stretched throughout the social and business community. "Hell," Momchilov told Lewis as they sat in the sparsely furnished detectives' office early one morning, reviewing the reports they had compiled in the previous few days, "I haven't met anybody yet who doesn't qualify as a suspect. Seems like everyone we talk to would have benefited, one way or another, from Dean Milo's death."

On the basis of the slim evidence they had gathered, they had decided to focus their efforts in three areas: the Milo family, business associates and competitors, and anyone, male or female, who might have been involved with Dean in an extramarital affair.

Which is to say they were scattershooting, running everywhere and seemingly getting nowhere.

It was a state of affairs that frustrated Maggie Milo to fits of screaming anger as the days following her husband's death seemed to drag endlessly. Finally, convinced that the local police were both inept and only mildly interested in the case, she contacted George Tsarnas and told him to hire a private investigator immediately.

Tsarnas said that he had little knowledge of private investigators qualified to work murder cases but would make some calls.

"I don't care who you hire, or what the company has to pay him," Maggie said, her voice more firm and authoritative than Tsarnas had heard it since her return home from Florida, "so long as he's the best there is."

In a matter of days, Paul Vaughn, comptroller of Milo Barber and Beauty Supply, was on the phone, placing a long distance call to Texas in an attempt to locate the man Tsarnas had recommended.

By the time Vaughn got in touch with the detective, Dean Milo had been dead almost four weeks.

2

On the morning of September 2, 1980, private investigator William C. Dear drove from his isolated country home in Texas, en route to the Dallas—Fort Worth International Airport. Instead of taking the long-awaited vacation he had planned to spend at his beachfront condo in the Florida Keys, Dear had agreed to travel to Ohio and look into the death of Dean Milo.

Persuading him had been no easy task for Paul Vaughn. Dear had recently been on a succession of demanding assignments, including the trailing of a drug smuggler throughout the Orient and a lengthy, headline-making search for a sixteen-year-old boy genius named James Dallas Egbert III, who had mysteriously disappeared from the Michigan State University campus in a bizarre Dungeons & Dragons scenario. He was physically and emotionally drained.

He was also feeling a growing concern that his recent marriage might suffer irreparable damage from another extended absence.

He could, he had told Vaughn, spend no more than a week on the case. His fee would be five thousand dollars plus expenses.

Few private investigators in the country had attained a higher profile than Dear. Flamboyant, handsome, self-promoting, and a man who made no apologies for the size of his ego, Dear was called by some in the media America's answer to the fictional James Bond. Dear had become a millionaire by the time he reached forty and would readily admit that his well-groomed image was good for business. It was not, however, his opulent lifestyle that attracted troubled families seeking lost children, or companies wanting to locate embezzlers, or law enforcement agencies wearied of getting nowhere on murder investigations.

Rather, it was his remarkable track record of success.

Any prospective client who contacted him at his split-level home surrounded by twenty-eight wooded acres could not fail to be impressed. Even those who disliked him personally and resented his often unorthodox approach to his job stopped short of criticizing his talent for solving cases.

Dear's law enforcement career began when he was a seventeen-year-old patrolman, the youngest man ever hired by the state of Florida. Within two years, he had been promoted to the position of chief deputy constable of Dade County and had caught the attention of the media. He had been in uniform only a few months when he ticketed Teamsters Union head Jimmy Hoffa for driving the wrong way on one of Miami's one-way streets.

Jealousy among his fellow officers developed and grew as Dear's success in solving highly publicized crimes in the Miami area earned him continued public praise and media notice. By the time he had reached the age of twenty-two, a half-dozen cases he had successfully investigated had been chronicled in various true crime magazines. He had been honored as Miami's peace officer of the year.

In time, however, the thrill of the chase and the personal reward of seeing criminals brought to justice were outweighed by the constant petty jealousy that Dear found to flourish within the ranks of organized law enforcement. He was, he knew, unpopular with most of those he worked alongside and therefore had become something of a loner, often working dangerous cases without a partner and never certain that back-up would arrive in the event he needed help. Disillusioned after a decade of success too often tempered with the frustration of criticism from his fellow officers, Dear made the decision to turn in his badge.

Moving to Texas, he worked for a time as a bodyguard for millionaire H. H. Coffield, one of Lyndon Johnson's primary financial supporters. When Coffield died, Dear applied to the Texas Board of Private Investigators for a license and went to work for himself. Vowing not to follow the traditional path taken by most beginning in the profession, Dear turned down offers to follow wayward husbands for spouses anxious for quick, handsome divorce settlements and concentrated on cases the police and other private investigators had given up on.

Adopting a workaholic routine, he quickly built a reputation. He aided in the investigation of homicides; assured clients of healthy insurance settlements by proving that deaths ruled as suicides had, in fact, been murders; and succeeded in locating scores of children who had either run away from home or had been kidnaped. His travels took him into the seedy opium dens of Bangkok, throughout Europe, and to all corners of the United States. Near-escapes from death—he was once stabbed in the back and on another occasion had his throat cut—failed to slow him. With each case the Bill Dear mystique grew. Aware that self-promotion was the best form of advertisement, he was never hesitant to detail his exploits for a television talk show host or journalists, whether they were calling from the *Dallas Morning News* or *True Detective*, *Playboy* or the *National Enquirer*. Each round of publicity, he quickly learned, resulted in a new series of calls from prospective clients.

When forced during an interview to admit that he had never attended college, Dear became so concerned that his lack of academic credentials might damage his image that he quietly enrolled in night courses at North Texas State University for a semester. In time his business grew to the point where he oversaw a staff of investigators who had access to the most sophisticated equipment on the market. Bill Dear and Associates was off and running at high speed.

And even as his income rose well above the comfort level, he continued a hard sell of the "real James Bond" image the media had so willingly applied to his lifestyle.

He moved into a 6,200-square-foot, million-dollar home just a short drive south of Dallas and furnished it in a manner that would cause envy in the heart of a Saudi prince. The bathroom featured a sunken tub of Italian marble with 14-karat gold fixtures. An indoor swimming canal led from the house to the outdoor heated pool.

In his closet were 150 suits and forty pairs of custom-fitted boots.

The centerpiece of his bedroom was a massive circular bed.

Mirrors adorned the walls and ceiling. Imported furniture and an elaborate gun collection decorated the living area. There were rooms for a hot tub, a sauna, and exercise equipment. The house was guarded by an elaborate electronic security system.

On the well-kept grounds were a tennis court, riding stable, pool, servants' quarters, and a helicopter landing pad. His fleet of fourteen automobiles included a thirty-thousand-dollar van customized to include the most advanced surveillance equipment available.

Just a short drive away, a private airport housed his plane.

Dick Merket, a former Ohio Highway Patrol officer who had recently retired to private investigation work, had agreed to pick up Dear at Cleveland's Hopkins Airport. Several years earlier the two had worked together to locate a missing child in the Akron area and a friendship and mutual respect had developed. Immediately after agreeing to take the case, Dear had telephoned Merket and asked that he gather as much information as possible on the Milo case.

Merket smiled as he saw his old friend nearing the baggage claim area. Dear wore a dark blue three-piece suit and ostrich-skin boots. His tanned, angular face was partially hidden by sunglasses. Merket immediately took inventory of several obviously expensive rings and a heavy gold bracelet as the arriving passenger shook his hand.

"Looks like you're managing to get by," Merket said. "Anybody on the plane mistake you for ol' J.R. and ask for your autograph?"

Dear dismissed the good-natured kidding and began searching through his briefcase for baggage claim tickets. "What am I getting into up here?" he asked.

"You're going to earn your money on this one," Merket said with a warning tone in his voice. "From what I've heard, the investigation isn't going anywhere. I've got some things in the car for you to look over."

For the first few minutes of the thirty-mile drive to Stow, another Akron suburb where the headquarters of the Milo Barber and Beauty Supply Corporation was located, Dear thumbed through a folder of newspaper clippings Merket had assembled. He was a bit surprised to read that the case was being referred to as the most sensational in the state since the infamous 1954 killing of Dr. Sam Sheppard's wife.

Paying little attention to the gently rolling contours of the Ohio countryside, Dear began to question his companion about Dean Milo.

"Strange guy," Merket began as he sipped from a Styrofoam cup of coffee he'd purchased at the airport. "Ambitious, domineering, persuasive, reasonably good-looking, and evidently ruthless as hell. People loved him or hated his guts; no in-between. From what I can gather, even his family isn't all that torn up over the fact he bought the farm.

"What you're going to find, I'm afraid, is a whole lot of bad blood in the Milo family."

Anticipating Dear's next question, he quickly launched into a brief history of the Milo family and its business success.

Sotir Milo and his wife, Katina, had emigrated to the United States from Albania just before World War II and had operated a small barber supply business out of the basement of their Akron home. Sotir would hand-deliver his supplies to local barber and beauty shops in a basket. Though the work was hard and the frequent deliveries and bookkeeping demanding, the business provided a comfortable living for the family, which would eventually include sons Dean and Fred and daughter Sophie.

It was when the children grew old enough to participate in the business, allowing their aging father to ease into semi-retirement, that things began to change dramatically. Though the elder Milo retained legal control of his company long after he turned much of the operation over to the children, it was Dean Milo who saw to it that the company flourished.

Taking over as president of the firm in 1969, Dean Milo quickly did away with the full-service operation his father had favored for over two decades and adopted a discount approach to the business. He expanded at a rapid rate and began opening stores stocked with the cosmetics and beauty supplies at drastically reduced prices. This revolutionary approach immediately angered cosmetics dealers who had exclusive distribution contracts with manufacturers.

Dean Milo's brainchild was as unique as it was controversial. Traditionally, distributors, including the Milo Corporation, sent salesmen out to call on the thousands of beauty and barber shops, extending credit for purchases and permitting returns if the shops didn't sell all of their inventory. Dean Milo cut out the middleman, the salesman, and sold everything on a cash-on-delivery basis either by direct mail or at the growing chain of discount stores he had opened. By eliminating the salary of a sales force, Milo Barber and Beauty Supply was able to offer deep discounts that the full-service companies could not afford to match.

Within the tradition-steeped industry there were angry cries of foul play. Even as the Milo Corporation expanded at an incredible rate there were accusations that what Dean Milo was doing was not only unethical but illegal. Some beauty product manufacturers, in fact, began refusing to sell to Milo Barber and Beauty Supply.

Dean Milo, proving his business sense, quickly found a solution to that problem by purchasing two full-service wholesale dealerships, one in nearby Columbus and another in Charleston, West Virginia, which bought the needed supplies in bulk and at reduced prices directly from the manufacturers, then funneled them to Milo. The wholesale dealerships, in effect, served as legal bootlegging operations for the Milo Corporation.

By 1980, Milo B&B was opening a new store every four weeks and almost without exception each was showing a profit in the first six months of operation. Dean Milo was making both money and enemies at remarkable speed.

His father had maintained control of the company until as late as 1975 and continued to own most of the stock. Then, however, Dean had proposed an unusual recapitalization plan to his parents, brother Fred, sister Sophie, and Sophie's husband, Lonnie Curtis.

Dean proposed that despite the fact he and his brother and sister would hold equal one-third shares in the company, he alone would have voting power on all matters relating to the operation. In effect, Dean Milo was telling the rest of the family to get out of his way. He was certain he could turn Milo B&B into a multimillion-dollar-a-year operation and wanted no interference from a brother and sister who, he felt, had precious little business sense. To his surprise, the family readily agreed to his terms.

By 1980, Milo B&B had grown into a sizable corporation with ninety-two stores in seventeen states and was continuing to expand. It had grossed over $45 million the previous year and would likely soon surpass the $50 million mark.

Dean Milo was seeing his dreamed-of empire become a reality. His salary in 1979 had been $260,000 and he anticipated making as much as $400,000 in 1980. Under his unique partnership arrangement, brother Fred was to earn 75 percent of what Dean made annually and sister Sophie would receive 50 percent. If, for instance, Dean's yearly earnings were $100,000, Fred would receive $75,000 and Sophie could expect to earn $50,000. Though the traditional business world might have considered the salary structure as odd in view of the fact each of the Milo children owned equal shares, the earnings of Fred and Sophie, who, along with Lonnie Curtis, were vice presidents of the company, were handsome indeed, since they were required to do virtually nothing except stay out of Dean Milo's way.

Dear said nothing, only listening to the figures Merket was reciting.

"Things really got strange a while back," Merket continued. "See, the way things were set up, Dean had voting power only in matters directly relating to the Milo Corporation. But when it came to matters involving the subsidiary companies it was still a one-third, one-third, one-third deal; Dean, his brother, and his sister.

"When Fred and Sophie finally snapped on the fact that big brother was easing them out of all the decision-making, they used their votes to take over the corporation's subsidiaries and started firing anyone and everyone who had shown any loyalty to Dean. Fred became president of one of the subsidiaries, Lovelace Beauty Supply, and Sophie's husband, Lonnie, was named to head up Capital Beauty Supply. The first thing both of them did was to refuse to allow their companies to continue serving as the bootleggers for Milo B&B.

"That's when the shit really hit the fan."

In late August 1979, Merket said, Dean Milo had fired his brother and sister and her husband. The dismissals set in motion a series of lawsuits against Dean. Joining his brother and sister in the suits were Sotir and his wife, Katina, all charging that Dean Milo had fraudulently taken control of the company. The suit was still pending when the murder occurred.

"Just one big, happy family," Dear observed.

"And steeped in tradition," Merket acknowledged. "From what I was able to find out, old man Sotir, who still pulls down fifty grand a year as chairman of the board, did the same number on his father about thirty years ago. Took control from Daddy and battled tooth and toenail to keep it."

"Did Dean Milo actually defraud the family?"

"Not that I can tell. Hell, none of it makes much sense when you sit back and think it over. There was Dean, working his ass off, making the business successful and earning a ton of money for everybody. The guy was everybody's free ticket to ride. Fred and Sophie could have never lifted a finger and it would have suited their brother perfectly. Fact is, that's the way he wanted it. If I'd been in their position, I'd have taken the money and run like hell. Gone fishing and never come back."

"Maybe they thought the business could prosper even more with their input," Dear suggested.

"If so, they were dreaming. I haven't talked to a soul who thinks either Fred or Sophie has a lick of business sense. And Lonnie, the brother-in-law, got where he is by marrying the boss's daughter. I understand he's ambitious enough, but it's hardly likely he'd have gotten where he is today on ambition alone. You've heard his story before: One day the guy's walking around in a fifty-dollar polyester leisure suit, wishing to hell payday would hurry up and get here, and the next day he's buying five-hundred-dollar silk suits and driving a fancy new car. From what I hear he went to work for the Milo company right out of high school, back when Dean had just taken over and was shifting things into high gear."

For the remainder of the trip Dear's attention alternated between the folder of newspaper clippings in his lap and the fertile countryside. In marked contrast to the parched browns and dismal grays of the Texas mesquite and scrub oaks, rural Ohio was bursting into a rainbow of fall colors as leaves turned to rich reds, deep oranges, and yellows. The pictorial setting somehow seemed out of keeping with the violent crime he was there to investigate.

Having reread one of the newspaper accounts of the crime scene, Dear asked about organized crime activity in the Akron area. The murder, it appeared, had been a professional job. Had the motive been robbery, the valuables in the house would not have gone untouched.

"The mob is thriving in Cleveland and goes into Canton, which is just down the highway from Akron," Merket said, "but there's little evidence of activity anywhere else up here.

"There are plenty of rumors that Dean Milo might have been connected with organized crime, but nothing solid. He moved a lot of money around and never seemed to have trouble getting financing. But I think that was just because he was a good businessman. Hell, banks were lining up to loan the guy money. Frankly, I don't think he needed the Mafia's financing."

Dear hoped that was the case. The dangers that go along with any investigation of organized crime, he well knew, were greater than he wanted to encounter.

Still, on the basis of the sketchy details already gathered, it appeared very likely that Dean Milo's murder had been carried out by a paid killer. Someone, he was certain, had wanted Milo dead but lacked the courage or ability to do the job himself.

Thinking aloud, Dear said, "These days it's not difficult to hire a killer if you know the right place to look."

Merket briefly turned his attention from the highway to look over at his passenger and laugh. "Hey, I know a guy over in Pittsburgh who swears he can get somebody popped for fifty bucks. Evidently, it's a pretty damn competitive business."

Minutes later Merket pulled into the parking lot of the sprawling new complex that served as the headquarters of Milo Barber and Beauty Supply. "Dean Milo's monument," he said.

Inside, Bill Dear was quickly ushered into the office of Paul

Vaughn. The comptroller wasted little time on pleasantries, launching into an update on the situation even as he was shaking the investigator's hand.

He was, he explained, temporarily in charge of the operation at the request of Dean Milo's widow, Maggie. There was, however, a growing concern over the legal campaign launched by Fred Milo and Sophie and Lonnie Curtis to take over the company.

"At present," Vaughn said, "Dean's attorney, George Tsarnas, has them temporarily stalemated, but he may not be able to hold them off much longer."

The reception was far from what Dear had expected. Vaughn's concern, it was clear, was more for the future of the company than finding a solution to Dean Milo's murder.

"Do you have any reason to believe that Dean Milo's death might be family- or business-related?" the investigator asked.

"It could be anything," Vaughn said wearily. "That's why we've asked you to come. See, Dean moved awfully fast. He moved into the financial big leagues very quickly. The truth is, the growth of this company came at the expense of a lot of other people. He stepped on competitors' toes; he made a number of enemies."

Rising from his desk, Vaughn began pacing the carpeted floor as he continued. "Don't get me wrong. I greatly admired Dean's spunk, his energy and his inventiveness. He was a man who got things done. He was a tough man who refused to let people get in his way. On the other hand, he was quick to reward those who did their jobs well.

"I'm in a bit of an awkward position so far as this family fight is concerned. I own no stock in the company but, at the request of Maggie Milo, I find myself in charge. I work for the Milo Corporation—and the corporation is the family—so you must understand why I'm uncomfortable discussing the battle over control of the business.

"I do want you to know, however, that Dean's widow wholeheartedly supported the idea of hiring you."

Dear then asked a question to which he already knew the answer.

Vaughn smiled weakly for the first time since the meeting had begun. "I'd have to say the others—Fred, Sophie and Lonnie, and maybe even Dean's parents—won't be happy to learn you're here. But I doubt it will have anything to do with your investigation of the murder. Rather, it will be because of the current legal battle. They aren't likely to support anything Maggie Milo does at this point."

Dear briefly contemplated the irony of the matter. As stockholders in the company, all of the Milos, even those who were less than thrilled at his presence, would be paying him for his investigation.

"Before we go any further," Dear said to the pacing comptroller, "I want one thing understood. Since I've agreed to take this case, it will be to solve it."

Vaughn stopped and fixed his tired eyes on his visitor, looking directly at him for the first time since they had met. "Mr. Dear," he said, "we want to know who killed Dean Milo. What can we do to help you?"

"As long as I'm here, I'd like to spend a few minutes looking around Dean Milo's office."

"Certainly," Vaughn said. "I'll show you the way."

It was a large, functional room, tastefully furnished but not nearly as ostentatious as Dear had expected. Obviously, it was the office of a man who used it for business. It was unlikely that much time was wasted here in discussing golf handicaps or upcoming country club cocktail parties.

The collection of neatly framed photographs that filled one wall showed Milo completing a business transaction with a smiling client, Milo shaking hands with some employee being rewarded for superior work, Milo front and center at the grand opening of a new store. In each photograph it was no chore to pick out the man in charge.

From the pictures, Dear judged that Dean Milo had been just under six feet tall and weighed in the neighborhood of 220 pounds; stocky but with little sign of the flab that many men in their early forties acquire.

Prominently displayed on Milo's uncluttered oak desk was a color photograph of a pretty woman Dear assumed was

Maggie Milo, surrounded by three smiling, expensively dressed children.

Dear sat at the desk for several minutes, staring at the mementos of a man no longer alive to savor them. Already it was clear to him that the crime had no lack of suspects. The family infighting over the business had escalated to a point where murder might be someone's misguided solution. The fact that Dean Milo had made enemies in the business world offered chances for further speculation. Then there were questions about Milo's social life. According to Merket there were rumors—nothing more—that Dean Milo had not been completely faithful to the woman who smiled from the photograph on his desk. If that proved to be the case, the investigation could take yet another course. Too, Dear could not dismiss the fact that the murder had all the classic elements of a mob hit. It had been what experienced homicide investigators call a "clean kill," no signs of forced entry, little struggle, and few clues left behind.

It was the possibility of a professional hit that most troubled him. In truth, such murders are rarely solved. Since the early twenties, the city of Chicago alone had been the site of literally thousands of murders linked to organized crime. And there had been only two convictions resulting from all the cases. A competent professional killer is difficult to trace. Often hired in another part of the country, he makes a quick trip to wherever the victim is, carries out the murder cleanly with no apparent motive, and is thousands of miles away before the murder is even discovered.

Already Dear was feeling that the week he had agreed to would hardly be enough to answer the questions he'd begun to list.

Turning his attention to one of the pictures that showed a smiling Dean Milo with a group of chamber of commerce Officials, Dear decided on his first step. As he had so often done in previous cases, he would acquaint himself with the victim as thoroughly as possible. He would learn his motivations, his habits, how he thought and had moved about in his daily life. Dear knew that some of his critics laughed at this approach as nothing more than one of his "hot dog" routines, but he had confidence because he had made it work before.

Just a year earlier he had been hired to locate the missing James Dallas Egbert, a sixteen-year-old Michigan State sophomore with an IQ of over 180. The gifted youngster had simply vanished from the campus during the noon hour in August 1979, leaving behind a bizarre series of clues that indicated his disappearance might well be tied to the highly popular fantasy role-playing game Dungeons & Dragons. Many felt the brilliant but lonely youngster had perpetrated a massive hoax and was actually hiding in a maze of steam tunnels that wound beneath the campus.

By the time Dear entered the case, the unsuccessful search had made headlines in such faraway places as South Africa and the Soviet Union. The approach Dear brought to the investigation was far removed from that employed by local law officers and the campus police. He made a concerted effort to adopt the personality of the lost teenager. He persuaded students to teach him the fantasy game that had so consumed Egbert. He crawled through musty, dark tunnels where he knew the young man had played his games. He learned much about the East Lansing gay community frequented by the youngster. And he even participated in the maddening, dangerous game called trestling, wherein Egbert and his friends had lain on a railroad track as a train approached, jumping to safety only at the last minute.

Long after others had given up hope that James Dallas Egbert was alive, Dear ultimately tracked him down and found him in hiding in rural Louisiana. He had managed to do so, he strongly believed, only because he had spent the time to learn the thought processes of the troubled young man.

Now, he felt, he would have to do the same in the case of the late Dean Milo.

Rising from the desk, Dear looked out the window, lost in thought for several minutes. Had Milo been apprehensive in those final days before his violent death, maybe even aware that his life was in danger? And, if so, had he shared that fear with anyone? Had there been secret transgressions, personal or professional, so extreme as to give cause for his murder? Was there a dark, private side of the man where lay an unsuspected motive for his death?

Walking to a nearby bookshelf, Dear quickly glanced at the titles of the few books there. They told him nothing new. Without exception they were books that promised better sales methods and better administration. It was the library of a man with a single, driving passion.

Sitting again at the desk, Dear was idly browsing through a drawer when he happened on a soft leather pouch. Removing it, he huddled over the writing pad in front of him and emptied its contents. Two sparkling diamonds suddenly spilled onto the desk top. Dear estimated their worth to be easily in the ten-thousand-dollar range.

He stared at the jewels, puzzled. For Milo to leave them so casually in an unlocked desk drawer, vulnerable to theft, aroused even more questions. Had he been as financially careless as this suggested? Were there more jewels elsewhere, kept to hide assets or maybe even avoid taxes? Was it possible that whoever killed Dean Milo was a jewel thief?

A few minutes later, Dear left the office, convinced that Dean Milo was not going to be an easy man to get to know.

Paul Vaughn was genuinely surprised when he looked into the leather pouch Dear handed to him. Milo had never mentioned the diamonds to him. Nor was he aware of any other gems that might be hidden elsewhere.

"What can you tell me about the Milo home?" Dear asked.

"As far as I know," Vaughn answered, "it's just as it was the day Dean's body was found. The police sealed it off."

"Is there someone who can let me in so I can look around?"

Vaughn explained that Bud Eisenhart, a boyhood friend of Dean Milo's who had worked as his personal aide, had a key. He offered to call him and have him meet Dear there.

"But, like I told you," Vaughn said, "the police have sealed it off. No one is allowed to go in."

"I understand," Dear smiled.

Dick Merket whistled softly as he turned into the circular drive in front of the Milo house. "I'd say this guy had a helluva lot to live for," he observed.

Almost immediately a second car pulled into the driveway and a plump, bearded man who appeared to be in his early forties got out. His hand extended, he introduced himself as Bud Eisenhart. "You must be Bill Dear," he said.

"I can't tell you how much I hope you will be able to solve this case," Eisenhart said. "I grew up with Dean. We lived next door to each other when we were kids. Went to grade school, high school, and college together. Played football on the same teams. Joined the army at the same time. He was like a brother to me." He spoke rapidly, as if worried that he had a minimum amount of time to establish himself as a loyal friend. He spoke in a breaking voice, and his distress seemed genuine.

"Do you have any idea who might have wanted to kill Dean Milo?" Dear asked.

"If I did, I'd probably go after him myself. No, I have no idea who would want to do something like this. It just doesn't make any sense," he said as he dug into the pocket of his jacket and handed Dear the house key.

Eisenhart followed as Dear walked to the porch and unlocked the door.

Even before entering the house Dear stopped and shook his head. "I don't believe this," he said, looking down at the markings that indicated where Milo's body had been found on the tile floor of the foyer. He had not known that the murder had taken place just a few feet from the doorway.

As Dear stood staring down at the chalked outline, Eisenhart staggered away, back toward the driveway. His face had turned ashen; agony was etched in his features. Tears had formed in the corners of his eyes. The last time he had entered the house his friend had been alive. It had rung with the happy sounds of children and the daily routine of family activities. Now it was cold and joyless; that chalk outline had more graphic finality than even Dean Milo's wake.

As he started to enter the house, Dear heard a car pull up and then a yell. Detective Richard Munsey of the Bath police made no attempt at pleasantries as he stepped from his car. "Who the hell are you?"

Turning and extending a hand—which Munsey displayed no interest in shaking—Dear said, "I'm a private investigator retained by the Milo company to look into the murder of Dean Milo."

"That doesn't mean shit to me," Munsey snapped. "You've got no business here, so I suggest you lock that door real tight and get the hell away from this house." It was a reception familiar to Dear and most private investigators. Seldom do members of law enforcement welcome outsiders into their investigations.

"Look," said Dear, "I've been hired to investigate this case. And that's what I'm going to do."

Munsey, his eyes squinted into an angry glare, waited several seconds before he replied. "You're not going to do shit here until you get an official okay from the agency in charge of this case," he said.

"The county sheriff's office?"

"That's right."

"I'm on my way."

"Don't expect a brass band to be waiting," Munsey said, staying only long enough to see that Dear pulled the door to the Milo house shut and locked it.

3

Seated in one of the cheerless cubicles in the detectives' office, Larry Momchilov was on the phone with John Hastings, a longtime friend with whom he had gone through the FBI Academy. His feet propped on the desk, resting on a stack of telephone books tattered from use, Momchilov omitted any small talk and went directly to the point.

For several minutes he generally outlined the frustrating sequence of difficulties he had encountered during his three weeks of investigation into the death of Dean Milo. "The damn case is already about to drive me to serious drink," he said, "and yesterday I heard there's some private investigator in town, talking like he's going to take over and teach us all how to be good cops. I need a background check on him."

"What's his name?"

Momchilov pulled out the business card that Richard Munsey had passed on to him the previous afternoon and read the name aloud. "Dear. Bill Dear. He's from somewhere down in Texas."

Momchilov was surprised when Hastings replied that he knew something about the man. Though he had not met Dear personally, Hastings explained, he knew several in the bureau who had previously worked with him on cases. "Have you seen him?"

"Not yet," Momchilov replied. "What can you tell me?"

The FBI agent began a quick, shorthand biography of Dear. "He's cocky as hell, I hear; a hot dog. The guy's a perfectionist who doesn't have much tolerance for anyone who isn't. And he's evidently got a temper that's a real beauty."

Momchilov scratched hurried notes onto a yellow legal pad that rested on his lap and made no response as Hastings continued. "He apparently thinks he's James fucking Bond. His lifestyle's a cliché. The press loves him. Big-assed house, fancy cars, all kinds of expensive, high-tech electronic gadgets. Dresses damn well and wears about as much jewelry as some of the guys playing in the NBA.

"He's got a half-dozen people on his staff, including, I understand, a rather colorful guy named Boots Hinton, whose father tracked down Bonnie and Clyde back in the good old days.

"Dear generally makes his living taking cases other people have given up on. He finds a lot of lost kids and hunts down businessmen who have suddenly disappeared into the night with a shitload of company money in a suitcase, stuff like that. He's also managed to prove that several apparent suicides were actually cold-blooded murder. That never makes the insurance folks too happy, but his clients generally wind up satisfied and pay him damn well to prove it.

"From all indications the guy's got brass balls. When he gets on a case he doesn't give up until he's solved it. And he generally seems to be able to get along with local agencies despite the fact he's eccentric as hell and his techniques seem to come out of deep left field at times.

"The bottom line, Larry, is the guy's apparently good. What I hear is he's honest and, beneath all the bullshit, a pretty class act."

Momchilov, the phone cradled on his shoulder, drew meaningless circles on his legal pad as he contemplated the information his friend was supplying. "The last thing I need right now," he said, "is for some high roller to come in here and turn this thing into an even bigger circus than it already is. I don't need another nut in this asylum. I don't like it."

Hastings could hear Momchilov's deep, resigned sigh. "Shit, John, it sounds like the guy's seen too many PI shows on TV."

"Well, from what you've told me, you could use some help on this one. If you're asking my advice, I'd say cut the guy in."

"I think I'm glad that decision isn't up to me," Momchilov said.

In truth, Larry Momchilov was desperately in search of allies. Never before in his career had he run up against so much angry resistance from people with no apparent reason to be uncooperative with law enforcement.

In the days that followed the discovery of Dean Milo's body, he had talked with dozens of people—Milo B&B employees, family members, attorneys involved in the takeover attempt, neighbors—most of whom seemed inexplicably determined to keep the investigation moving at a snail's pace.

Those assisting him, Detective Sergeant Munsey from the Bath Police Department, and Detective Lieutenant Bill Lewis and Detective Sergeant David Bailey from the Summit County sheriff's office, were crashing into the same hostile brick walls. Each, in fact, had expressed surprise at the direction from which some of the hostility had come. Too many people, they had already agreed, weren't telling all they knew about Dean Milo, obviously protecting his reputation—or their own.

The most troubling encounter Momchilov had experienced was one with County Coroner A. H. Kyriakides, who had been out of town the day Milo's body had been found. Momchilov's first opportunity to talk with him had come just after the autopsy. It was then that Momchilov learned that the coroner and Milo had been close friends. The performance of the autopsy, in fact, had been particularly difficult for Kyriakides.

A highly regarded pathologist who had served Summit County for seventeen years, the white-haired Kyriakides had viewed the result of violent death in every hideous form imaginable, but the performance of an autopsy on a friend clearly had unnerved him.

Momchilov and Lewis had watched the procedure in silence, listening to the anger boil in the doctor's voice as he spoke into a recorder, detailing his findings: powder burns near the wounds. ... Second entrance wound in back of neck five millimeters long, three millimeters wide.... Death resulted from cardiorespiratory failure, due to penetrating, perforating gunshot wound to the brain."

The coroner completed his report with an angry observation

that the victim, though probably unconscious, had likely lived as long as a half hour after being shot. Then, ripping away his rubber gloves, he had officially ruled that Dean Milo had been murdered.

Kyriakides' indignation, Momchilov assumed, would make him anxious to cooperate in the investigation. Yet when he had requested the contents of the briefcase that had been taken from Milo's bedroom by officials from the coroner's office, Kyriakides had immediately refused. The coroner said brusquely that at a later time, Momchilov would be allowed to review the contents and photocopies of whatever he wanted would be made.

Momchilov's argument that the materials contained in the briefcase might be vital to the investigation met with arrogant dismissal. He would, Kyriakides said, get only copies of whatever papers he requested.

When he did return to collect the copies that had been made for him by a clerk in Kyriakides' office, the stack of papers given him was far smaller than the original one he had requested. What he had, the clerk told him, was all that the doctor had requested that she copy.

It was but another in a growing list of events that made no sense, adding to an already uncontrollable list of questions without answers. Momchilov thought back to the fact that Dr. Kyriakides' son Rod, chief buyer for the Milo company, had been one of the first employees to arrive at the crime scene and wondered if there were private matters he might have shared with his father about the dead man both had been close to. Momchilov could also not help wondering what secrets he might have learned had he been given access to all the papers in Dean Milo's briefcase.

The puzzle scattered before him, he had told his wife during one of their increasingly rare dinners together, seemed to have nothing but black pieces. "This one," he had admitted to her, "is going to be damn hard to put together."

When Bill Dear walked into his office, Larry Momchilov's first thought was that John Hastings had described him well. Several of the secretaries had demonstrated more than casual interest when Dear stepped from the fourth-floor elevator and asked directions to the detective's office.

Momchilov's interest was several degrees cooler. "How do you figure into this?" he asked immediately after Dear introduced himself.

"I've been retained by Milo Barber and Beauty Supply," Dear replied. "They're not happy with the progress being made on the case."

"And you're going to show us the way."

Momchilov's sarcasm was not lost on his visitor. "I'd like to help," Dear said. "I want to cooperate with you people in every way possible. From what I gather, you've got big problems with this case. I've got twenty years' experience, I've got manpower, and I've got time you and your department don't. I'm here to work exclusively on this case. Unless you have a crime rate here that's unique, I suspect you can't afford that same luxury."

It was a speech Bill Dear had made a number of times before, trying to establish a rapport with local law officials not at all happy to have him invading their carefully guarded turf. "It seems to me the important thing here," he continued, "is that someone find the person who murdered Dean Milo. That's what I've been hired to do. I'd like to help you in any way I can."

"I don't think we want your help, Mr. Dear," Momchilov said. Yet even as he spoke he could not help mentally agreeing with the points the private investigator was making. It was certainly true that the case was already tangled with problems. And, while every available man was currently working it, experience told Momchilov that soon there would be pressing matters that would force officers' attention to other investigations. Crime in Summit County would not come to a standstill simply because a prominent citizen had been murdered. Also, Momchilov was one of those rare law enforcement officers whose ego had remained in check. It made no difference to him who got credit for solving a crime. Unlike the man standing before him, Larry Momchilov had spent his career making a concerted effort to keep his name and picture out of the newspapers and off the ten o'clock news.

Sipping from his first cup of coffee of the day, Momchilov

looked at Dear and shrugged. "There's no point in us dancing," he said. "I'm in charge of this investigation, but I'm not the man who decides whether you're in or out. So what I think of you doesn't really amount to shit."

Dear laughed. "At least you don't beat around the bush." Momchilov then led him across the hall and into the office of Ed Duvall, chief of detectives. Waiting with Duvall were Momchilov's partner, Bill Lewis; Summit County Sheriff David Troutman; assistant prosecutor Michael Wolff; and Sergeant Munsey from the Bath police.

Munsey's warning from the previous day proved prophetic. While Momchilov's reception had been cool, the one in Duvall's office would have frozen beef.

Duvall opened the conversation by asking, "What makes you feel you will be able to do something we can't?"

Dear did not answer immediately. Instead, he surveyed his surroundings, taking stock of the men who had gathered to judge him. It was going to be like the interrogation of a suspect. Munsey, seated in a chair near the wall, nervously clenched and unclenched his fists, never taking his eyes off the visitor. Duvall, a former street cop who had climbed the ladder to his current position, sat with arms folded, his expression challenging. Wolff, dressed in the three-piece suit favored by young assistant prosecutors, appeared impatient, as if to signal Dear and the others that his valuable time could be better spent elsewhere.

Dear measured his words carefully as he repeated what he had said to Momchilov earlier. "I'm not here offering any guarantees that I will be able to do anything more than what you people have done. I'm sure you're doing everything that can be expected. But the fact of the matter is I've got resources you can't possibly have. I'm adequately financed by the people who have hired me. I can work this thing around the clock.

"I'll go back to square one and begin my investigation just as if nobody's asked a question. There's always the chance that someone might suddenly remember something. Or that something might have been overlooked."

Dear was aware that Munsey visibly stiffened at the suggestion but continued. "I've got people working for me who are just a phone call away if they're needed; four men and a woman all with impressive backgrounds in police work. That's five more people to work this thing if necessary."

He was speaking rapidly, presenting his case as quickly as possible, in an attempt to ward off refusal of his offer. "In addition to manpower and financing, I have a private plane available. If this case carries the investigation somewhere else, I can be there and back before you people can even get the paperwork requesting approval started."

Duvall's expression did not change as Dear spoke. "The important thing here is that Dean Milo's murderer be found. And I think I can help you people do that," the private investigator said in a firm voice.

The chief of detectives, who Dear had already realized would have the final say in the matter, rocked forward in his chair, placing his elbows on the desk in front of him. Looking squarely at Dear, he asked, "And what do you plan to do if we decide we don't want anything to do with you or your airplanes or your other investigators?"

Dear did not need time to think of his answer. "With or without your cooperation," he said, "I go ahead."

Duvall looked around the crowded office as if trying to measure the reactions of his fellow officers. Finally, he returned his attention to Dear. "If you don't mind," he said, "I'd like for you to step outside for a minute or two."

For the next several minutes, Dear wandered aimlessly in the large room that served as the headquarters for the detectives. It was no different from most he'd seen before: desks with stacks of manila folder case files, a framed picture of a wife and children here and there, coffee cups. The most common element all seemed to share was a lack of order or neatness.

On one wall was a bulletin board that featured a montage of wanted felons, meeting notices, yellowing newspaper articles, and several humorous snapshots of people Dear assumed to be office personnel, obviously taken at lighter moments.

Dear called the front desk of the Holiday Inn Cascade, where he was staying, to see if he had received any phone messages since leaving earlier that morning, then stepped into the hall for a drink of water he really had no desire for. Killing time did not come easy for him. He was beginning to feel like an attorney awaiting a jury's decision when, finally, Duvall, still soberfaced, opened his office door and beckoned him back inside.

"Okay, Mr. Dear," Duvall said, "we've decided to work with you."

Dear smiled. "I'm glad to hear it."

"But only under certain guidelines."

"Which are ..."

"There are just two," Duvall said. "But they are part of a take-it-or-leave-it deal. First, we get together and decide what the press is going to be told about this investigation. I understand your name gets in the papers quite a lot. But there'll be no press conferences on this case until we've got something we all think's important."

Dear did not bother to explain to the chief his belief that the powers of the press could be used to great advantage in certain investigative situations. Criminals also read newspapers and often, based on what they read, react in a way that causes them to make some mistake that might prove helpful to an investigation.

"That's no problem," he said.

Duvall then outlined the second requirement. "Second, we share all information. And when I say all, I mean all. It'll work both ways; you can count on that. What we've got to have here is a team effort. Our people will shoot straight with you and provide you everything we have. You do the same with us. If you learn something, we want to be the first to know."

"Sounds fair to me," Dear said.

Duvall rose from his desk and extended his hand. "I suggest you and Larry Momchilov get your heads together on this thing as quickly as possible. You've got a helluva lot of catching up to do."

Seated at Momchilov's desk, Dear looked at a stack of file folders that was easily a foot high. "It's all there," Momchilov said, "statements that have been taken, crime scene pictures, the autopsy report, records of the physical evidence collected. So far about all it amounts to is just a big stack of papers."

The tone of the lieutenant's voice was not lost on Dear. For the first time since they had met, Momchilov had allowed his frustration to show.

Dear read through the remainder of the morning, through lunch and well into the afternoon. Going through the daily reports filed by those assigned to the case, he quickly saw that the investigation had been thorough and professional. Generally written in a dry manner with oft times inventive punctuation and spelling, police reports can, to the trained eye, evoke the fascination of a well-plotted mystery novel. Dear found need at times to remind himself to make notes as he pored over the material. Though the reports gave him far more information and insight than the collection of newspaper clippings Dick Merket had provided, it was easy to see the reason for Momchilov's frustration. What he was looking into was a case with too many suspects and too little evidence. And now, almost four weeks after the murder, time had become an adversary. There is an unwritten rule in police work that most homicides not solved within forty-eight hours are never solved.

As if on cue, Momchilov reappeared after Dear had closed the final folder. The issue of the private investigator's involvement taken care of, he was congenial and relaxed. "Got it solved?" he asked.

Dear replied with a question of his own. "Larry, do you even have a gut feeling on this thing?"

"I don't really know what to think. There are times when I think it has to have been someone in the family, but it's hard to make that wash when you look at the fact there's no indication of a really strong motive. They may have been fighting over control of the company, but that whole matter seemed closer to resolution than ever at the time Milo was shot. Their day in court was apparently right around the corner. If the family had decided to get rid of the guy, why hadn't it happened sooner?

"Then, there's the matter of financial gain. Hell, even if Dean Milo had won and controlled the company lock, stock, and barrel, everyone was going to make more money than they could possibly spend. That's the part that really doesn't make any sense to me. I'm damned if I would be pitching a fit and going through a court battle to work at a job that paid me more if I never went near the office."

Dear flipped the pages of his notebook until he found a notation he had made from one of the reports about Milo's financial involvement in a restaurant chain. "How many shares of stock did he have?" he asked.

"Something in the neighborhood of twenty-six thousand," Momchilov said. "Sounds like a lot to me, but as I understand it amounted to about two percent." He anticipated Dear's next question. "Word is, the chain is mob-controlled. But you know how that goes. Even if that's the case it would be hard as hell to prove. Trying to wade through all the dummy corporations and camouflages is like digging a hole in the sand. But the FBI's been working on it. In fact, they were looking into it long before Milo's death.

"What interests me is the timing of all this. As a member of the chain's board of directors, Dean Milo was scheduled to give a deposition on August twelfth—the day after his body was found. It could be someone was worried about what he might say."

"Who's the major figure in the chain?"

"A guy named Jake Solazo. Lotta rumors about him but nothing you could make a case on. He was at the wake and Milo's widow evidently made quite a scene. She just marched straight up to him and asked him who had killed her husband—like there was no doubt in her mind he would know, Solazo swore he didn't have any idea."

"Tell me about the wake," Dear said.

"Strange affair, I've been told. Members of Maggie Milo's family were subdued, quiet; the way you would expect mourners to be. Most of Dean Milo's family seemed to be having a pretty good time, smiling and laughing. The noticeable exception was Dean's brother, Fred. He was evidently pretty broken up, crying a lot, talking to the casket."

At one point during the wake, Momchilov related, Katina Milo had approached her daughter-in-law and mentioned that it was time for all the family differences to be set aside and everyone reunited. Maggie Milo replied with a glare and the suggestion that Katina return to her own group.

"There's no question in Maggie Milo's mind," Momchilov added, "that the responsibility for her husband's death somehow rests with his family."

"Does she have a prime suspect?"

Momchilov shook his head. "Not really. But my guess right now is she wouldn't have a lot of trouble imagining everybody in the whole damn family standing over her husband's body, each holding a smoking pistol."

"Everything you have here," Dear observed, "points to a professional hit. Evidently there was nothing taken despite the fact there were valuables literally on display, ready for a robbery. The only thing somebody wanted was Dean Milo dead.

"There's one thing that really bothers me about this, though," Dear continued.

Momchilov smiled. "The gun," he said.

"Yeah," Dear said. "If the killer was a real pro, why was he using a .32 automatic? It's one of the most unreliable handguns you can buy. They're always jamming or misfiring. I would hate to have stuck a gun like that in the face of someone built like Dean Milo and it not go off when I pulled the trigger.

"It's just not the type weapon a contract killer would have anything to do with. Unless the mobsters you've got up here in Ohio are really second-rate."

"Oh no," Momchilov said, "our mobsters are first class all the way. Top of the line."

Both men laughed. Already they were beginning to feel comfortable in each other's company.

Momchilov wanted to know what Dear thought of the most puzzling of the physical evidence that had been collected. "What do you make of the cotton in the victim's mouth?"

"You want guesses?"

"Why not? That's all we're coming up with at this point."

Dear shifted in his chair, crossing his long legs, and stared down at his boots as he launched into a hypothetical sequence of events. "According to the reports, a tissue with semen was found near Milo's bed upstairs," he began. "Let's say he was up there with a lover when someone knocked at the door. The lover—he or she—remains in the bedroom, hears the shots, and then rushes down to find Milo mortally wounded and finds some cotton to swab some of the blood from Milo's face.

"Which, of course, would mean that we've got a witness running around here somewhere. The trouble with that theory, though, is it would mean we get lucky. And there's little to indicate that luck is going to play much of a role in this investigation. If there had been a witness, you guys would probably have got wind of it by now."

Momchilov nodded in agreement. "We've checked, believe me. There's some talk on the streets that Milo might have been a switch hitter, but I have a hard time buying that. Just bullshit talk. The guy might have played around a little, but not with the boys."

"Okay," Dear said. "Theory two: The cotton was placed over Milo's mouth to keep him from yelling for help—which would point to the assailant being a large, strong man. And he could have been reasoning with Milo, telling him he was there to rob him, not kill him. That would give you an edge. A victim would be more apt to allow someone to gag him if he thought that by not struggling he was saving his life.

"That theory gets pretty well blown out of the water by the fact the intruder apparently didn't get too concerned about noise until he'd already fired the first shot. Using the cushion to muffle the second shot seems to be almost an afterthought."

"You think it was the second shot that went through the cushion?" Momchilov interrupted.

"Had to be. It's hard to imagine Dean Milo stretching out on the floor and passively letting somebody put a pillow over his head and blow his brains out. In a situation like that, you're going to put up some kind of struggle, regardless of how slim your chances are. But there was no sign of a struggle where the body was found, right?"

"And, why muffle the first shot with the cushion and not the second?"

"We do have a few psychos in this part of the country," Momchilov said. "There's a file cabinet over there against the wall filled with crimes committed by people who didn't bother to use a great deal of logic. It just could be that we're looking for a crazy sonuvabitch."

"There was some degree of logic and planning applied to this one," Dear said. "The blank telegram points to that. That has to be the way the killer got into the house. This had to be a hit of some kind. Everything points to it."

"Any more theories?"

"Assuming this was the work of an amateur, someone who didn't know the shortcomings of the .32 automatic, it could have been that the cotton was used as some kind of silencer. Maybe it was wrapped around the barrel of the gun. Or even stuffed up into the barrel, which would really have been crazy. If he did something like that, he's lucky he wasn't found lying next to Milo after the gun blew up in his face.

"But, as long as we're playing 'what if,' it could explain the lack of concern over noise made by a first shot and the need to use the cushion on the second one. It could be that some of the cotton landed on Milo."

Dear then shrugged. "But that doesn't tell us how the cotton got into his mouth, does it?"

Momchilov only nodded. Versions of the same theories Dear had outlined had been running through his head, stealing his sleep, for weeks. "This thing doesn't make much sense right now," he said, "but it will before it's all over. I don't know what conclusions you might have drawn about Dean Milo so far, but regardless of what kind of person he was, he didn't deserve what happened to him."

Picking up one of the crime scene pictures from the desk, he looked at it for a moment, then pitched it back onto the stack of file folders. "Nobody deserves that."

"I'm going to start knocking on some doors," Dear said as he placed his notebook into his briefcase and began walking toward the door. "I'll be in touch."

Momchilov handed him a business card. "My home number's on there," he said. "Call me anytime, day or night."

As he drove in the direction of Bath, ready to begin meeting some of the people he had only read or heard about, Dear found himself wondering just how well even those who called themselves his friends had really known the late Dean Milo.

One of the things he had read, then reread, as he went through the case file was a handwritten letter found in Milo's briefcase. Though it had included no salutation, it had apparently been written to his wife.

Dear had copied part of the letter into his notebook:

I bought you a new home. You didn't like it. I get you a babysitter. You don't take enough time with the kids. I entertain your family in Florida and when you come back to Akron you won't even call my mother or my family. What kind of person am I? The guy that just pays the bills?

One thing Dear already knew for certain about Dean Milo. He had not died a happy man.

4

Though established in 1810, Bath Township displays all the glittering trappings of new wealth. Geographically, it is detached from the city of Akron by the winding Cuyahoga River, which meanders northward until it empties into Lake Erie. The distance from downtown Akron to the quiet, peaceful suburb is just over ten miles, and the differences one encounters across the Cuyahoga River Bridge are dramatic. Akron is a weary, graceless factory town, a town of blue-collar workers, shop owners, and students at the university whose campus sprawls on the edge of the downtown area. With few exceptions, moneyed society has retreated to the suburbs, to escape the riotous beer joints, topless bars, and crammed-together duplexes and apartment villages where so much of the city's crime is bred.

In Bath, as in other townships around Akron, modern shopping centers, complete with grocery stores, movie theaters, and a wide variety of specialty boutiques, make it unnecessary for shopping housewives to ever travel into Akron.

Bath is primarily residential and its homes are architecturally creative. Those who live in them pay high into the six-figure range to own a house that does not look like the one next door.

Lawyers, doctors, and executives of the billion-dollar corporations that earned Akron the status of Rubber Capital of the World—Goodyear, Firestone, BF Goodrich, and General Tire—retreat to Bath when their workdays are done. So, too, do presidents of many of the 150-odd trucking companies headquartered in the area—as well as the directors of smaller successful businesses like the Milo Barber and Beauty Supply Corporation.

Once there, however, most prefer the isolation of their homes to any social involvement in the community. Aside from those whose paths cross at local parent-teacher school functions, Little League games, or Sunday church services, few Bath neighbors know much about each other.

For the Milos, the arm's-length distance that most Bath residents seem to have adopted was ideal. Still holding to many of the Old Country philosophies taught by his Greek Orthodox father, Sotir Milo had jealously guarded his privacy from the first day he arrived in America. He and his wife forever suspected anyone who expressed even the most innocent interest in their family concerns. The same reservations had been passed along to their children. If there was a backyard barbecue at the home of any of the Milos, the only ones invited would be other members of the family and perhaps a few close business associates who could be trusted.

Son-in-law Lonnie Curtis knew his membership card to the family inner circle had been granted—somewhat begrudgingly—only as a result of his marriage to Sophie Milo.

Now Bill Dear hoped to penetrate this family barrier, to learn more about Dean Milo and possibly find some clue that would lead him closer to Milo's killer. Walking up the Curtis driveway, which led to a garage where two Mercedes were parked, Dear pulled a business card from his coat pocket. There was a quickness to his step as he anticipated his first encounter with a member of the Milo family and the surge of excitement he always felt at the beginning of an investigation.

Curtis, trim, athletic, and well dressed, answered the door and listened as the visitor identified himself and asked if he could talk with him and his wife.

Lonnie Curtis made no gesture of hospitality. "I'm afraid I can't talk to you," he said in a voice devoid of warmth. "Why?"

"My lawyer has told me—and my wife—not to talk with anyone."

"Mr. Curtis," Dear replied, "I'm afraid I don't understand. I would think you would be eager to talk with me. I've been hired by Milo B&B to solve the murder of your brother-in-law. I would think our interests in this matter are one and the same.

As you know, this was a cold-blooded, vicious killing."

Curtis was clearly having none of Dear's charm or reason. "I pay good money to my lawyer for advice," he said, "and I'd be a fool not to follow it. I'm not talking with you." Puzzled by the defensive stance Lonnie Curtis was taking, Dear ignored the proclamation. "Mr. Curtis," he asked, "is your attorney a criminal lawyer?"

Curtis nodded.

"I find that a bit confusing. Why would you need a criminal lawyer in a matter like this? Do you have something to hide?"

"I don't want to talk to you anymore," Curtis said.

He was beginning to close the door when a woman's voice came from the hallway behind him. "I would like to talk with you, Mr. Dear."

Sophie Milo, a pretty woman of medium height and a dark complexion, smiled at Dear over her husband's shoulder. "Please come in," she said in a soft voice.

"No," her husband said, glaring at her. "We're not talking to anybody!" With that, he slammed the door in Bill Dear's face.

Minutes later, still troubled by the mixed reception, Dear was at the front door of Dean Milo's brother. Fred Milo answered, but he kept a closed screen door between them.

"I'm Bill Dear …"

"I know who you are," Fred Milo said.

Again the voice Dear was hearing was unwelcoming. The shadowed figure behind the door wore horn-rimmed glasses and stood no more than five-eight. Fred Milo had no physical characteristics that would suggest a kinship with his dead brother. He avoided direct eye contact with his visitor and seemed almost timid as he spoke. "I can't talk with you," he said.

"On the advice of your attorney?"

"That's right," Fred Milo said. "Your name has been mentioned specifically to me. I've been instructed not to speak with you."

"I assume you have the same lawyer who is advising Lonnie Curtis," Dear said.

"Yes, George Pappas."

Dear shook his head in genuine disbelief. "I don't understand this at all. Not one little bit. I would have thought all of you people would want to find out who killed your brother."

"I want that very much," Milo said, making a frail attempt at indignation. "You have no idea how much. But you have to understand my situation in this matter. I'm under a great deal of pressure. Family pressure."

Dear felt himself tense. "Look, I'm not here to talk about pressure. I'm here to talk about your brother. What about him?"

Milo replied in a voice that was barely audible. "You're not going to frighten me."

"I'm not here to frighten you, for Pete's sake. This is a business card I'm holding, not a gun. What you're saying just doesn't make sense. You should want to talk to me. And frankly, the fact that you don't looks pretty damn suspicious."

"It's my lawyer ..."

"It's your brother."

"I'm closing the door."

Dear, who rarely used profanity, felt his anger building as he looked through the mesh screen at the man he had already decided to dislike. "What the hell kind of man are you? Damn, I seem to care more about the death of your own flesh and blood than you do. Why? Enlighten me."

"I can't," Fred Milo said, looking down at the floor as he gently closed the door.

Back in his car, Dear sat for some time, stunned by the sequence of events. He had been hired by Milo Barber and Beauty Supply to solve the murder of the company's president. Yet the very people who were paying his fee were adamantly refusing to talk with him. Two of the people who had known Dean Milo intimately would say nothing. Why?

Fred Milo's words thundered in his mind: "Mr. Dear, you don't understand."

Indeed he didn't.

Having failed in his first two attempts to interview family members, Dear was not ready for what he feared might be a quick third strike and chose to leave Dean's widow and Sotir and Katina Milo for later. More than once during his career he had been hired by hostile clients whose only motive had been to divert attention from themselves. There had been the widow of a murder victim in Texas who had sought his services, then immediately began acting suspicious when Dear questioned her about her husband's death. It had quickly become apparent that she had no interest in his doing a thorough investigation. Before resigning from the case, in fact, he had provided police with information that made the woman the prime suspect in the murder of three previous husbands. Which is to say it is not only the innocent who hire private investigators. Dear would have to know a lot more about the Milo family before he eliminated them as suspects, even if they were paying his salary.

But for now he decided first to spend some time looking around the neighborhood without the intrusion of the Bath police. Soon he was again standing on the front porch of Dean Milo's home, but he did not try to enter. Rather, he looked intently at his watch as the second hand ticked to the beginning of a new minute. As it did, he began to walk briskly down the walk, headed back in the direction of the nearby Curtis home. Hurrying along his course, Dear was unaware of the warm breeze that had blown away the morning chill. For most Bath residents, it was a welcome sunny day, perfect for an afternoon walk in the neighborhood. For Dear, lost in concentration, it was just another workday.

As he arrived at the walk leading up to the front door Lonnie Curtis had closed earlier, Dear checked his watch. It had taken him three minutes and thirty seconds to make the trip. Hands in his pockets, Dear stood on the sidewalk for a moment, looking up at the Curtis house, wondering if there were eyes watching him from inside. He hoped so. Lonnie, he thought, could have shot Dean Milo and been back in the safety and seclusion of his own home even before the victim had died. If he had run instead of walked, he could have made it even more quickly. And if shortcuts were taken through the open-spaced neighborhood, he could have whittled the time even more.

Mr. Curtis, Dear thought as he turned to retrace his steps

back to the Milo house, I'm going to get to know you a whole lot better—whether you or your lawyer like it or not.

Returning to the Milo house, Dear again checked his watch carefully, then began another brisk walk, this time in the direction of Fred Milo's house. It took him seven minutes and forty-eight seconds. Yet even as he walked, Dear considered this little more than exercise. It was impossible for him to call up a mental picture of the timid, boyish-looking Fred Milo standing up to his big brother, putting a bullet in his head, then firing another shot into the body. On the assumption that such an act of violence took some twisted form of courage, Dear was certain he could rule out Fred Milo as the man who pulled the trigger. Courage and Fred Milo, he was sure, had never met.

He soon found that this was not something he could say about the recently widowed Maggie Milo.

Dear drove to the home of lawyer George Tsarnas and finally encountered a friendly face. Tsarnas, almost a caricature of the shrewd and prosperous corporation lawyer, immediately extended a handshake and escorted the investigator into the den where Maggie Milo sat watching television.

She was even more attractive, more petite, than she had appeared in the photograph Dear had seen of her on her husband's desk. She was, he knew, thirty-four. Her features spoke of her Greek ancestry and her eyes, dark as onyx, fascinated him. In another time and under less tense circumstances, Dear assumed, she would have been warm and friendly. Now, however, she wore anger and bitterness on her sleeve and wasted no time with small talk.

"I realize you haven't been here long," she said, "but have you learned anything?"

Dear smiled. "I've learned that Lonnie Curtis and Fred Milo aren't interested in talking to me."

The mention of their names clearly angered Mrs. Milo. "Both shut the door in my face," Dear explained.

"You should know, Mr. Dear, that I don't care much for Lonnie Curtis. He's a carnivore who married Sophie only to solidify his position in the company. Just look at where he is now. He started out working in the warehouse ... and now he fully expects to become the president of Milo B&B. The very idea makes me furious."

Maggie Milo, Dear thought, was a woman who could be a formidable adversary if she chose. He was relieved that they were on the same side. "What about Fred?" he asked.

Before answering she returned to her place on the sofa and motioned for Dear to sit down. The anger faded from her voice as she spoke of her brother-in-law. "The man is dominated by his mother," she began. "When you meet Katina you will find out quickly that she runs the family. She has always had total control, and will have it no other way. It bothered her that my husband and I objected to being under her thumb. Frankly, she has no use for me or anyone in my family. We're outsiders and, consequently, the enemy. That's just the way the woman thinks.

"She managed to convince her husband that he had made a grave mistake by letting control of the company slip from his hands and into Dean's. So she began to plot a way to get back the control. She convinced Fred, along with Lonnie and Sophie, that they were being cheated by my husband. All of them ganged up on him. It was sick.

"Instead of being grateful for what Dean had done, making them all wealthy, they plotted against him. For Fred and Lonnie, it was the first time they had ever felt they were important in Katina's eyes. And they've loved every minute of it."

Anxious for her to continue the review of the family background, Dear interrupted only to ask about the relationship between Dean Milo and his mother.

"They used to be extremely close. But as Dean and I grew closer, she became increasingly resentful. She's never said so, but I think she resented the fact my husband placed greater emphasis on me and the children than he did on the rest of the family. The more apparent that became, the more Katina resented it. In time her relationship with Dean turned sour.

"Let me give you an example: At the company Christmas party last year she spent the entire evening mingling with the employees, saying awful things about Dean—how Dean's ambition would be the destruction of the company, how he would cost them all their jobs, how his deceit was ruining the family. Cruel, unfounded, awful things.

"After a while, Dean went over to her and asked her to please stop and not spoil the party. Katina just got louder and more abusive. Finally Dean had had enough and asked her to leave. He had to ask his own mother to leave the Christmas party.

"Bud Eisenhart, Dean's best friend, said he would drive Katina and Sotir home. When they got out to the parking lot, Fred was sitting there in his car, waiting for them. He had driven them to the party, knowing full well what Katina had planned to do. Hell, he had probably helped plan it.

"That's just a typical example of how this family has been torn apart because of the company. They had become like a pack of hungry dogs, fighting over the same bone."

Dear shook his head. "From what I've heard, no one was going hungry. Wasn't there any way for them to patch things up?"

Maggie replied with an incredulous look. "With so many people involved," she said, "it's hard to point a finger at anyone and say he is the main culprit."

"Give it a try," Dear urged.

Rising from the couch, Maggie Milo began pacing in the deep carpet of the den as she contemplated the challenge. Turning to Dear she spoke in a controlled, even voice. "I blame Lonnie Curtis for stirring up a lot of it. He seemed to delight in fanning the flames. He'd go over to see Sotir and Katina and cry about how badly Dean was mistreating him. And they would believe him and sympathize. They decided it was terrible that Dean was operating their company like he was. Or like they were led to believe he was."

"But your husband did fire Lonnie," Dear interjected. "And his wife, and Fred."

Maggie Milo nodded. "On August thirty-first of last year," she said. "And he should have. Let me explain: See, the family owns Mico, an independent company that sells supplies to Milo Barber and Beauty Supply. Dean had put Fred and Lonnie in charge of Mico, to give them something to do and keep them out of his hair.

"The reason he fired them was they wrote two checks,

totaling three hundred thousand dollars, to Mico from the Milo B&B account without Dean knowing. It was nothing more than a way for them to get their hands on some of the company money that they felt Dean was controlling unfairly. When my husband found out about what they had done, he fired them.

"What you have to understand, Mr. Dear, is that even by firing them Dean assured them they would be comfortable for life. With him running the company—which was growing by leaps and bounds—their one-third shares would keep going up. By firing them, he in effect gave them a lifetime pass to run and play while never having to worry about money ever again."

"Did your husband have enemies within the company?"

"I can only think of a couple," Maggie replied. "A man named Ray Sesic and another named Tony Ridle. Dean fired Sesic after learning that he was leaking confidential company information to Fred and Lonnie. Dean finally tricked him and found out what he was doing. He gave Sesic some information that wasn't true and, sure enough, it came back to him on the grapevine in just a matter of days. Dean knew that Sesic was the only one who could have spread the story.

"Tony Ridle quit because he didn't think he was getting the promotions he deserved. He was very bitter, as I understand. He and Dean had words."

Dear studied the pretty brunette carefully as she spoke. There was a strength in her posture and attitude that he liked. Maggie Milo, he thought, was the first person he had talked with since his arrival who seemed to be reacting to Dean Milo's murder in a predictable way. She made no attempt to hide the hurt and anger she was feeling. And, even more important to the investigator, she was not hesitant to haul the family skeletons from the closet for him to view.

It was only when he began to question her about the personal relationship she and her husband had had that tears formed in the corners of her eyes, suddenly dulling their black sparkle.

"I hope you understand," Dear said, "that there are questions that I need to ask …"

"I understand." Even before she had buried her husband, her attorney had explained that she, like everyone else in the family, would likely be looked upon as a suspect. "The fact you and the kids were away, in Florida, when Dean was killed won't eliminate you," George Tsarnas had pointed out. "In fact, that might cause even more questions. Police don't like for people to have alibis that seem too convenient. They're going to get pretty imaginative if they don't solve this thing pretty quickly. So prepare yourself."

Maggie, at first angered that anyone might suspect her of having anything to do with the death of her husband, had, in the days just past, come to grips with the fact that investigators had to explore even the most remote possibilities. Thus she answered Dear's first question before it was even asked.

"We had a good marriage," she said. "We were in love."

"Did you have any concern that your husband might be seeing other women?"

Maggie tensed at the question but looked Dear squarely in the eyes as she answered. "No. Absolutely not. We cared deeply about each other. I knew my husband very well." She paused, then added, "I think I would have known if there was another woman."

If she was aware of the rumors about her husband's extramarital affairs, she had chosen to ignore them.

"There was a letter found in his briefcase," Dear continued, probing into areas that he knew were painfully personal, "that indicated there were some problems."

"I'm aware of the letter," she said. "It doesn't paint a true picture. It was the result of a great deal of strain, from pressures at work, the lawsuit, and the problems with his family which I've already mentioned. I can only assume that he wrote it in an attempt to relieve some of the tension he was feeling. But I know it didn't reflect his true feelings.

"Every marriage has its ups and downs, you know. But Dean and I loved each other. We were planning to build a beautiful new home. It was going to be our dream house. Does that sound like a man unhappy in his marriage?"

Dear studied Maggie Milo carefully as she spoke. Again, her strength impressed him. He liked her.

As she continued talking, it was obvious that her attorney,

who stood quietly near a bookshelf, had explained to her the need to provide the investigator with as much information on her husband as possible. Her husband, she volunteered, was a man troubled by fears that she had never completely understood. The dark had frightened him from childhood. A light sleeper, he would awaken at the slightest sound. He had kept a heavy wooden walking cane near the bed and, if awakened during the night, would walk from room to room, checking for intruders, carrying the cane as a weapon. Being alone—even eating a meal by himself—bothered him. He drank only moderately and used no drugs. To her knowledge he didn't gamble.

"How do you think he might have reacted to a knock at the door on the night he was murdered?" Dear asked.

Maggie hesitated, as if gathering the courage to imagine the sequence of events that had led to the horror of her husband's death. It was something she had contemplated numerous times since that evening she had received the phone call in Florida, advising her to return home as quickly as possible.

Taking a deep breath, she turned away from Dear, looking out the window toward the Tsarnas back yard. "First, he would have looked out the bedroom window to see who it might be. But if the person was standing on the front porch, near the door, Dean wouldn't have been able to see him because of the overhang of the roof. He would probably have gotten his cane and gone downstairs. But he would not have opened the door to a stranger late at night. I'm sure of that.

"Unless," she added almost as an afterthought, "whoever it was convinced him there was something urgently important; perhaps that something had happened to me or one of the children." Their oldest son, she explained, suffered from a blood disease that, although controlled with medication, was a constant source of worry. "If someone had come to the door and told Dean that our son was sick, there's a good chance he might have opened the door without even thinking." Particularly, Dear thought, if the caller had identified himself as a messenger from Western Union and shown him what appeared to be a telegram.

"Would he normally have gone to the door wearing only his shorts?" the investigator asked.

Maggie shook her head. "Not unless it was some kind of emergency. My husband wasn't the best in the world about picking up his clothes. There were always trousers or cut-offs or a robe lying on the floor on his side of the bed. He would have put something on before going downstairs. Probably the cut-offs that he liked to wear around the house in the evening."

She could offer no explanation for the fact the boxer shorts that Milo had been wearing were on backwards.

When Dear mentioned the fact that tests had revealed traces of sperm in a tissue near the bed, she folded her arms around her as if trying to ward off a sudden chill. "We had a good sex life," she said. "It's possible he could have masturbated. I don't understand that part of it at all."

"Did you keep cotton in the house?"

"Yes, cotton balls, in our bedroom and the bath."

She had, she said, last spoken with her husband at approximately 4:30 p.m. on the Saturday prior to his death. He had called with good news. His brother, Fred, had contacted him about a meeting. They had agreed to get together the following day. "He sounded very upbeat," she said as she again began to cry softly. "He was convinced that a settlement was about to take place and that all the squabbling over control of the company was going to be put to rest. I had expected him to call Sunday and let me know how the meeting went, but I never heard from him. I just assumed things hadn't worked out. I thought about calling him several times, but I was busy with the children most of the day and, frankly, I didn't want to hear anything more about the legal feud unless it was good news. And if there had been good news, Dean would have called."

Instead, the news she ultimately received was the worst imaginable. The financial infighting, so much a topic of concern at the Milo home in recent days, seemed suddenly insignificant when compared to the far greater tragedy.

It was late when Bill Dear left the George Tsarnas home. Once again he drove to Everest Circle and parked in front of the deserted Milo house. For some time he sat, staring up at the bedroom window where the drapes were still slightly parted, perhaps last opened to see who might be calling at a late hour.

He reviewed the things Maggie Milo had told him about her husband. Why would a man of Dean Milo's confidence and build be afraid of the dark? What was it that concerned him so about being alone? What unknown demons had haunted him?

To find answers to his questions, Dear knew, he would have to get to know Dean Milo much better.

5

Larry Momchilov reacted just as Bill Dear expected he might when they met the following day at the Summit County sheriff's office to compare notes. "You're going to do what?" Momchilov asked after Dear advised him of what his next investigative step would be. There was an amused tone to his question.

"I'm going to move into Dean Milo's place for a while," Dear replied. Once Momchilov realized the plan was serious, he could not make up his mind whether it was a showboat move Dear was making to put an exclamation mark to the fact he delighted in using unorthodox methods or whether the man was simply a certifiable nut case. The idea reminded him of long-ago nighttime dares he and his friends had laid down in the neighborhood where he'd grown up. There had been an old, abandoned two-story house rumored to be haunted by the ghosts of former residents who had been mysteriously ax-murdered in their beds. Neither Momchilov nor any of his preteen pals had ever mustered the courage to get any closer than the tangled rosebushes that grew along the fence of the house's unattended front yard.

Dear made no attempt to explain his motivations. Nor did he point out that he had done similar things in the past and as a result managed to understand better the case on which he was working. Even had he wanted to make Momchilov understand, he doubted he could. All he knew was that to get a better grasp of the circumstances under which Dean Milo had met his sudden death, he needed a feel for the victim and his environment. To do so, he would have to try to think as Dean Milo thought, feel what he might have felt, see what he might have seen.

It wasn't something he could do from his room at the Holiday Inn.

The September moon was a rich orange ball on the evening horizon as Dear, having left his luggage behind at the Holiday Inn, stepped from his car and again walked toward the door of the Milo home on Everest Circle.

A stuffy smell greeted him as he entered through the front door, sidestepping the chalk outline on the floor in the entry hall. The chill inside the deserted house seemed more biting than any he had experienced since his arrival in Ohio.

Not bothering to turn on lights, Dear used the last gray remnants of the fading twilight to find his way to the stairs and slowly proceeded toward the master bedroom. The only sound he was aware of was his own breathing.

Once in the Milo bedroom, he slowly undressed, hanging his clothing on a valet stand near the closet where Dean Milo's expensive suits, silk ties, and starched shirts hung.

For several minutes, the investigator stood in the center of the room, looking at every detail. He was trying to mesmerize himself into his Dean Milo role—as if this were his own sanctuary. It was here he and his wife had retreated at the end of each day, to talk, to make love, to share secrets, perhaps argue. But Dear had the sudden feeling of being an interloper, of intruding on a privacy he had no right to invade. Still, if his plan was to work, he had to achieve that sense of identification with the unwitting man who was about to be murdered.

He walked to the king-sized bed, which had remained unmade, and lay down on the left side, where Dean Milo had obviously slept. Just a few feet away was the window where the parted drapes allowed the last faint light of day into the room. His head propped on a pillow, Dear tried to relax and allow himself to construct a hypothetical scenario of the events that preceded Milo's death.

For a moment he tried to imagine someone on the bed beside him. A woman? Perhaps another man?

Dear realized he was hardly breathing and that his body was tense, rigid with anticipation. He was waiting for the knock at the door which he imagined Milo had heard. For a moment he thought back to Larry Momchilov's reaction to his plan. Maybe this was crazy. How could he possibly explain the fact that he was lying in a dead man's bed, dressed only in a pair of shorts—which he had purposely put on backwards?

But, determined to lose himself in an imaginary world, he waited for whatever sound had urgently summoned Dean Milo. He lay there in the dark that Milo had feared, aware of the slow passage of long, silent minutes. Then he conjured up a frantic knock at the door below.

An involuntary jerk of fear accompanied the imagined sound and he looked to his right. Was there someone there to share his alarm? Did he say anything to that person? Lifting himself from the bed he silently walked to the window and stood at arm's length to avoid being seen by anyone from outside. Parting the drapes a few more inches, he saw again that the front porch was blocked from his view. It was impossible to see who might be there, calling with some urgent news. Normally, he thought, a visitor will knock or ring the doorbell, then step back to await the arrival of whoever answers. This visitor was remaining close to the door.

Trying to follow the thought processes of Milo, Dear returned to the bed, reached for the cane that Milo used for protection, then pulled his hand back. It was still there. That night Dean Milo had not carried the cane downstairs with him.

For a moment the fact the cane still stood near the bed raised the possibility of another scenario. Perhaps the caller had, in fact, stepped back from the door and Milo had been able to see him. Maybe it was someone he knew; someone he had no reason to fear or dress to greet. If so, there would have been no reason for the protection of the cane.

Dear walked quietly from the bedroom into the hallway and down the carpeted stairway. As he moved on tiptoes, he wondered if Dean Milo had entertained even the slightest suspicion that there was something sinister about this call.

Standing at the door, he waited several seconds before opening it, holding his breath in an attempt to hear or even sense a presence on the other side. Dear lifted himself to the balls of his feet to try to see through the small window set high in the front door. Though considerably taller than Dean Milo had been, he still would not have been able to see the visitor's face from that vantage point.

Now in an almost hypnotic state, Dear, still standing silently near the door, imagined a sudden, thundering series of knocks.

"Who is it?" Dear heard himself call out. The words had come from his mouth in an unconscious reaction, as if spoken by someone else.

"Western Union," he imagined the voice saying. "I have a telegram for Dean Milo. From Florida ... Clearwater, Florida."

How, Dear wondered, would Milo have reacted to such an announcement? To most people a late-night telegram could bring only bad news. Maybe something had happened to his ill son, Sotir. Had his condition worsened? Was he dying? Perhaps, God forbid, even dead? Why hadn't someone called? Why a goddamn telegram?

Feeling an unexpected panic tightening in his chest, Dear opened the door to what he imagined would be a large man; powerful, brutish, evil, pointing a gun. He imagined the man placing a rough hand with something in it over his mouth. The intruder quickly forced himself into the house, kicking the door closed behind him. He had, Dear thought, come to rob Dean Milo. But then he imagined his head exploding.

The investigator stumbled to his knees, puzzled and confused, trying to imagine the searing pain that the victim must have felt. So absorbed in his scenario was Dear that he experienced a sudden, sick dizziness. The floor where he lay seemed to be slowly revolving, drawing him down like quicksand. He heard himself groan even though he sensed no pain. The sound he made echoed in the dark hallway.

Then his mind conjured rustling nearby and he felt something soft—the pillow—being placed on the back of his head. There was another quick, cracking sound, which seemed to be coming from far away.

Then, nothing.

As he pulled himself from the floor, Dear realized that his knees were shaking, his entire body trembling. A clammy sweat clung to his body as he slowly made his way back upstairs. He took a shower in an attempt to wash away the sour odor of fear. As the stinging needles of hot water bathed his body he still shuddered. Though he had investigated more homicides than he could remember, the awareness of how quickly and unexpectedly it could happen had seemed sharper in that dark hallway. Now he knew how Dean Milo could have gone from the warmth of his bed to cold and sudden death.

Again stretched out on the bed, Dear tried to clear his head and review the moves he had made since "hearing" the knock at the door. There were, he knew, pieces of his re-enactment that didn't fit, but there was something else, some incident, that seemed important but elusive, that flirted just beyond mind's reach. It was like trying to recall the name of some silent movie star. It is there but the harder you try to recall it, the more difficult the maddening process becomes. He forced himself to relax and went limp on the bed.

It was in the early morning hours when it finally came to him. When he had looked out the window in an attempt to see the front porch, his peripheral vision had registered the fact that nearby homes on each side were within easy earshot and eyeshot of the Milo front porch.

He returned to the window again, this time looking for something not imagined.

The house to his left was no more than sixty feet away, the one to the right no more than thirty. Though aware that the police had already interviewed neighbors, Dear decided to talk with them again in the morning. The night of August 9, he knew, had been warm, and it was likely that windows were left open to allow the cool night breezes—and possibly some unusual sounds—in. Even if that were not the case, how could the loud, insistent knocking or the ringing of the doorbell that must have taken place not have been heard by someone? And what of two gunshots?

Unable to sleep, he set about to better acquaint himself with the Milo house. For the next few hours he inspected every square foot, making himself used to the surroundings he would live in for the next several days.

The house spoke volumes about its owner. As he looked in the bedroom closet he saw what must have been Maggie Milo's handiwork. Each suit had the proper color-coordinated shirt hanging next to it. Each of the ties was pre-knotted. Dean Milo, the tough, hard-driving businessman, had apparently been totally lacking in fashion sense or the ability to choose his own wardrobe. Hell, he couldn't even properly knot a tie. Dear recalled Maggie's insistence that her husband had feared the dark and being alone. In many ways Dean Milo had been a dependent child.

On the nightstands near the bed Dear now noticed, as the police had found earlier, evidence that the left-side sleeper and the right-side sleeper had quite different tastes in bedtime reading. Stacked beneath the small reading lamp on Dean Milo's side were copies of *Playboy, Penthouse, Gallery*, and *Hustler*. Near Maggie's pillow were a Bible and several Christian magazines. Dear thumbed through some of the magazines from each stack. What different dreams on the two sides of the bed.

Down the hall were the bedrooms of the children, each colorfully decorated with posters, toys, and stuffed animals. Going from room to room, Dear sensed a genuine parental devotion. In each room he felt a warmth that seemed absent in the master bedroom.

The first floor of the Milo house could have served as the set for one of television's popular family sitcoms. There was a friendliness about the casually decorated den with its comfortable couch and stuffed chairs, a large, brightly lit aquarium and numerous framed family photographs. The kitchen was obviously one of the primary gathering places of the Milo family. It was there they ate most of their meals, where hurried notes to each other were attached to the door of the Refrigerator. Dear imagined Maggie seated at the breakfast bar, drinking coffee and reading the morning paper after her husband had hurried away to work.

Just a few steps away was a formal dining room, spotless and obviously seldom used. Standing on the thick carpet, Dear assumed it was reserved for special occasions like Thanksgiving and Christmas, or those times when Dean Milo entertained business guests.

Downstairs was a full-sized basement, where Maggie did laundry and the children played on bad weather days.

As he roamed the house, casually flipping through record albums, Dean Milo's business papers, notes Maggie had made to herself about school activities and grocery needs, Dear's thoughts kept retreating to the master bedroom. Unlike any other part of the house, it was cold. There was a feeling of tension there that seemed somehow isolated from the rest of the home.

It was four in the morning before Dear returned to Milo's bed and finally dropped off to a sleep made restless by images of an ominous intruder waiting at the door and the wounded body lying in the foyer. By six, Dear was up, eager to search for answers to new questions. He showered, then, in an attempt to further assume the role of Milo, tried on one of his suits. That only confirmed the fact that he was much taller and thinner than the murder victim. The clothes he had worn the previous evening would have to suffice.

Stepping from the door, he sat down on the front porch, looking at the houses on the left and right, then out the cul-de-sac to where it spilled onto Bath Hills Boulevard. There, directly in line with the Milo home, was a two-story house with an open upstairs window. Sitting there, Dear realized he was directly in the line of vision of anyone who might be standing near the window. So, too, might have been a late-night caller to the Milo front door. Dear remained seated on the porch, considering the task that awaited him, for almost two hours. Finally, he rose.

It was time to begin the tedious task of knocking on doors.

The home to the left of the Milos belonged to a middle-aged couple who insisted they had heard or seen nothing in the early morning hours of August 10. The wife, obviously weary of answering the same questions as had been posed to her earlier by Bath police officials, once again pointed out that she had been up late that night, packing for a trip to Europe. If there had been any unusual occurrences next door, she said, she would likely have heard something.

One of the troubling aspects of the crime was the speculation on the part of the coroner about the time at which Milo had been murdered. Basing his judgment on the state of rigor mortis, which is not always a reliable gauge, Dr. A. H. Kyriakides had insisted the time of death was late afternoon or early evening of August 10. Dear, on the other hand, felt strongly that Milo's death had occurred much earlier—probably between one and four in the morning. Why, for instance, would he have been in bed, then dressed only in shorts, in the afternoon? And wasn't it far more likely that someone would have seen a killer coming or going during the daylight hours? Wouldn't a killer wait until late at night?

The investigator was aware that several people had telephoned Dean at home during the morning and afternoon of August 10 and had got no answer. And Dean had made several engagements for that day, none of which he kept. One of those had been for lunch, a time when he hated to be alone.

If not already dead, where had Dean Milo been? The murder *could* have occurred during the time frame advanced by the coroner, yet Dear, who had battled against stubborn medical examiners most of his professional life, held to his own theory. The business of determining the time of death was not the exact science detective novels and television police shows would have the public believe.

Thus he concentrated his questioning on the theory that Milo had been assaulted in the early morning hours of August 10.

An older woman who lived in the house on the other side of the Milos recalled that she had been battling the flu during the early hours of the tenth hardly sleeping at all. "Even if I had nodded off," she insisted, "I'm a very light sleeper and would have heard any unusual activity in the neighborhood, particularly if it had been right next door."

Dear had no reason not to believe her but was troubled by the fact two people very near the Milo house had, in all likelihood, been awake at the time of the murder but had heard nothing. Perhaps a knocking at the door, even in the early morning hours, would have raised no suspicion and therefore not been memorable. But gunshots, even if muffled by a silencer, should have been a different matter.

Dear spent the entire day knocking at doors, asking questions he knew the residents had already heard. Experience, however, had convinced him that the everyday citizen is more apt to confide in a private investigator promising to keep the conversation confidential than a police officer whose visit might result in a grand jury appearance or names and pictures in the newspaper.

Several whom Dear spoke with speculated that the murder had been a mob hit but offered no basis for that theory. That such rumors were spreading, however, worried Dear. People wary of being involved in any kind of criminal investigation were doubly shy if there might be reason to fear the Mafia.

The litany Dear was hearing became more predictable with each visit to houses in the neighborhood: "I wish I could help you, but ..."

He purposely waited before trying the house he had so carefully studied earlier from the Milo front porch. He was convinced that it had the best vantage point from which to see anyone knocking at the door. The man who answered Dear's knock was R. D. Hall, a tall, handsome man in his early forties.

"As I've already told the police," he said, "I didn't see anything." There was a firm politeness in his voice that indicated he was eager for the questioning to be finished. His wife stood next to him in the doorway, wearing a worried expression that signaled an alert Dear had hoped for. He noticed that her hands were shaking slightly as her husband spoke.

Dear, smiling and friendly, pressed the matter. "If you had seen something, anything at all, would you tell me?"

Hall hesitated briefly before answering. "Frankly," he said, "I'd have to think about it. The word going around, you know, is that the mob was probably involved in this. I have a family to consider, you understand."

Dear did understand. No authority can guarantee protection against a criminal bent on silencing a witness. It was a truth he had learned firsthand.

As a fourteen-year-old in Miami, Dear had once seen a couple fleeing the scene of a grocery store holdup as he rode his bicycle along his predawn paper route. He had followed the couple to their destination, taken down the address, and called the police. After the arrests were made, the *Miami Herald* had run a story that portrayed him as a "hero." The story had also printed information about where he and his family lived.

Ultimately, the holdup couple were released on bail and, just a few days later, attempted to run him down with their car. Again the police were called. They assured the Dear family that their son would be watched carefully. Two days later the couple again tried to run him down. Dear and his parents were unable to relax until the pair was tried and sent to prison.

"I don't think you have anything to worry about," Dear told Hall. "I frankly don't believe that any kind of organized crime is responsible for what happened to Dean Milo." Even as he spoke he could read Hall's unspoken reaction: You don't think I have anything to worry about? Dean Milo's murder had brought a rude awakening to the neighborhood. In today's violent society, death could be just around the corner, regardless of the neighborhood. Milo's money and status hadn't saved him. Neither had the fact he lived in a neighborhood populated by upstanding citizens.

Hall smiled for the first time since Dear's arrival. "Well," he said, "I guess I don't have to worry about it one way or another, do I? I didn't see anything."

"Mr. Hall, I guarantee you confidentiality ..."

"That's nice," Hall replied, sarcasm seeping into his voice.

Hall's mention of the fact he had a family to protect and the anxiety Dear had sensed in Hall's wife hinted that the couple might know something they were refusing to admit. Already certain he would visit again, he turned the subject from his investigation. Hall told him he had one son in college and another who would be attending the following fall. Dear and Hall also compared the Ohio weather to that back in Texas.

Returning to the Holiday Inn late in the afternoon, Dear checked his telephone messages. Maggie Milo had called, as had Paul Vaughn and George Tsarnas. Dennis McEaneney, a reporter from the *Akron Beacon Journal*, had also left his number. In view of the no-publicity agreement he had struck with Chief of Detectives Duvall, Dear quickly dismissed the last.

Among the stack of messages were two unfamiliar names. One had called more than a dozen times. Returning the calls of the unknowns headed his list of priorities.

6

Attorney George Tsarnas, using his law firm's financing, had posted an attention-getting twenty-five-thousand-dollar reward "for information leading to the arrest and conviction of the person or persons involved in the death of Constantine R. (Dean) Milo."

The announcement, which had received prominent play in the *Beacon Journal* and had been broadcast on numerous occasions by the electronic media, had urged anyone with information to contact Dear or the police. Tsarnas had agreed to include the private investigator's name after Dear explained to him the difficulty many informants have with talking to law enforcement officials. For one thing, he pointed out, the police demand a written statement for their records, while a private investigator can and generally will agree to nothing more than oral information. Additionally, police can be forced by a sharp attorney representing a defendant to adhere to the judicial procedure known as discovery to reveal the identity of an informant. A good private investigator, like a good journalist, will protect a source to the extent that he will accept jail time on a contempt of court charge before betraying a confidence.

The decision by Tsarnas to post the reward had pleased Dear greatly. Greed, he had long ago learned, was a tremendously effective tool to be used in the pursuit of criminals. Even the most close-mouthed informant, at one time dead set on protecting a friend or associate, can be drawn over the line by the prospect of earning a great deal of money for a minimum of effort. Such motivation overcomes conscience, fear, and rationality, setting friend against friend, family member against family member.

Dear had worked more than one case in which the information provided had resulted in the indictment of the informer's own brother.

And in Akron, where a downward-spiraling economy was a constant concern, the chances of someone coming forward in hopes of earning Tsarnas's reward were good.

Dear had argued with Tsarnas on only one point. He had lobbied to have the "conviction" part of the bargain eliminated. Streetwise snitches, generally familiar with judicial procedure, would be immediately aware that whatever information they might have could well lead to an arrest—but that conviction was a different matter. Before the final verdict, there were the obstacles of clever defense attorneys, jurors with poor judgment, ill-prepared prosecutors, or law officials who might not have carried out their investigative tasks competently. Even if the prosecution of the case was a textbook example of good police work, the judicial system was a maze of legal loopholes through which murderers often slipped.

"Look," Dear had argued to Tsarnas, "I know of a man who confronted his estranged wife in the driveway of their home and shot and killed her in cold blood. She was carrying their five-year-old daughter in her arms at the time. Police opened the guy's locked car and found a note he'd written, outlining his reasons for killing the woman. But his conviction was overturned on appeal—because his car had been searched for Pete's sake. The police didn't have a damn search warrant.

"Today that guy lives with and is raising the kid who watched him kill her mother."

He went on to explain that had an informant been needed to make a case against John Hinckley for the shooting of President Reagan, the informant could not have collected under the same conditions Tsarnas had set down because Hinckley had been found not guilty by reason of insanity.

"I'll be the last to argue that certain measures are necessary to keep our judicial system from going head-over-teakettle," Dear said, "but somewhere common sense has to come into play. If we're going to get any help on this thing, you've got to change the 'arrest and conviction' part of the deal to 'arrest and indictment.'"

Tsarnas, he knew, had little experience in such matters. He was viewing the matter as a businessman. By steadfastly sticking to the demand for a conviction before paying off, he was protecting his firm's money.

Dear was pleased that the attorney had agreed to reconsider the provisions if nothing materialized from the offer as it was originally worded. He decided to push the matter no further.

Now, seated on the edge of his motel room bed, Dear shuffled through the stack of phone messages several times, noting that someone named Glen Gosdin had been the most aggressive caller. The times listed on the message sheets indicated that some of his calls had come only ten minutes apart. In all, Gosdin had called fourteen times during Dear's twenty-two-hour absence from the motel.

Dialing the number, he waited through several rings before a raspy voice answered. "Checkmate Lounge."

Having expected to reach a home, Dear was taken aback momentarily. "Is there a Glen Gosdin there?" he finally asked.

"Hang on."

Dear heard the receiver land with a thud on what he assumed must be the bar. As he waited he could hear the mixture of crowd noises and the jangling sounds from a jukebox that seemed to be in competition with a nearby television set tuned to a baseball game.

He was conjuring a mental image of what the Checkmate Lounge might look like when Glen Gosdin's voice interrupted. "This Dear?"

Dear replied, "Is this Glen Gosdin?"

"Right. I'm calling about that reward business. Is it for real?"

"It depends on what kind of information you have."

"I've got all you need," Gosdin replied. Obviously enjoying the cat-and-mouse game, he began to laugh.

"Okay," Dear said, "I'm listening."

"Fuck that, buddy. My mama didn't raise no fool. I ain't talking about this kind of shit on the phone. It's gotta be eyeball-to-fucking-eyeball, pal." He said he would be at the Checkmate Lounge for the remainder of the evening and gave the address.

Dear agreed to meet him and hung up. Before leaving, however, he dialed the number of the other unknown caller. A man named Richard Eubanks answered, from what appeared to be his home phone. By the sound of the man's voice, Dear judged him to be in his early to mid-fifties.

"I'm calling about the Dean Milo case," Eubanks said. "The reward. I don't know how people usually go about these things, but I think I have some information that might be of use to you. What do I do?"

Dear briefly explained to him the sequence of events that would lead to an informant's being paid the twenty-five thousand dollars. "All I can tell you, really, is that if your information is good and meets the qualifications, you have my word you'll get the money." He was surprised at how willing the man on the other end of the line was to tell his story.

"Okay, look," he began. "I'm a cab driver here in Akron. This friend of mine, another cabby named Danny, is gay. And he's got this friend named Gypsy who dates this bartender at one of the clubs on Market Street. Now, I heard this Gypsy telling his bartender friend that he'd been turning tricks for this guy Dean Milo."

Dear tried to mask the fact that the information interested him; that it might possibly lend some credence to his earlier notion that Milo might have been with a gay lover on the night he was killed. "So what does this lead you to believe?" he asked the cab driver.

"It wouldn't surprise me if Gypsy's roommate killed Milo. The guy's mean and jealous and has a terrible temper. In fact, I wouldn't be that surprised if Gypsy himself did the guy in, particularly if this Milo guy beat him out of some money. Gypsy is the kind who would rather do something than argue, if you know what I mean."

"Are you telling me that Dean Milo was gay?"

"No, I'm not saying any such thing. I wouldn't have known the man if he walked into my living room. I'm just telling you what I've heard."

Dear wrote down the address of the Market Street club where the bartender worked, the informant's address, and the name of the cab company he worked for. He promised he would be back in touch.

The conversation had opened a new avenue of possibilities for Dear. Suppose Dean Milo was involved with members of the gay community? What if there had been no one at the door that night? What if the killer, someone named Gypsy or whatever, had been in the house, maybe even in Milo's bed?

On the other hand, the caller might have been someone's jealous lover. Maybe Milo had known the man at the door and had answered in hopes of reasoning through a lovers' quarrel. Perhaps the caller had been a third party invited for a threesome. Each scenario, Dear realized, was more bizarre than the last. And each produced another list of unanswered questions. That's the way the whole investigation had gone.

He hoped a visit to the Checkmate Lounge would lift his spirits.

Dear drove to the 800 block of North Main Street and pulled into the congested parking lot adjacent to the Checkmate, a striptease go-go joint that had managed to hang on long after the music the women undressed to had lost its popularity. It was just after six in the afternoon as he walked into the darkened club, which was obviously a stopover for many Akron blue-collar workers before going home to wives and kids. For much of the clientele, a few beers while watching expressionless teenage girls gyrate and show their breasts offered a welcome postponement of the two-dollar woes and second-mortgage worries that waited at home.

Dear had barely taken a seat at the bar when Gosdin approached him. He stood no more than five-eight and had no doubt given up on his weight problem long ago. He wore a Cleveland Indians baseball cap and a red T-shirt with the message "Kill 'em all, Let God sort 'em out" printed across the front. Even in the semidarkness of the club, it was easy to tell that his faded jeans and well-worn tennis shoes had not seen the inside of a washing machine in some time.

"You Dear?" he asked aggressively.

Even before Dear could answer, Gosdin had turned his

back, motioning in the direction of a table in the corner near the small stage where the strip show was going on.

For the first several minutes Dear had to reassure the thirty-year-old man sitting across from him that he would, indeed, be given the reward if his information led to Dean Milo's killer. He did, however, stop short of giving Gosdin the fifty dollars he asked for up front.

Two watery Scotches and several tiresome songs later, Gosdin hunched forward, his face just inches from Dear's, and began to tell his story.

"Word I get," he said in a conspiratorial voice, "is that this asshole Milo was heavy into dealing drugs. That's how he got so rich so fast. The guy had a helluva cash flow, thanks to folks who like to stuff shit up their noses."

Dear made little attempt to show interest in yet another theory. Generally, if someone is involved with drugs, either as a user or a pusher, that is the first information investigators get wind of. There had been no one, not friends, family, or business associates, who had even hinted that Dean Milo was involved in drugs.

"Who told you Milo dealt drugs?"

Gosdin feigned shock. "Are you fucking crazy? I'm a dead man if I tell you that."

"You could be in big trouble if you don't."

"Yeah, but not dead, man. Besides, what are you gonna do? You run and tell the cops that I told you this shit and I'm gonna deny I ever seen your ass. Your word against mine, man; that simple."

Gosdin's words had been spoken rapidly. But he seemed to sense that he was having no luck in intimidating the man across from him, and he slowed his speech, spreading his hands in front of him, palms up, in the gesture of a man coming clean. "Look," he said, "just hear me out, okay? If you're gonna learn who wasted Dean Milo, you've got to look into the drug business. You need a guy like me to get you started down the right road; somebody to tell you what rocks you gotta look under. See what I'm saying?"

Dear did not change expression. "You'll do it for the reward…"

"You got it, man. See, this Milo dude, he owned a piece of a mob restaurant here in town. I know that. He—"

"How do you know it's mob-owned?" Dear interrupted.

"Come off it, man. Everybody knows. Fucking everybody."

Dear winced as Led Zeppelin took over for Alice Cooper on the jukebox. "The difference in what you're saying and what can be proven is like night and day," he told Gosdin.

"Hey, you're supposed to be the hot-shit detective. Poke around. I know what I know. And I know a drug-related mob hit when I read about it. Think about this: Dean traveled all over hell and gone, right? Places like Miami, Tampa, Philadelphia, Chicago, Detroit, Phoenix, not to mention Cleveland which, in case you ain't aware, is right up the fucking highway. All those places got mob people and drug dealing running out the ass. You figure it."

Gosdin was retreating back to the belligerence he had shown when they first sat down. Tired from his long day of walking the Milo neighborhood, knocking on doors, Dear considered ending the interview. But, he decided, why not play out this fool's game?

"The Milos had stores in all those cities," Dear pointed out.

"Yeah, and why was that? I'll tell you. It was so the families could be kept informed about whatever was shaking with their business, man. They wanted to keep an eye on their investment."

"So, you're saying the Mafia owns part of Milo Barber and Beauty Supply?" Dear asked. This time there was sarcasm in his voice. Gosdin, he had decided, was a man on a fishing expedition, casting in all directions in hopes of pulling out a big, fat reward.

It was neither the first nor would it be the last time the investigator had wasted his time on the ramblings of an informer who had nothing worthwhile to tell. Almost without exception, when the authorities or the family of a victim post a reward the hustlers, con men, and screwballs come running with their five-and-dime, shot-in-the-dark theories.

There was an elementary logic to Gosdin's theory. And if on the off chance it turned out that Dean Milo's death had been somehow drug-related, he and some ambulance-chasing lawyer could come running, insisting that the reward money was his because he had provided the information.

Throughout his career, when reward money had been involved, Dear had always sought to be fair. If anything, he had bent over backward to see that those who had legitimately earned rewards were paid. More than once he'd battled with people who had put up rewards and then tried to avoid payment on some trumped-up technicality. Dear had, during his years of investigative work, earned a reputation for paying off as promised.

Though he thought it unlikely, he considered the possibility that Gosdin had luckily hit the nail on the head. There seemed to be some question over exactly where Dean Milo had obtained the financing necessary to expand the company from what amounted to a cottage industry into a ninety-seven-store chain virtually overnight. Perhaps his desire to eliminate the others from the family business was not, as people were insisting, to clear away the deadwood but, instead, to prevent their learning about the darker side of his business. Dealings with organized crime could explain Milo's strange fears of the dark and being alone.

Gosdin, sensing that Dear's interest was waning, began talking in hurried sentences again. "Hey, I don't know if the mob owned any of the guy's businesses for sure. But, shit, it just makes sense, doesn't it? They gotta have legitimate fronts, right? They gotta hide their money somewhere.

"Maybe they loaned this dude money to get his business going big time. If that was the case, they would have wanted a piece of the action. You can bet on that."

"I don't bet," Dear answered dryly. "And I don't particularly like this place—or you—so I'm getting out of here."

"Hey, wait a minute, man ..."

Standing to leave, Dear looked down on the disappointed face beneath the baseball cap. The macho, wise-cracking Gosdin had suddenly taken on the look of a child whose lollipop had been taken away.

Pulling on his jacket, Dear allowed his informant one final chance. "Listen," he said, "you told me that Dean Milo dealt drugs. Give me a name."

Gosdin shook his head, staring down at the drink in front

of him. "Man, I told you. I can't tell you that. I ain't putting my neck in the noose for anybody. Not even for your fucking twenty-five grand."

Dear shrugged. "You haven't told me a thing," he said.

"Okay, asshole, believe what you want. Doesn't make a shit to me. But when you look into what I'm telling you, you'll hit paydirt. I guaran-damn-tee it. I know the score, man. I know a drug-related hit when I hear about it."

Dear turned to leave as Gosdin continued talking. "Don't worry, man, I'll be around. Remember that. When all this shit gets settled we won't forget who told you where to look, will we?"

Not until he stepped into the cool night air of the parking lot did Dear realize how mind-numbing the music and the sound of Glen Gosdin's voice had been. He took several deep breaths before getting into the car, tuning the radio to an "easy listening" station, and heading in the direction of Everest Circle and another night in the Milo house.

7

Over the next three weeks the investigation settled into a demanding routine of interviews with friends and business associates of Dean Milo, and the reading and rereading of case reports in the hope that someone, somewhere might have overlooked something that would give new direction to the pursuit.

In an effort to cover as much ground as possible and still maintain the coordination the investigation required, the four men working the case full-time agreed to break into teams. Momchilov would continue as the Summit County Sheriff's Department's man in charge and would work in partnership with Dear. Lieutenant Lewis of the sheriff's office and Sergeant Munsey, the only Bath police officer still assigned to the case, would work together. Lewis and Munsey, who were given their assignments by Momchilov, would not have liked the whispered observations in the courthouse that the investigation now had an A team and a B team.

For Dear, whose penchant for organization bordered on the fanatic, the arrangement was ideal. With each passing day, his admiration for Momchilov's low-key but dogged pursuit of the investigation grew. At the same time, Momchilov's respect for Dear had steadily increased as he took note of the long hours the private investigator was putting in on the case. The relationship, now on a first-name basis, was fast growing beyond professional admiration into genuine friendship.

Dear had spent a week living in the Milo home before moving back into the Holiday Inn. Though nothing in the spacious, lonely house pointed to a motive for murder, he had, he felt, learned a good deal about the victim. He had thumbed through the books and record collection in the den, gaining some insight into Milo's tastes. He read through stacks of complicated business papers that Dean had been working on at home. If Dean Milo wasn't a workaholic, Dear assumed, he was well on the way.

There was nothing that would indicate Milo had sensed he might be in danger. Even the relatively harmless cane had remained in its place near the bed that night.

And while the house served up small bits of understanding, it also produced puzzling questions. The fact that tapes of pornographic movies had been found hidden in Milo's closet troubled Dear. Nowhere in the house was there a videocassette recorder that would have allowed Milo to view them.

On the last night that Dear had stayed at Everest Circle, a friend of Milo's had driven by and, noticing lights burning, had stopped. Thinking that Maggie might have moved back in, he wanted to say hello. When Dear answered the door, the caller was speechless for a moment. "For just a second there," he told the investigator, "I thought you were Dean. The way you were standing, the gestures you made when you opened the door. Your voice even sounds a little like his."

Dear had followed up on the information provided by the taxi driver who had suggested Milo was involved in the gay community. He located and talked with the homosexual known as Gypsy. A frightened, meek youngster barely out of his teens, he admitted having said that he turned tricks for Milo but insisted it was only idle boasting, an attempt to add some degree of status to his miserable life. "I just read about the murder in the paper," he explained, "and came up with the story. I thought it would make my roommate jealous." With that he smiled weakly. "You know," he continued, "it really would have been something if somebody like this rich Milo guy had been paying me."

Dear shook his head at the pathetic confession. Gypsy's reward from his lover had been a black eye and several loosened teeth. Obviously, the idea of making him jealous had worked.

After visits to hangouts favored by Akron's gay community, Dear found no evidence to suggest Dean Milo had ever traveled the same route. It was time, the investigator determined, to lay aside the theory. The fact the boxer shorts he wore to his death had been on backwards indicated nothing more than the haste with which he had put them on before going downstairs to answer the door.

Using names provided him by Momchilov, Dear had discreetly gotten in touch with several figures reported to be familiar with local organized crime activity. Promising confidentiality, Dear pointed out to those he spoke with that all indications were that Milo's murderer had been a professional hit man. Much of the investigation, he informed them, was centering on the possibility of mob involvement with Milo B&B.

The message he took away from each of the conversations was that the state's Mafia activities were headquartered in Cleveland but that there was no indication anyone there had been involved in Milo's murder. If Milo's murder was, indeed, a mob hit, it had been organized and done by out-of-state talent.

After spending several days at the Bank of Ohio, poring over Milo's financial transactions and talking with loan officers, Dear could find nothing that pointed to organized crime financing of the company. Milo, he determined, had no trouble borrowing large sums of money because he paid back his loans on time. Officials at the Bank of Ohio pointed out that Milo had, over the years, borrowed escalating amounts and there had never been a problem. They had, in fact, been prepared to lend him more whenever he asked.

It was a situation Dear had seen before. The bank executives had viewed Dean Milo as a rising financial star and eagerly hatched their interest-earning wagon to him. "It was thrilling to watch how Dean built that business," one loan officer admitted.

Among Milo's banking records were papers showing his 2 percent interest in the restaurant chain that several people had indicated was mob-controlled. Dear noted as he read through the documents that Dean's brother, Fred, also owned a small interest in the chain as did Summit County Coroner Kyriakides. Though Dear felt no warmth for the coroner after arguments over the time of Milo's death and the knowledge he had withheld evidence from Momchilov, he was not ready to believe that the doctor was financially involved with organized crime.

All of which put the investigation back to square one. It was time, Dear decided, to call in more help. There was just too much to be done, too much ground to cover, for the number of people working the case. Already there was grumbling from the press and many of the community's prominent citizens about the evident lack of progress.

If this investigation failed, Dear thought, it was not going to be because of a lack of manpower.

In response to a telephone call to his office in Dallas, three men from Dear's investigative agency were immediately en route to Akron. Dick Riddle and Joe Villanueva drove company cars, while Frank Lambert piloted the company-owned C55 Baron.

Each of the men summoned by Dear had a unique investigative talent.

The thirty-eight-year-old Riddle, a former police lieutenant who had left his position with a department in the Louisville, Kentucky, suburbs, was best described as the person who acted out the good cop role in any good cop—bad cop interrogation. Nature had equipped him with the ideal personality for the part. His sincere smile and easy habit of being a genuinely sympathetic listener made people look on him as a favorite uncle. Along with that, he was persistent. If he didn't succeed at first, he would try again, and again, until the job was completed.

Upon his arrival, Riddle was assigned the task of around-the-clock surveillance of Fred Milo. "The guy bothers me," Dear explained, "but I don't have a handle on him. That's your job. Time your sleep schedule to coincide with his. Shadow him wherever he goes. We need to know what makes this guy tick."

Joe Villanueva, a tall, husky, handsome twenty-three-year-old, was a street-smart Mexican-American who could blend into areas where others might stick out like a sore thumb. He had been trained by Dear since his teenage years and had polished his ability to appear comfortable at the most posh country club gathering one night and a seedy back-alley nightclub the next. His courage, tempered with caution and good judgment, had made him the man Dear called on most often when facing potentially dangerous situations.

Villanueva's assignment was to keep tabs on Lonnie Curtis.

Frank Lambert, thirty-one, had served in Vietnam as a Green Beret, spending much of his time as a tunnel rat. One of the most hazardous jobs the army offered, it called for him to crawl down into the maze of underground tunnels dug by the Vietcong, seeking out enemy troops. He was a man of great physical strength, and he hid a fierce temper beneath his quiet, soft-spoken demeanor.

An expert pilot capable of landing a plane on small, rugged surfaces, Lambert was assigned by Dear to take aerial photographs of Bath. A much better picture of what might have transpired—how the killer got to and from his Everest Circle destination—could be seen from the air. The finest topographic map available could not compare to the value of the shots Lambert would take from the air.

The arrival of this personnel freed Dear of the frustration of needing to be in several places at the same time, and allowed him the opportunity to pursue other avenues.

One of the things he had been wanting to do since his arrival in Ohio was to re-enact the crime. The Bath Police Department and Summit County sheriff's office at last agreed to participate. Only Larry Momchilov seemed to feel there was genuine merit to the idea.

Still, even he was surprised at the elaborate preparation they found as they arrived at the Milo house.

Dear had purchased a six-foot manikin, dressed it in a pair of Milo's boxer shorts, and had carefully positioned it in the chalked outline of the body.

At Dear's instruction, police officers stationed themselves inside the houses and in the yards on each side of the Milo residence. Another officer was positioned at the entrance of the cul-de-sac, near the front of R. D. Hall's home. Their job was to determine what, if any, noises might have carried to other points in the neighborhood. And the officer near the Hall house was to be alert to whatever might have been seen from that vantage point.

Another officer was sent to the Milo back yard with special instructions to pay attention to the back yard of a neighbor directly behind the Milo house, where a dog had been penned outside on the night of the murder. The Saint Bernard's owner had assured Dear during an interview that the dog could hear leaves drop, yet he had not heard it barking on the night of August 9. Dear wanted to know why.

Despite the elaborate preparations and cooperation from the local law enforcement agencies, Dear had not managed to persuade them to carry out the re-enactment just as he wanted. He had argued that the drama should be played out at two in the morning—the approximate time of the murder according to Dear—but the Bath police had insisted on doing it during the day to coincide with the coroner's estimated time of death. Additionally, there was concern over a late-night disruption of an already uneasy neighborhood that felt the crime should long ago have been solved.

Dear, who had given himself the role of Dean Milo, explained the parts others would be expected to play. David Bailey, a detective from the sheriff's office, would be the hit man. Others would be stationed at strategic points in the house to observe.

Assignments made, Dear excused himself and walked up the stairs to the master bedroom.

Lying on the bed, he did not hear the first knock at the door by Detective Bailey. Not until the officer pounded a second time did Dear get up and move to the window, where he parted the drapes slightly. No matter what angle he tried, he could not see the man knocking at the door.

From the top of the stairs he shouted, "Who's there?"

"Western Union."

At the door, Dear stood on tiptoes just as he had done that first night alone in the house, straining to see who was on the other side of the door. Though easily four inches taller than Milo, he was able to see only the top of Bailey's head. The observing detectives watched the play-acting in silence.

Again trying to conjure the thought patterns of Dean Milo,

Dear forced himself to think of what a telegram at such an hour might mean. He waited several seconds before opening the door.

David Bailey ad-libbed his part expertly. The killer, he knew, would have no way of knowing exactly what to expect from the man responding to his knock. He would have had to play things by ear.

As Dear reached out for the telegram, Bailey handed it to him, then hurriedly pushed forward into the house, catching Dear off balance. He had play-acted the element of surprise perfectly and quickly pointed an unloaded .32 pistol at Dear's head.

Bailey then spun Dear around, putting his left hand, in which he held a wad of cotton, over Dear's mouth. Exerting a strength that Dear had not anticipated, Bailey applied pressure that immediately brought him to his knees.

"Don't panic," Bailey said. "This is a robbery."

Then he said "Bang!"

Dear never had a chance; neither had Dean Milo.

The investigator sank to the tiled floor in the hallway, waiting as Bailey found a pillow, placed it over his head, and feigned a second shot. Then he was quickly out the door, closing it behind him, racing down the cul-de-sac to his car. Dear lay still until he heard the sound of Bailey driving away.

If it hadn't happened that way, he was confident it was close. The nagging question of Dean Milo's offering no resistance was answered. Totally caught off guard by the intruder, he had not had an opportunity. No matter how suspicious someone might be, regardless of precautions he might take, there was no way to prepare for the violent act of a determined killer who had speed and the element of surprise on his side.

They ran through the scene several more times, using the manikin and real bullets so the officers stationed outside might measure the noise level from the shots. Dear wanted to determine the position of Milo at the time he had been shot. By seeing where the spent shell casings landed, it seemed most likely that Milo had been kneeling or lying face down at the time the bullets were fired.

Almost without exception, the officers who participated in and witnessed the elaborate re-creation of the crime would call it the strangest—and most fascinating—thing they had taken part in during their law enforcement careers.

"I'm surprised," one said after the drama had been acted out, "that Dear didn't insist on digging Dean Milo up so he could use the real body."

"Well," a fellow officer replied, "you have to give the guy points for one thing: He's the most thorough sonuvabitch I've ever seen work a case."

The experiment convinced Dear that he could eliminate any member of Dean Milo's family as the possible triggerman. Although there are frequently murders within families, he could not imagine a scenario in which a close relative of the victim could summon the courage to collect a pillow to be used as a makeshift silencer, then methodically fire the second shot, execution-style. The time lapse that had to occur as the killer sought the pillow in the den was the key. A brother, even a wife, might stab a family member repeatedly, inflicting dozens of wounds, but in mad, nonstop fashion, without pause for thought. One might empty every bullet in the chamber of a pistol, but the shots would be fired as quickly as the trigger could be pulled. Only after the crime had been completed and the murderous insanity past would the person realize fully what he had done. Only on the rarest occasions would a family killer make certain the victim was dead with a final coup de grace. In the case of Dean Milo, the killer had obviously wanted to be certain.

As they sat in the den of the Milo home, reviewing the sequence of events, several detectives shook their heads as they offered their contributions to the discussion. Those stationed outside had clearly heard the shots. Even had the shots been muffled by some kind of silencer, they felt they would likely have been aware of some noise because of the close proximity of the other houses to the Milo home. At two in the morning, without competition from the normal daytime noises, the sounds must have been even louder. The dog in the yard behind the Milos most certainly would have gone crazy as soon as he heard the first shot.

Dear was more certain than ever that someone in the neighborhood must have seen or heard something but for whatever reason remained fearful of coming forward.

And what of the cotton particles found on Milo's body?

Was it remotely possible that a professional killer would have planned to use cotton to gag his victim? Did the possibility remain that there was someone else in the house that night who had come downstairs and found Dean Milo mortally wounded and tried to wipe away the blood with cotton balls retrieved from Maggie Milo's dressing table? Or had cotton somehow been used as a makeshift silencer when the first shot was fired?

The idea of a trained killer resorting to such an amateurish method did not set well with any of the officers. Still, given the alternatives, it seemed the most logical guess. On the other hand, the possibility that an inexperienced killer was responsible could not be dismissed.

While the discussion continued, Dick Riddle and Joe Villanueva, relieved of their surveillance duties for the afternoon, carefully combed the Milo yard with powerful metal detectors brought from Texas, hoping an overlooked murder weapon might be found. Later joined by Dear, they also searched the neighborhood near Fred Milo's and Lonnie Curtis's homes, peered into drainage gutters, and lifted manhole covers. All they got for their efforts were strange looks from passersby and a lot of questions from inquisitive children playing in front yards.

While Dear and his associates were conducting their fruitless search, Frank Lambert was flying Lieutenant Lewis and Sergeant Munsey to Richmond, Virginia. Momchilov's check of Dean Milo's telephone records had revealed that several calls had been made to a residence there. Further checking showed that the number belonged to a woman named Patsy Caldwell, who had been a sweetheart of Milo's before he and Maggie had married.

The report Lewis and Munsey returned with added another

angle to the life Dean Milo had led.

Reluctant to talk at first, Patsy Caldwell finally explained that she and Dean had gone together for some time prior to his marriage. Only recently, she said, they had begun seeing each other again when he was in Richmond on business. Though she was married she had agreed on several occasions to have dinner with him, flattered by the intensity of his pursuit. In time, she admitted, the relationship had become physical.

The officers had outlined for her the sequence of events they assumed took place on the night of Milo's death, including the fact that a tissue with semen had been found on the floor near the bed.

They were surprised when the woman nodded at the information. It was not out of the ordinary, she told them in a matter-of-fact manner, for Dean to masturbate as they talked on the phone. In fact, she added, she was reasonably certain he had done so the last time they had talked.

"Shit," Momchilov said as he stood up from his desk and stretched. "At the rate we're going our list of suspects in this thing is going to equal the population of mainland China. What about this woman's husband? Did he know what was going on with his wife and Milo?"

Munsey said she had strongly indicated that he hadn't known. "And the way she talked, he wouldn't have cared all that much if he had. I don't think they've got one of those marriages made in heaven.

"But if what she says is true—and I had the feeling it was—he's got a pretty good alibi."

"What's that?" Momchilov asked.

Munsey smiled. "He was at home with his old lady."

The following afternoon Dear sat in the downtown Akron office of George Tsarnas, providing the attorney and Maggie Milo with an update on the progress of the investigation. Neither attempted to hide the fact that they were displeased with his report.

Directing his words to Maggie, Dear said, "I'm relatively certain that your husband had no idea there was anyone stalking him or planning to take his life. If I'm right on the approximate time of death, I can account for most of his movements from around six-thirty on the afternoon of August ninth until about one in the morning."

Looking at Tsarnas, Dean said, "It was at six-thirty when he had dinner at your house, right?"

Tsarnas nodded.

"He attended a wedding reception from eight-thirty until approximately ten-thirty before joining you and your wife and another couple for coffee at Bill Crocker's Restaurant. You told me he left there at a few minutes past midnight.

"Neither you nor your wife sensed any apprehension or fear when you were with Dean that night. A number of people who were at the wedding reception have said that he seemed in excellent spirits.

"All of which says he had no idea someone wanted to kill him."

Tsarnas rocked back in his thickly stuffed leather chair and eyed Dear carefully. "Which tells us nothing really new," he observed.

Dear did not acknowledge the remark. If George Tsarnas was waiting for an admission that the investigation was going nowhere, he would be gravely disappointed.

It was Maggie Milo who finally broke the icy silence. "What are your plans?" she asked.

Still focusing on Tsarnas, Dear wasted no time turning the conversation to the reward being offered. "We need something dramatic if we're going to get a breakthrough on this thing," he said. "I think we need to change the conditions of the reward—and raise the amount."

Tsarnas remained silent as Dear continued. "The truth is, George, nobody with any sense is going to risk his neck as long as a conviction remains part of the condition for collecting the money. We could grow old waiting for that to happen."

Straightening in his chair, Tsarnas folded his arms. A look of concern crossed his face. "You really think people's opinion of the legal system is that negative?"

"I'm afraid so."

"How much are we talking about?"

"Fifty thousand," Dear replied, "for information leading to an arrest and indictment."

"Can we be offered any assurance that the killer will be punished?" Tsarnas asked.

"There's no way I can offer such assurances," Dear admitted, "but I strongly feel that your local law enforcement and the prosecutor's office want very badly to solve this case. So I would assume they stand ready to do everything possible to see that justice is served.

"I can tell you this: As things stand now, I can promise you that no one is going to come forward with the information we need. If that were going to happen, it would have happened by now. We're at a stalemate—unless we can do something that will make us a break."

It was Maggie Milo who first spoke out in support of Dear's plan. She was, after all, guaranteeing the reward money, she pointed out. "I think we should do it. Fifty thousand dollars, and make it for the arrest and indictment."

The attorney looked at Maggie, then Dear. Then he nodded.

It was agreed that a press conference to announce the new reward would be held jointly with the Summit County Sheriff's Department.

The concession greatly pleased Dear, who felt the breakthrough so badly needed just might finally be possible.

8

Ray Lemon was a man still lost in the sixties, a flower child who had never completely grown up. At age thirty-four, he still wore his hair in a long ponytail, would eagerly pontificate on his vague concepts of peace, love, and brotherhood at the slightest show of interest, and freely admitted there were few, if any, drugs he had not at least experimented with. From the time he graduated from high school in 1965, he had drifted in and out of a variety of jobs. He had done menial work at several of the Akron rubber plants and most recently had been a distributor for Amway products. Between jobs he had spent time in several drug rehabilitation centers and mental hospitals.

He was out of work and living at home with his parents when he heard of the increased reward on a local radio station newscast. Despite the overwhelming amount of local publicity about the murder, the September 25 newscast was the first Lemon had heard of the investigation.

An enterprising radio reporter, aware that something big was in the wind, had prowled the halls of the courthouse earlier in the day, seeking out his regular sources to see if he could get a jump on the competition. His mission had been successful, thus his station was reporting news of the increased reward and the relaxed conditions even as other newsmen were gathering for the official announcement.

It was while Sheriff David Troutman, Larry Momchilov, and Bill Dear spoke to a room filled with reporters that Chief of Detectives Ed Duvall answered the call from a man who refused to identify himself. He knew, he said, who had killed Dean Milo.

Duvall's tone was a mixture of skepticism and politeness as he listened to the droning voice of his caller. After a lengthy conversation, in which he learned little about what the man might know of the crime, Duvall finally managed to arrange a meeting in the coffee shop of the Greyhound bus station across the street from the sheriff's office.

As soon as he hung up the phone, he returned to the room where the press conference had just been completed. Calling Momchilov and Dear away from the remaining reporters, Duvall smiled. "You're not going to believe this," he whispered, "but I think we may already have something." Quickly recapping the conversation, Duvall outlined his plan for his meeting with the caller. He would wear a wire and have another officer monitor the conversation from a car parked outside the bus station.

"Don't press him too hard," Momchilov suggested. "Convince him to come on over here and talk with us."

Duvall winked and nodded. "I've got a feeling about this one," he said. "Know what? The damn guy said he really wasn't calling because of the reward. But he did say that if we wanted to give it to him he would take it."

"I'll bet," Dear said.

In the Greyhound coffee shop the two men seated at one of the tables near the window offered a marked contrast in Akron society. Lemon, his drooping eyelids hiding blue eyes dulled by too many drugs, was dressed in torn jeans and T-shirt despite the crispness of the weather. Duvall looked every bit the establishment Lemon had spent his adult life speaking out against: three-piece suit and a crew cut. The detective's eyes sparkled with an enthusiasm he hadn't felt in some time.

He was surprised at how quickly Lemon admitted his identity and agreed to accompany him across the street to the sheriff's office.

Even before Lemon was ushered into Momchilov's office, a computer check had been run on him. Dear was looking at a print-out that indicated Ray Lemon had no criminal record, when Duvall escorted him in and introduced him to the investigators.

After a few minutes of casual conversation, Momchilov shifted his weight in his chair and looked at Lemon for several silent seconds. "Okay, Mr. Lemon," he said, "why don't you just tell us what you know. We're in no hurry here, so take your time; think carefully before you answer any questions." Lemon had clearly begun to have second thoughts about involving himself in the investigation. His hands were shaking as he looked across the desk at Momchilov, saying nothing.

Dear spoke up, hoping to coax Lemon to begin talking. "I understand," he said, "that what you have to tell us occurred at an address different from where you now live ..."

Lemon nodded his head. "That's right," he said in a high-pitched voice that surprised those in the room. "It all happened at 288 Gordon Avenue. I was staying there at the time."

"Who else was living there?" Dear asked.

"This dude named Denny King and his wife, Terry Lea, rented the place. It was them and their little daughter who lived there. I was having some financial problems at the time and they let me stay with them. I slept on the couch down in the living room."

Without further urging he went on to describe the strange living arrangement of Denny and Terry Lea King. The husband and daughter, Lemon volunteered, slept in a bedroom on the second floor of the apartment, while Terry Lea King isolated herself in the attic, which had been remodeled into a bedroom. "What kind of arrangement was that?" Dear asked.

"Strange," Lemon admitted, smiling faintly for the first time since his arrival. "See, Terry Lea, she had a boyfriend living over in Medina. Her husband knew all about it and just kinda accepted it. Denny King was that kind of guy. He knew their marriage wasn't going nowhere but he cared about Terry Lea—he wanted to help her with her problems—and he loved his little girl. He's a good guy, one of those people whose door's always open to somebody needing help. Hell, he helped me plenty." Lemon fell silent for a moment, looking down at the floor. "I just wish his old lady had treated him better."

He began to detail the strange lifestyle of Terry Lea King. He had, he said, jokingly called her Princess because she loved to hold court whenever an audience was available. She was either very flamboyant or very introverted, with little in between. At times, he said, she would lock herself in the attic room, keeping it padlocked and off-limits even to her own daughter. The steady stream of people who visited the house indicated to him that she dealt drugs. She did so, he surmised, to feed her own drug addiction which, she had insisted, had evolved into a twenty-five-thousand-dollar-a-year habit.

She had worked off and on as a go-go dancer at most of the clubs in Akron and occasionally performed at private parties, including one held in Cleveland by the Cleveland Browns football team.

If there was any sexual contact between her and her husband, Lemon was unaware of it.

Dear, who had been leaning against the wall, moved to a chair next to Lemon. "Tell us," he said, "what you know about the death of Dean Milo."

Lemon took a deep breath, as if to compose himself. "It was sometime in late February, maybe early March," he said. "I was laying on the couch when Terry Lea came down from the attic. Straight out of the blue, she asks me how would I like to make five thousand dollars. I figured she was joking, so I played along. I asked her who I had to kill. She didn't even crack a smile. She said there was some rich dude in Akron who was hurting a lot of people. She told me it was worth five thousand dollars to kill him. I was dumfounded. I knew she did a lot of crazy things and joked around a lot. But this time she wasn't joking, man. She was dead-assed serious. It was scary."

"What did you tell her?" Momchilov asked.

"I told her I would think about it. But I never had no idea about getting involved in any shit like that. I wouldn't hurt nobody. I just figured she would forget the whole thing. See, what you gotta understand is that Terry Lea's a little crazy."

"Did she forget about it?"

Lemon shook his head. "About two weeks later she came down from the attic one evening. I was stretched out on the couch again. Without saying a word she tosses me this package.

Inside was a big stack of money, all hundred-dollar bills, and a gun. She said there was five thousand there. Then she said, 'I think I can get you five thousand more when the job's done.'"

"What kind of gun was it?" Momchilov asked.

"Shit, I don't know. Like a policeman's gun, I guess. I don't know much about guns. They're not my thing, you know."

"Like this?" Momchilov said, pulling his .38 from its holster and showing it to Lemon.

"I don't think so," Lemon said.

"Did it have a revolving chamber?"

"I don't think so."

"Was it more like this?" Dear asked, showing his .380 automatic.

"That's more like it, but the one she showed me was smaller."

Dear popped the clip from his gun. As he did so, Lemon nodded and pointed. "That's it. There was a clip like that inside the package."

"Tell me more about the package," Momchilov said.

"I looked inside it, like Terry Lea wanted me to do, then I just put it under the couch for a couple of days. See, I didn't want to piss her off. I thought I'd just play along until I could figure out some way to get the hell out of there. I know this sounds crazy, but Terry Lea's a tough lady. All she would have had to do was throw a fit and tell her husband she didn't want me around and I'd be out in a minute. I didn't want to get her all upset and get myself thrown out. See, I was kinda in a tight spot; I didn't have any place else to go.

"But after a couple of days of worry about it, I finally got up the courage to give the package back to her. I told her that I needed money bad, but not bad enough to kill anybody. I told her I wasn't interested. She just shrugged and took the package back like it was no big deal. Surprised the shit out of me."

"Did you and Terry Lea King ever talk about killing the rich man again?" Dear asked.

"Yeah, a few weeks ago."

Momchilov shot a quick glance in Dear's direction before asking his next question. "I want you to think carefully about this," the detective said. "Would it have been sometime in early September?"

"Man, I can't remember exactly. I ain't shit at dates. But I'd guess it was more like late August. I was driving Terry Lea to a car wash that day. She was really uptight. I asked her what was wrong and she said she guessed it was hearing Barry's name on the radio—"

Dear immediately interrupted. "Who's Barry?"

"Barry Boyd. This lawyer. He's a friend of Terry Lea's; used to come over to the house now and then."

"Okay, so what else did she say that day?"

"She said she'd been feeling a lot of pressure," Lemon said. "Then she just kind of opened up and let it all out. She said, 'You remember that guy I wanted you to kill?' I told her I did and she said, 'Well, it's been done. He's dead.' She said the guy's name was Dean Milo. I was shocked. I asked her if this dude Barry had done it, and she said he had just been a middleman or something. When I asked her again who did it, she said it was this Milo dude's family."

"She wasn't any more specific?" Momchilov asked.

"No she just said 'his family.' Man, I was freaked out. All I could think was that Terry Lea had gotten herself into some deep shit in the past, but nothing like this."

"Did she say anything more about this Barry Boyd?" Dear asked.

"After we left the car wash she asked me to drive her to his office downtown. I circled the block for ten, maybe fifteen minutes, while she went inside. When she came out she seemed to be feeling a lot better. Like she had taken an upper.

"She said Boyd had told her there was nothing to worry about. Everything was cool. The hit man had left town and the police would never find him. I mean, she was like a different person when she got back in the car."

Dear asked Lemon if Terry Lea King had specifically said "hit man." Lemon said he remembered her using the phrase. "Did she know his name?"

"I don't think so. If she did, she didn't tell me."

"Did you get the impression that Barry Boyd knew who he was?"

"I'd imagine so."

"You think if you talked with Barry he'd tell you?" Dear asked.

The question unnerved Lemon. He shook his head. "Maybe if Terry Lea King was with you," Dear continued. Lemon rose from his chair and began to pace in a small circle. He was wishing he'd never made that phone call after hearing the reward announcement on the radio. "Oh, man, I can't imagine him giving me—or anybody—the name of a fucking hit man. That would be pretty crazy, wouldn't it? Why would he do something like that? The guy's no dumbass."

"Would you be willing to give it a try?"

"Man, I don't think so. That's a helluva lot more than I bargained for when I came over here."

Momchilov, aware of the reluctance that was sweeping over Lemon, hurriedly changed the direction of the conversation.

"Let's talk some more about the gun Terry Lea gave you," he said. "Did you ever see it again after you gave it back to her?"

"No."

"You have any idea what happened to it?"

Lemon shook his head from side to side.

"Do you have any idea what Terry Lea was to be paid for her role in this killing?"

Lemon, calmed somewhat, returned to his chair. "This is where the whole thing gets really crazy," he said. "She had this idea of getting the Milo family to set up a trust fund for her daughter. Something like fifty or a hundred thousand dollars. In exchange, she was going to take the blame for the murder. She'd say that it was all the result of some kind of fucked-up lovers' quarrel she and this Milo guy had.

"See, Terry Lea was pretty messed up then. Said she didn't much care about living anyway. By confessing, she said, she could get the Milo family off the hook and provide for her daughter. Said it would feel nice to do something good for a change. She had it all figured out. After making the financial arrangements and then confessing, she was going to kill herself. That way no one could prove she'd been lying. She said it would be perfect."

"Are you sure she didn't do the killing?" Dear asked.

"Oh, I'm positive. Naw, Terry Lea couldn't do something like that. No fucking way."

Later in the day, Ray Lemon took a polygraph test at which many of the same questions posed during the interrogation were asked. He passed with flying colors.

He was sent home with instructions to say nothing about the conversation in Momchilov's office. In hopes of insuring his silence, it was pointed out to him that his life could be in danger if the killer of Dean Milo learned of his knowledge of the crime.

Dear immediately called Frank Lambert and assigned him the task of shadowing Lemon's every move. "This guy," Dear said, "sounds like the real thing. But there's always the possibility he's working both sides of the street. I don't want to wake up some morning and suddenly find out that he was sent here by the Milo family or this guy Boyd, to see if he could find out what we know. If he contacts someone, I want to know about it."

Despite his caution, Dear, for the first time during the investigation, felt optimistic.

With Lambert assigned to keep track of Lemon, all three of the men Dear had summoned from Texas to Akron were working surveillance full-time. Dick Riddle had continued following Fred Milo while Joe Villanueva kept tabs on Lonnie Curtis. To their boss's disappointment their jobs had been dull and nonproductive. If the men they were following were, indeed, criminals, they seemed blithely unconcerned about being watched. Now, however, with new characters thrown into the cast, Dear felt the need for additional help. He placed a call to his office and arranged for Terry Hurley and Carl Lilly to join the investigative team.

Lilly a black former Michigan police officer, was assigned to follow Fred Milo, while Riddle took over on Lonnie Curtis, thus freeing Villanueva to begin a watch on Barry Boyd. Terry

Hurley, a young, pretty former prosecutor's investigator, would begin visiting the bars and clubs that had most likely been frequented by Terry Lea King in an attempt to learn more about the woman. Dear and Momchilov had agreed they would shadow Terry Lea King themselves.

While waiting for the arrival of the additional manpower, Dear decided to visit the office of Barry Boyd at One Main Street. He was eager to get a look at the man whom Ray Lemon had described as a "straight arrow." The only thing Lemon had found unusual about Boyd was his interest in Terry Lea King and the fact he drank too much at times.

Boyd greeted Dear with a firm handshake. He was a thin, balding man in his mid-thirties, with a scholarly look about him. He was pale and appeared nervous but smiled warmly as the investigator introduced himself.

"I'm investigating the death of Dean Milo," he said.

"What can I do to help you?" Boyd asked from behind his desk.

"Do you represent either Fred Milo or Lonnie Curtis in any legal matters?" The directness of the question clearly unnerved Boyd. Noticing that the lawyer's hands, folded in front of him on his desk, trembled, Dear wondered if that was evidence of guilt or booze.

Boyd cleared his throat. "Yes, sir, I've been counsel for both of them for a number of years. A few oil deals. Some civic matters. All pretty minor stuff, really. I'm working on a small matter for them now, but I'm afraid I'm not at liberty to discuss it. Lawyer-client privilege, you understand."

"You haven't been connected with the litigation involving Fred Milo and Curtis's wife against Dean Milo over control of the company?"

"No," Boyd answered. There was a tone to his reply that strongly hinted disappointment over the fact.

"How long have you known Fred and Lonnie?"

"I went to college with Fred. I met Lonnie a few years ago through him."

"Were you friends with Dean Milo?"

"I knew him just to say hello. He was older than the rest of us and traveled in different circles, if you understand what I mean."

"Can you tell me where you were on August ninth and tenth?"

"I spent the day with my son. I'm divorced. My former wife now lives in Florida. I have custody of the boy for most of the summer."

Dear continued his terse line of questioning, making no attempt to establish any warmth. "Would you be willing to take a polygraph exam?"

"Certainly," Boyd said. The sound of the reply was far more confident than the man appeared to be.

Dear nodded and rose from his chair to leave. "I appreciate your time," he said as he turned toward the door. "I'm sure we'll be seeing each other again. I'm here until this murder is solved. I'll stay as long as it takes. I just thought you should know that."

Joe Villanueva waited outside the building where Boyd's office was located. He only nodded as Dear walked from the front door, headed in the direction of his car.

Both shared the hope that a nervous Barry Boyd would soon be leaving, perhaps to share newborn concerns with some member of the Milo family.

It was late that evening when Dear and Momchilov sat in the detective's office, taking stock of the dizzying speed at which things had happened during the day.

Frowning at the sip of cold coffee he had just swallowed, Momchilov asked what impressions Dear had taken away from his meeting with Boyd.

"I think he's hoping time is on his side," Dear said. "The guy probably doesn't really have the stomach for all this, but he's got enough snap to know that the longer the investigation goes on, the less likely the murder will be solved. He's smart, but he's scared. I just wanted to make him a little uncomfortable.

"My guess is that if he is involved, he's one of the weakest links in the chain. Enough pressure and he'll roll over."

"So ..."

"So, I'm going to become Barry Boyd's worst nightmare.

He's going to go to bed thinking about me and then wake up wondering what the hell I'm up to next."

Momchilov laughed. "This asshole's going to think the sky is falling on him all of a sudden. I did a little checking on him myself today. He's evidently in trouble over some funny stuff he tried to pull on a DWI case the police department has against him. And evidently a couple of credit card companies are tired of waiting for money he owes them and about to begin legal action.

"If you ask me, it sounds like he needs to start looking for a good lawyer." With that the detective suggested they go for a ride.

"Hey, why don't you get out of here and go home to see Joan?" Dear suggested, aware that Momchilov had been able to spend little time with his new wife in recent weeks.

"Hell, she probably wouldn't recognize me," Larry joked. "I just wanted to drive by Boyd's house for a minute."

"I've got nothing better to do," Dear replied.

The attorney's Tudor-style home sat on the corner in a quiet, tree-lined neighborhood, looking cold and unwelcoming. Momchilov drove slowly past the unlit house, then parked his unmarked car down the block. In silence he and Dear made their way to the driveway at the back of the house and up to the open garage. Parked inside was an antique Jaguar. Momchilov knelt down behind the car and quickly wrote the number of the Ohio license plate in his notebook.

Back at his car he radioed for a motor vehicle check on license plate number D 4447 L. In less than a minute the radio crackled back the information he sought.

The Jaguar was registered to Lonnie Curtis.

9

The rain had returned, promising to change to sleet before morning, as Bill Dear paced his motel room. When working a case he fought sleep as if it were his enemy, begrudging those still, silent hours when there was little to do but wait for the next day's creeping arrival.

From his eleventh-floor window he had a view of downtown with its lonely yellow streetlights straining against the steady downpour. There was no movement along Main Street; no street cleaner, no garbage collector. Nothing. It was as if all life had abandoned the city.

The scene sent a shiver of sadness through Dear. He checked his watch and briefly contemplated calling home. He and Jan had been married only six months and already too much of that time had been spent apart. He knew that she resented being left alone so much, and he felt the sudden urge to call and try once more to explain. But he knew there was no satisfactory explanation. This was what he did. It was so simple—until he tried to make someone else understand.

It was just as well that it was too late to call. Jan would already be sleeping.

As he stood looking out on the cold, rainy street, Dear came to the conclusion that he did not like Akron, Ohio, at all.

Neither did he like the fact that his case had a cast of characters that grew with each passing day. Every answer he found raised a dozen new questions. Every person he talked with pointed him toward others.

Finally stretching out on the bed, he replayed his conversation with Barry Boyd. Just beneath the lawyer's composure was a ticking time bomb. Dear had sensed fear in the man as soon as he had walked into his office. Boyd, he was convinced, was the key to unlocking the mystery of Dean Milo's death. But even that feeling of certainty troubled him. What he had learned of Barry Boyd did not point to the degree of desperation that would lead him to involve himself in murder.

In his younger days Boyd had been an idealistic man, a VISTA volunteer and a civil rights activist. His law practice had begun to flourish even before he married into the wealth and social power of the Firestone family. The marriage had assured him status among the social, political, and industrial elite of Akron. His debutante wife was educated at one of the finest finishing schools in the East and had traveled throughout Europe. She loved to sail and to tell the stories her mother and father brought home after attending White House parties or spending vacations on the sixty-foot sailboat they docked behind their inland waterway home in Fort Lauderdale.

Then, however, the marriage had gone sour, ending in divorce. Boyd, once a rising young lawyer, began to let his business slide. In recent months he had begun to drink heavily. A man who once seemed to have it all now showed all the signs of self-destruction. But had he fallen low enough to become a participant in cold-blooded murder?

This was but one of the questions that kept Dear from sleeping.

The hostility of Lonnie Curtis in that first front-door encounter also bothered him. On one hand, Curtis's actions on the weekend Dean Milo was murdered seemed anything but suspicious. He had spent most of Saturday at home, leaving only briefly during the afternoon to help Sotir Milo with some minor repair work. Then that evening Lonnie and Sophie had taken their son to visit Sea World. They were all in bed by midnight.

Sunday, too, had evidently been routine. Lonnie cleaned the swimming pool during the morning and watched television. Sophie had gone shopping and dropped her son off for a visit with Fred and Kathy Milo. That afternoon, Lonnie had spoken on the phone briefly with Barry Boyd about business matters, then took a drive to inspect some property he owned in Sand Run Park. At about 6:00 p.m. Fred had stopped by the Curtis house, returning their son and visiting briefly. Shortly thereafter the Curtis family left home, first stopping at Fred Milo's, where Lonnie delivered some papers he had forgotten to give Fred earlier, then driving to Sophie's parents' home, where they stayed until about 9:00 p.m. before leaving for a planned trip to Columbus.

Dear could not help wondering if the combined business and pleasure trip to Columbus had been made to avoid being in town when Dean Milo's murder was discovered. By the same token, if Lonnie had knowledge of the murder plot, why didn't he arrange to be out of town for the entire weekend? And why would Curtis be so unwilling to cooperate with his investigation?

The only out-of-the-ordinary thing Curtis had done was to telephone a neighbor and tell him that they were going out of town and that his family would be welcome to use the swimming pool while they were gone. The gesture had surprised the neighbor, who had never so much as been in the Curtis home. His relationship with Lonnie Curtis, in fact, had never consisted of more than an occasional quick hello if they met at the shopping center.

Dear, grasping for any scenario that might make some sense, considered the possibility that Lonnie had been under the impression that his brother-in-law was to be killed on Sunday night and had established an alibi by leaving town when he did. Dear well knew that a casual acquaintance cast in the role of an alibi witness was far more believable, less likely to invent a story, than a close friend, who might be persuaded to lie.

Lonnie Curtis reinforced a fact that was gnawing at the investigator: He was, he knew, collecting far more questions than answers.

Then there was Fred Milo. On the Monday morning before his brother's body was found, Fred had called home to leave a message for his wife, Kathy, on the answering machine. "Tell Lonnie I got him the best birthday present he could want," he had said. No one in the family could recall Fred Milo's having ever remembered his brother-in-law's birthday before. Dear wondered if that "present" had been the elimination of Dean Milo.

One of the investigator's first rules when entering a case is to look for any change in behavior patterns by anyone who might qualify as a suspect. The sudden displays of generosity by Lonnie and Fred interested Dear a great deal.

So did the relationships of the two men with the elder Milos.

The picture had emerged of Fred Milo as a mama's boy, dominated by Katina Milo and his brother. There was little doubt that Dean Milo had been the favored child. He had inherited the characteristics of his mother and had developed them into the forceful, hard-driving businessman she had once hoped his father might be but never was. Even Sotir Milo seemed awed by the powerful personality of his older son.

On the occasions when Fred Milo made suggestions about the operation of the company during family gatherings, Dean had been quick to dismiss them, with Katina's obvious approval. Even in the corporation where he was a one-third owner, Fred Milo was referred to by employees as "Dean's brother" or "Freddie," often in his presence.

Fred, then, was a man without an identity, playing tennis on weekday afternoons, driving around town in his shiny Mercedes, and all the while failing miserably in his attempt to give the public impression of an effectual businessman who had devised a way of earning his six-figure income without getting his hands dirty.

To keep Fred removed from the day-to-day running of the business, Dean made a habit of sending him on "special assignments." It was when Fred had returned from a three-month tour of the company stores that he learned Dean had taken all corporate decision-making powers into his own hands. His resentment boiled into an anger he had never before displayed.

While Fred Milo was "Dean's brother," Lonnie Curtis was "the man who married the boss's daughter."

Though Dean had served as best man at the wedding of Lonnie and Sophie, he made little attempt to hide his disapproval of the man his sister had chosen as a husband. Dean Milo felt strongly about having employees with skill, education, and experience and resented the fact that Curtis had moved into a high-ranking position in the company using a marriage license as his ticket.

As Dean became increasingly critical of Lonnie's handling of his department, Lonnie countered by attempting to gather support from members of the organization. If there was to be a family war, the ambitious Curtis decided, a divide-and-conquer tactic was his best weapon.

When he saw his power dwindling, Lonnie had solicited a buyer for the company named Ray Sesic to serve as an inner-office spy who would keep him abreast of the management decisions Dean was no longer sharing with others. But Dean soon unmasked Sesic as a corporate spy and fired him.

Just as quickly, Curtis hired him to work at a Milo B&B subsidiary.

It had been Lonnie Curtis who kindled the fire and fanned the flames of the family feud, enlisting the sympathy of Katina. Dean, he insisted, had become an autocratic lone wolf, turning the family business into a dictatorship. On one hand, Katina admired the aggressive manner in which her son ran the business. But when it became apparent to her that he no longer relied on her decisions, she too became angered. Having long enjoyed being the power behind the throne, she felt betrayed by her favorite son.

Even Sotir lent a sympathetic ear to the complaints of Lonnie and Sophie. To him the solidarity of the family unit took precedence over business success. If Dean was dealing unfairly with the others in the family, something had to be done.

Ultimately it was agreed that legal action was the only course.

Lying on his bed, Dear contemplated the personal conflicts that had divided the Milo family. Outside, the rain had turned to sleet, tapping gently against the window. The first gray hint of dawn was arriving when he finally fell into a fitful sleep. In his dreams he saw a figure standing at a doorway, a telegram in his hand. The man had no face.

On September 26 the Akron police, who had been interested in Barry Boyd for reasons that had nothing to do with the Milo murder investigation, arrested the attorney for tampering with court records. A court clerk had witnessed him removing documents from a file related to his own arrest on a DWI charge and had reported what she had seen. In an attempt to stop prosecution on one charge, Barry Boyd was now facing one even more serious.

Even as Boyd was being released on bond, news of the arrest brought smiles to the faces of Dear and Larry Momchilov. "The timing is perfect—absolutely perfect," Dear said. "I don't see him as a guy who can handle a lot of pressure. Now, all of a sudden, the whole world's falling down around his bald head. What we do now is show him what real pressure is. If he did have something to do with Dean Milo's death, we're going to convince him that confessing to it is preferable to the living hell we're going to make for him."

The sparkle in Momchilov's eyes signaled his agreement.

In the meantime, however, Dear and Momchilov wanted to learn more about Terry Lea King. They arranged for Ray Lemon to come to the sheriff's office and place a call to her in an attempt to get her to elaborate on the murder plot and to discuss her relationship with Boyd.

Both were surprised at the calm demeanor of Lemon as he sat in Momchilov's office, listening to their instructions. They explained that the conversation would be taped and that he should try to be as casual as possible. "Don't rush it," Dear advised. "We've got lots of time and plenty of tape. Try to make her comfortable; let her do the talking."

Lemon nodded and dialed the number of the apartment on Gordon Avenue, letting the phone ring for several minutes before hanging up. He then called the number of the house in Medina where he knew she was spending a good deal of time with her new boyfriend. A faint smile crossed his face when he heard Terry Lea's voice answer.

For several minutes they chatted about mundane occurrences in their respective lives since they had last seen each other. For

Terry Lea, things had not been going well.

"I'm in a spot," she said. "Got any money I could borrow?"

"Hey, I still owe you twenty bucks," Lemon replied. "I should have already paid you. Will that help?"

"I'm two hundred short," she said.

"Damn, you sound bad off. When could you get it back to me? I'd have to have it pretty quick. Two, three days. A week tops. I'm running a little low myself."

"I can get it back to you in just a few days," she said. There was a new warmth in her voice. Suddenly, Ray Lemon had become her angel of mercy calling.

"Look, when are you coming to town?" he asked.

"I'll be there tomorrow. I could have come in today but Barry just left."

Lemon shot a quick glance at Dear and Momchilov at the mention of the name. "Barry Boyd?" he asked.

"Yeah."

"From what I've been hearing on the radio the last couple of days—caught trying to fix a ticket or something—he should get on the wagon or something. I worry about Barry." Terry Lea King's voice took on a sharp edge. "He went on the wagon right after that DWI business. Barry worries about Barry."

"Yeah, but, like I was telling you, there's all that shit in the papers about the Milo business and—"

"Barry's cool," Terry Lea snapped. It was time to change the subject.

After setting up a time to call her about the loan, Lemon said his goodbyes. He shrugged his shoulders as Momchilov pushed the button to turn off the recorder. "Sorry," he said. "I guess I'm not too good at this."

"Naw, you did fine," Momchilov said. "Real good." Dear, a man with less patience, did not share Momchilov's tolerance of the muffed opportunity.

After Lemon left, the detective and the investigator replayed the tape several times. "Barry's cool."

"Barry worries about Barry." Close, but nothing, really.

Aware that Boyd's attorney had sent word to the sheriff's department that his client would speak with no one until his current legal difficulties were resolved, Momchilov suggested they get a little better acquainted with Terry Lea King.

It was the time when most of those living along narrow Gordon Avenue were watching the late news or preparing for bed when Momchilov parked near a corner that provided a good view of the apartment where Terry Lea lived.

For an hour they watched as a steady stream of people entered and left the house. There was little doubt they were there to make drug buys, because Momchilov recognized several of Akron's known drug users. All the while the light in the attic, Terry Lea's private kingdom, shone brightly.

It was shortly after midnight when Terry Lea emerged from the house and got into a Thunderbird parked in front. Momchilov waited until she had driven to the end of the short block before he began to follow at a safe distance.

She led them to the outskirts of town, then onto the highway, where she picked up speed as she headed in the direction of the picturesque little community of Medina, twenty miles away. Shortly after entering the city limits she made a left turn into a residential area and parked in the driveway of a house which, unknown to the men trailing her, belonged to a suspected gun dealer and drug pusher.

Momchilov drove to a house several hundred yards away and pulled into the driveway. The For Sale sign in the front yard and evidence that builders were still in the finishing stages offered the assurance that no one inside would awake and wonder what a strange car was doing parked in front at such a late hour.

"That house isn't going anywhere," said Dear after they had been sitting in the darkened car for a half hour. "What we need to know is what's going on inside." They agreed to make alternate forays to the modest frame house. Dear, a nonsmoker eager to escape the stifling smell of Momchilov's cigarettes, volunteered to make the first trip.

Reaching the yard, he lay down and silently belly-crawled toward the shadow of the row of hedges that surrounded the house. Looking in the window, he could see three men seated, talking and smoking what appeared to be marijuana. Terry Lea appeared briefly, a hypodermic syringe in her hand, but then carried it into another room and out of Dear's view.

As he crawled from window to window a succession of cars began to arrive. Each time a new visitor entered the house Dear would make his way to the driveway, using the shadows for protection against the revealing light of a near-full moon, and write down the license plate number in a small notebook he carried in his hip pocket.

He was recording a number when an arriving car caught him by surprise. Just seconds before its headlights would have focused on him, Dear dove in a quick roll across the ground and huddled beneath Terry Lea King's Thunderbird. He didn't even breathe as the new arrivals climbed from their car and made their way toward the front porch. Lying there, Dear silently cursed the position he found himself in. *This is great,* he thought. *Now all I need is for her to come running out, start the car, and run over me.*

Even as the absurd scenario played in his mind, the front door opened and Terry Lea came out, walking hurriedly in the direction of her car. Dear lay motionless, quickly deciding to wait until the last minute before rolling from his hideaway. What he would do after that, he had no idea.

Terry Lea opened the door, leaned inside for several long seconds, then stood up, slammed the door shut, and returned to the house. Obviously, she had come only to get something. Dear closed his eyes and felt the tension drain from his body.

When he returned to the car, dirty and with a rip in one pant leg, Momchilov began to laugh. "Damn," he said, "did you get in a fight with somebody?"

Dear ignored the question and related what had just happened.

Momchilov was still laughing. "You know," he said, "if she had run over you, I'd have this case all to myself. Too damn bad."

"Maybe so," Dear added, "but just think how embarrassing it would have been for you to have to go in and tell your boss how you brought me out here and got me killed."

"I'd have figured something out," the detective replied.

For the next five nights Momchilov and Dear followed Terry Lea King on a tour of the Akron area's subculture; to seamy bars and strip joints, skid row alleys and street corners and shabby houses, all apparent drops for the drugs she was delivering.

Streetwise and obviously paranoid about being followed, Terry Lea drove routes that a madman could have designed. She seldom traveled more than three blocks before doubling back, winding through miles of residential and industrial areas. Traffic lights regularly worked to her advantage, as though she possessed a sixth sense. She regularly hurried under yellow caution lights a split second before they turned red and halted all cars in her wake.

Momchilov, Dear decided, was the best surveillance man he had ever worked with. He never lost Terry Lea King and she was not alerted to the fact she was being followed.

They, on the other hand, were not as fortunate.

One evening they followed Terry Lea back to her home away from home in Medina and parked in a cul-de-sac directly behind the lot on which the house stood. Leaving their car, binoculars in hand, Momchilov and Dear had crept into a stand of small trees in hopes of getting a better vantage point from which to watch the comings and goings.

They had been there only a few minutes when they heard a gruff voice asking what they were doing. They turned to see two Medina police patrolmen, guns drawn and pointed in their direction.

They were told to walk to the patrol car and spread-eagle across the hood.

"We're investigators," Momchilov said, carefully pulling his badge from his jacket pocket. "We're with the sheriff's office.

Neither of the patrolmen even looked at the badge. "What sheriff's office?"

"Summit County," Momchilov said.

Dear remained silent, hoping he would not be asked to show some identification. If there was anything law enforcement personnel disliked more than having officers from another jurisdiction invade their territory, it was having an unfamiliar private investigator snoop around.

The patrolman who was doing all the talking continued to glare at Momchilov. "You're a little bit out of your territory, aren't you?"

"We're working a case."

"What kinda case?"

"We followed a car out here from Akron. We just wanted to see where it wound up."

"I guess it didn't occur to you to check in with the local police and let us know you were in town."

Momchilov, still stretched across the hood of the car, was straining to remain composed. "Hell, man, we were in pursuit of a fucking car. There just wasn't time to turn off and drive by the police department for a visit. We were going to stop in before we left town." With that he rose to a standing position, not bothering to ask the officer's permission.

"Which car were you following?"

"That's the hell of it," Momchilov answered. "It turned out to be the wrong car. We were just about to leave when you guys showed up." The detective's instinctive suspicion of law enforcement officers had taken over. There were, in fact, few in the business whom he trusted. He wasn't about to detail the case he was working on for two men he'd never seen before, even if they were carrying badges.

"Well, you realize you're on our turf," the patrolman again reminded him. "If you come to town again on any of your wild car chases I suggest you call us first."

"Count on it," Momchilov said.

The patrolmen returned to their car and waited until Momchilov and Dear were backing away before starting their engine.

Momchilov glanced into the rearview mirror at the patrol car as they pulled from the cul-de-sac. "Assholes," he said.

Since Terry Lea King worked nights and slept days, Dear used the daylight hours visiting the bars and go-go clubs where he hoped to find friends who might tell him more about her activities. He decided to pose as a businessman interested in hiring her to dance at a private party he was planning.

On his first few stops none of the few weary-looking daytime customers or any of the sad-eyed dancers knew anything about Terry Lea. Finally, however, a bartender had suggested he get in touch with a girl named Darlene Drake, a dancer who had worked for a while with Terry Lea.

Darlene had agreed to meet Dear at a waterside restaurant near Akron's Portage Lakes.

Wearing sunglasses and sipping on a drink, Dear explained his interest in hiring Terry Lea. "She's a hard lady to find," he said. "I'd like to get in touch with her."

"I don't think it's gonna do you any good. She quit dancing. Just like me. I don't think she'll be interested in what you've got in mind."

Dear listened as Darlene launched into a history of her dance career. For a while it had been fun. The go-go joints had paid between $8 and $20 an hour. For the private parties the fee went as high as $175. But in time the groping and obscene suggestions from men in the audience and the demands of owners and businessmen who felt they were owed something more than an honest night's work had worn on her. As she talked, recalling the days when she and Terry Lea King were two of the highest-paid dancers in the city, she casually mentioned several private parties the two had worked. One, she said, had been for the Milo B&B employees. Dean Milo, the man who had been killed recently, had hired them.

Dear said nothing, hoping his reaction to her offhand recollection was concealed behind his dark glasses.

"It got old real quick," Darlene said. "So I got out."

"Why did Terry Lea give it up?" Dear asked.

"She told me she's in love. Really hooked on some guy who lives out in Medina. And she's got other problems—drugs and stuff like that. I really shouldn't be talking about it."

"I understand," Dear said politely. "It's none of my business. I just got her name from Barry Boyd."

Darlene's eyes widened at the mention of the attorney's name. "You know Barry?" she asked.

"Yeah, we met a while back."

"He's a good friend of Terry Lea's. He's also one of her problems."

"How's that?"

"I'm not sure. She's all tied in knots about some deal she got involved in with him. She won't talk about it."

During the first week of October a meeting was held in the sheriff's office to discuss the progress being made on the case. Chief of Detectives Ed Duvall requested the presence of Momchilov and Bill Lewis from his staff, Bath detective Munsey, and Dear for an update of the progress being made.

With Boyd protected by an attorney who continued to refuse to allow him to be interviewed further, it was decided that the most likely break in the case would come from the pursuit of Terry Lea King. It was what Dear had hoped would be agreed on. He and Momchilov had already discussed it at great length.

Dear outlined the plan to the others in attendance. Since Ray Lemon was their most direct link to Terry Lea, they wanted to try one more time to have him lure her into an incriminating conversation about the plot to murder Dean Milo. "If we can get her to say the right things," Dear observed, "you'll have enough to take to a grand jury. I'm not crazy about using Lemon—the guy's a certified flake—but he's all we've got."

The plan called for Lemon to contact Terry Lea and set up a meeting to give her the money. Rather than have Lemon wear a wire and meet Terry Lea at her apartment, Dear suggested the transaction be made in a car on some public parking lot to avoid any suspicion on Terry Lea's part. A tape recorder could be concealed beneath the front seat.

It was the last step of Dear's plan that caused the others in the room to sit up in their chairs. He would, he said, ride in the trunk of Lemon's car, listening on earphones just in case something malfunctioned with the recording device.

Munsey rolled his eyes and said nothing. Momchilov finally broke the silence that had fallen on the room after Dear's outline. "Hell, sounds like fun to me," he said.

"Let's give it a try," Duvall said.

Momchilov had arrived early, driving an unmarked car, and located a parking space that would afford him a good view of the McDonald's restaurant where Lemon and Terry Lea had agreed to meet. On schedule, Lemon drove into the lot at three in the afternoon and parked. In the trunk, Dear was curled into a fetal position, trying to ignore his discomfort and concentrate on what he might be able to hear on the earphones he wore.

Momchilov, just yards away, alternately puffed on a cigarette and checked his watch, worried that Terry Lea might not show. He had been watching Lemon's car for less than fifteen minutes when he straightened from his slumped position, knocking cigarette ashes into his lap. He couldn't believe what he saw.

Approaching Lemon's car was Barry Boyd. Momchilov felt his pulse quicken. What the hell was going on?

In the trunk, Dear was unaware that the plan had taken a drastic detour until he heard Lemon's voice through the earphones As Boyd approached, Lemon dealt with the surprise well. "Barry Boyd," he said. "What the hell you doing here?"

Dear tensed at the signal that Boyd had somehow walked into the scenario and urgently pressed the earphones to his temples. The next voice he heard was Boyd's.

"Terry couldn't make it," he was saying. "She asked me to pick up the money for her."

Dear said a silent prayer that Lemon would somehow manage to take advantage of the rare opportunity that had literally fallen in their laps. Invite him to sit down in the car with you, for Pete's sake. Get him talking. Ask him about the Milo murder. Let the sonuvabitch hang himself.

The silent coaching was to no avail. Lemon, more unnerved than he had appeared, simply handed Boyd the money provided him by the sheriff's department and watched as he walked away.

Dear contained his rage until he felt sure Boyd had left, then exploded from the trunk. "Dammit to hell, Ray, what's the matter with you? We had it laid out for us; an opportunity we probably won't ever get again, and you blew it, you dumb bastard."

Momchilov moved quickly to Lemon's defense. "Hey, Bill,

ease off " he said. "This guy's not trained for this kind of shit. Things just got a little crazy and he reacted. It's done.

"And when you think about it, we did accomplish something. We've got another incident that ties our man Boyd to Terry Lea King."

Dear calmed and slumped against Lemon's car. He felt more dejected than he had at any time since his arrival in Akron. "But we could have had so much more," he said in a voice barely above a whisper.

Joe Villanueva, Dear's assistant who had been assigned to follow Boyd, had witnessed what had taken place at the McDonald's. Unaware of the planned meeting, he had simply been maintaining surveillance and Boyd had led him to the scene.

"The guy's a puzzle," Villanueva told Dear as he sat briefing him on Boyd's actions in recent days. "If you want this guy scared, I think you're succeeding. He's walking around in a fog, like he's got the weight of the world on his shoulders. He's completely ignoring his work."

When Dear asked whom Boyd had been in contact with, Villanueva said that he had followed him to the home of a nurse named Sally Reeves on several occasions. "I think she's his girlfriend these days.

"The only other people he's seen are old friends of yours—Fred Milo and Lonnie Curtis."

In a dramatic departure from standard surveillance procedure, Dear had instructed Villanueva to make certain that Boyd knew he was being followed. Adding more pressure took priority over the secret surveillance. "Does he know you're following him?" Dear asked.

"It's weird," Villanueva said. "I've been pretty obvious. I wear dark glasses and slink around like a bumbling idiot. I put a newspaper up to my face whenever he comes out of his building. I've made a half-dozen sudden stops right behind him when I've been following him in the car. I feel like I'm acting in some B detective movie.

"I've done everything but wear a damn sign, but I'm not

sure he knows I'm tailing him. It's like the guy sees me, but doesn't see me. He wanders around in a fog. He's so wrapped up in his own problems that a bomb could go off across the street and he'd never hear the boom."

Boyd's meetings with Fred Milo and Lonnie Curtis interested Dear.

"Boyd and Curtis got together once in some accountant's office. I figure they were discussing money. He's met Fred Milo twice on the street corner near his office. Both times they would chat for a minute, then go to a little coffee shop. Neither meeting lasted more than ten or fifteen minutes." Villanueva's report was much like those Dear had received from Carl Lilly and Dick Riddle, who had been charged with the duties of following Fred Milo and Lonnie Curtis. Lilly, in particular, was wishing he had been assigned to someone whose life was a bit more interesting. "Following Fred Milo around" he had written in one of his daily reports, "is only a notch above taking a sleeping pill."

Milo left the house at the same time each morning, went directly to work, then went home in the evenings. The two brief downtown meetings with Boyd had been the only deviation from the routine. He apparently didn't drink, had no interest in gambling, and saw no girlfriend on the side. Like Villanueva, Lilly had taken no special precautions to make certain Milo was unaware of his presence. But there had been no indication that the man he was assigned to follow had any notion he was being watched.

Dick Riddle, on the other hand, had been carefully instructed to make sure that Lonnie Curtis did not suspect he was the subject of around-the-clock surveillance. Dear's reasoning was self-serving. At that first encounter, he had quickly judged Curtis to be a person who would delight in calling his attorney and having him work up a harassment case against anyone he thought to be following him.

"If the guy's worried about anything," Riddle told Dear, "he doesn't show it. To see him, you would think he's got the world by the tail. The guy actually struts. He wears his three-piece suits and drives his fancy car and just goes about his business.

If you ask me, he's doing his damnedest to copy Dean Milo and pulling it off pretty well. I'll bet you a steak dinner he dreams about running that company when he goes to sleep at night."

The most interesting thing he'd done since Dear had given him the assignment, Riddle said, was to have a cup of coffee with Villanueva while Curtis and Barry Boyd had their meeting in the accountant's office.

Much of Terry Hurley's work had been done at night, observing the late-hour stops of Barry Boyd and Terry Lea King. She had talked to a number of people who had acknowledged that Boyd and King were often seen together. Too, there were any number of people who had expressed concern over Terry Lea's worsening drug problem. But from what she had heard and observed firsthand, Boyd's drinking might be even worse than Terry Lea King's drug habit. On several recent occasions Boyd had drunk so much at a bar called Night People that he became incoherent. One night he had sat at the bar for hours, silently crying as he drank himself into a stupor.

The information supplied by his investigators was evidence of solid, nuts-and-bolts detective work, but it did little to speed the pace of things. For all the long hours and manpower being applied to the case, Dear was left with an overwhelming, frustrating feeling of trying to dig a hole in dry sand.

Returning to his motel room to shower and change clothes after his ride in the trunk of Ray Lemon's car, Dear checked his telephone messages and saw that his wife had called earlier in the day.

He returned the call, knowing even as he dialed the number that the conversation would ultimately get around to the question of when he would be returning home. They had talked only a few minutes when Jan sensed something was wrong.

"Bill," she said, "you sound different. I've never heard you sound so mean. What's wrong?"

He thought briefly of detailing the frustrations of the day, then decided against it. "I'm just tired," he said.

"You get too involved in these cases," she said. "They

change you. 1 don't know who you are when you're like this."

And then she asked, as she did every time they spoke, when he would be coming home.

"In a month," he replied, "... maybe a month."

His answer was met with cold silence. Dear had been making such promises since they were married. An earlier case which he had assured her would last but a few days had turned into an international drug smuggling investigation, stretching to four weeks as his itinerary carried him from Dallas to Los Angeles, then to Hong Kong and Korea, and finally to Thailand and Tokyo.

His week in Akron had already stretched to six. He didn't need a calendar to realize that he had spent more time away from home than he had in Dallas with his wife since their wedding.

Jan finally responded. "I don't feel married anymore," she said. There was no anger in her voice, only a sigh of resignation. Then she hung up.

Bill Dear sat on the edge of the bed for some time, staring down at the carpet. Damn you, Dean Milo, he thought; you're costing me too much.

10

Ray Lemon could not shake the disappointment of his failure to lure Barry Boyd into conversation during their surprise encounter at McDonald's. For several days after, he hardly left the house. He had, he knew, blown an opportunity to make big points with the local cops and the private investigator from Texas who seemed to be someone pretty important.

Too, it had been more exciting than anything he'd ever done before. It had been like playing a role on one of those TV cop shows. Though he had been admittedly nervous about calling Terry Lea King and during the aborted meeting, the events had given him a rush no drug had ever provided.

He dug Detective Momchilov's card from his wallet and called him. He was, he said, willing to give it another try.

"We damn sure haven't got anything to lose," Momchilov said to Dear. Dear agreed.

In short order a new plan of attack was outlined. Aware that Terry Lea was spending most of her days in Medina with her boyfriend while her husband and eleven-year-old daughter remained at the Akron apartment, they decided that Lemon should drive to Medina unannounced and urge Terry Lea to go to lunch with him. Once he got her in the car, he was again to try to get her to talk about her involvement in Dean Milo's murder.

Again Bill Dear would be in the trunk, listening on the earphones.

Lemon, determined to make good on his second chance, followed Momchilov and Dear along the busy highway leading from Akron to Medina. A couple of miles before reaching the turnoff that led to the house where Terry Lea stayed, they turned onto an access road and drove to the back of an isolated service station. Dear left Momchilov's car and took his position in the cramped, filthy trunk of Lemon's automobile.

"All snug and comfy?" Momchilov grinned as he looked down on Dear's lanky, curled-up frame.

"Just shut the damn lid and let's get this over with," Dear replied.

"Night," Momchilov said.

The day was unseasonably warm, and exhaust fumes seeped into the trunk as Lemon drove. The fumes were something Dear had not considered. He was feeling weak and nauseated even before Lemon finally pulled into the driveway at the Medina house. He began to worry about falling into a peaceful, deadly sleep.

This time they had wired Lemon personally in the event Terry Lea refused to go with him in the car. If something incriminating was said while they talked in the house, on the front porch, or in the yard, the recording equipment and Dear's earphones would pick it up.

Surprised to see Lemon, Terry Lea quickly insisted that lunch was out of the question. She was not feeling well. Maybe some other time. She was grateful for the loan, by the way, and would try to repay him by the end of the week.

Several men Lemon did not know wandered about the house, in and out of the living room where he and Terry Lea talked. He felt a strange mixture of relief and disappointment at the knowledge that this mission, like the previous one, was doomed to failure.

He did manage a casual mention of Boyd, asking Terry Lea if she had "talked about anything" when he had delivered the money to her. She had answered with an uninterested shrug.

When a young man wearing cut-off jeans and a T-shirt came into the room, a beer in hand, and turned on the television, Lemon gave up.

Returning to his car he waved to Terry Lea, who stood on the porch, backed out of the driveway, and sped away, forcing a new blast of exhaust fumes into the trunk.

Dear's disappointment in the mission had become secondary. Ill and fearing for his life, he was anxious to escape his darkened hiding place. Dizzy and fast becoming disoriented, he again found himself sending mental messages to the driver. Just get a couple of blocks away and pull over, he thought, so someone can get me out of here.

Instead, Lemon continued driving. To Dear it seemed like miles. Damn, he thought, he's going to go all the way back to Akron. The investigator began yelling at the top of his lungs and urgently kicking against the back of the trunk. Lemon, unaware of any problem, drove on, carrying his passenger closer and closer to asphyxiation.

Momchilov, following in his unmarked car, honked his horn several times in an attempt to get the attention of the speeding Lemon. Finally, he placed the portable light atop his car and set it in motion. Lemon finally noticed it and pulled off the highway.

The detective rushed to the trunk, lifting the door to find Dear in a semiconscious state. Placing his arms around Dear's shoulders, he dragged him from the car and helped him to a standing position. Dear tried to focus on his savior but his eyes rolled drunkenly. "Thanks," he finally managed in a slurred voice.

Momchilov was furious. He glared at Lemon, who stood on the shoulder of the road with a hangdog expression, then turned his attention to Dear. "Pal, you're either incredibly brave or stupid as hell. I don't know which and really don't give a particular damn. But you almost bought it this time. This fucking case isn't worth losing your life over."

Dear finally managed a nod. Nothing more was said on the drive back to Akron. Momchilov took Dear to his motel room, sat while making sure he drank several cups of the hot tea delivered by room service, then suggested he get some rest. Dear slept the rest of the day, finally awakening early in the evening with the cloying, sweet smell of gas fumes still in his nostrils.

Back in his office, Momchilov was talking with Joe Villanueva, who had stopped by in search of Dear.

Momchilov related the events of the day without the usual touch of humor in his story-telling. "Your boss worries me," he said.

Villanueva nodded. "I've never seen him like this before. He needs to back off for a while. He gets so damn mad about this case that he literally shakes. I don't think he's getting much rest."

"Hell, how could he?" Momchilov answered. "He's out with me all night, then running all over Hell and half of Georgia during the day."

"Sounds to me like you're burning the candle at both ends, too," Villanueva suggested.

"I'm not letting this thing get to me like Bill is, though."

"That's just the way he is. He's only got one speed. I decided a long time ago he was burning a different kind of fuel than most folks."

"The sonuvabitch is obsessive," Momchilov offered. "Just like Dean Milo was."

Villanueva nodded.

By the end of the week, the Medina event had been forgotten and yet another plan set in motion. Since the investigation of Terry Lea King had produced evidence of interest to the narcotics division of the sheriff's office, Momchilov and Bill Lewis suggested that undercover agent Mark Martin join the case.

Dear suggested that the experienced Martin might be able to succeed where the drug-worn Lemon had failed. His plan was to have the undercover agent contact Terry Lea and pretend to possess information that would implicate her in the Milo murder, then give the impression his silence could be bought.

"Extortion," Momchilov said.

"Damn right," Dear said. "I think maybe that's a language this lady would understand."

When the plan was taken to the department's legal adviser, assistant prosecutor Michael Wolff, he warned of the dangers of illegal entrapment. "Something like this could get messy," he told the investigators.

"We've got all kinds of probable cause," Dear argued. "Let me toss it around with a couple of other attorneys and I'll get back to you," Wolff said. The following day he phoned Momchilov. "It's shaky, but if you think it's all you've got, I think we can give it a try."

Momchilov immediately relayed the good news to Mark Martin and Dear.

Placing a phone in one of the isolated interview rooms and connecting it to a tape recorder, Martin dialed the number handed him by Dear. When a woman's voice answered, he said, "Terry?"

"Yeah, who's this?"

"That's not important right now. I've got something to discuss with you."

"Tell me who this is or I'm hanging up."

"I don't think so. See, this concerns Dean Milo."

Terry Lea did not hesitate. "Who's Dean Milo?"

"The dude who was killed. You and Barry Boyd did a number on him."

"I don't know what the fuck you're talking about."

Martin pressed the issue, suggesting they should get together to talk about it, and Terry Lea kept insisting on her ignorance.

"Look," she said, "why are you calling me about this?"

"Because I'm kinda hurting for cash right now. For a small fee I'd be glad to keep my mouth shut. I won't tell that Texas dude who's been snooping around, asking all kinds of shit questions."

"This is absurd."

"Let me explain something to you," Martin continued, "They're offering a big reward, a helluva lot more money than I need. And, see, I don't want to be messing with the police because I've been in a little trouble myself. But I'll do what I have to. It's strictly up to you, babe."

When Terry Lea did not reply, the undercover agent continued. "You better get your act together real quick, because I don't have a lot of time to screw around. I'm just looking for enough cash to get the hell out of town. Five thousand, tops. So if you want to talk, we'd better set something up fast. You know where the Western Omelet is?"

"Yeah, it's just a few miles from here."

"Hey, I'm trying to make it convenient for you," Martin said, then laughed. "So here's the deal: If you want to talk, be damn sure you come by yourself. I don't want anybody with you, okay? Hell, you people already killed one person. I damn sure don't want to be next. Meet me there at two o'clock!."

"What time is it now?" Terry Lea asked. "I just woke up."

"It's twelve-thirty. Throw some water on your face and get your ass to the Western Omelet by two."

"This is crazy."

"I'm just trying to give you and your buddy Barry Boyd a chance. If you don't show, I'm talking to that PI from Texas. Count on it."

Again Terry Lea said she knew nothing about a murder, but she went on to ask for specific directions to the restaurant and how she would recognize him.

"I'll be wearing a yellow knit stocking cap and a green army jacket," he replied.

"Are you ... you sound like an adult."

"I am an adult, honey. Kids don't extort money." Two hours later, Mark Martin, wired for sound, sat alone in a booth at the Western Omelet. He stayed there until almost four in the afternoon before resigning himself to the fact that Terry Lea King was not going to keep the appointment.

When Martin called again the next day, Terry Lea made it clear that his bluff was not going to work. This time, she took the offensive. If he wanted to go to the police or some private investigator with his wild story about her being involved in a murder, she wanted to go along with him and discuss his extortion plans with the authorities.

"There are two things I want you to do," she yelled into the telephone. "First, leave me the fuck alone. And second, you tell Ray Lemon, who seems to be talking about this shit a lot, that his little joke's gone just about far enough. Goodbye."

Martin heard the connection broken and looked over at Dear and Momchilov. "She's tough," he said. "You guys sure this Lemon guy is shooting straight with you?"

For Bill Dear, the case was becoming a nightmare. Convinced that the maddening puzzle could be solved with only a few brief sentences of admission from either Terry Lea King or Barry Boyd, he was beginning to wonder if he would ever hear those words spoken. If there was anything more frustrating than not knowing who the guilty parties were, it was knowing who they were but not being able to connect them legally to the crime.

Dear placed calls to a number of law enforcement friends around the United States, detailing the investigation on which he was working, asking for suggestions they might have. None offered any ideas he had not already tried.

A veteran Texas lawman, whose opinions Dear had long respected, listened attentively as the frustrated investigator poured out a description of the winding trails the case had thus far led him down. "Sounds to me," the listener drawled after Dear's lengthy narrative, "like you're kinda snake-bit on this one. You know, there are cases that just don't get solved."

"This isn't going to be one of them," Dear replied.

Several days later Dear hurried into the sheriff's office in search of Momchilov. It was early morning but he had been up for some time. When Bill Lewis told him that Momchilov had not yet arrived, Dear asked for the lieutenant's help.

"You got time to spend an hour or so poking around with me over in Terry Lea King's neighborhood?"

"Sure. What you got in mind?"

Dear didn't detail his offbeat plan until he had Lewis in the car with him and headed toward Gordon Avenue. "Just a little snooping," Dear smiled. "Nothing we could get thrown in jail for."

Once at the corner he and Momchilov had used as a stakeout point to watch Terry Lea's movements, Dear asked Lewis if he remembered the Jack Anderson column about the evidence produced by a rummage through the contents of FBI director J. Edgar Hoover's garbage cans.

"It rings a bell," Lewis said.

"Well, today's garbage pickup day, so I thought maybe we'd

see what Terry Lea King's trash tells us."

"You re shitting me," Lewis said.

It was midmorning when Terry Lea, dressed in a bathrobe, appeared on the front porch with two plastic trash sacks. Instead of taking them to the curb as most others in the neighborhood had already done hours earlier, she left them on the porch and returned to the house.

"No garbage collector in Akron is going to walk up on the lady's porch to get that trash," Lewis offered.

Even as he spoke, Dear noticed a battered 1930s vintage truck, piled high with boxes, worn mattresses, and tangled parts of discarded bicycles. The driver, wearing dirty overalls and puffing on the stub of a cigar, was a scavenger who rummaged through the neighborhood trash for things he deemed valuable before the official collectors made their scheduled stops.

Dear, with Lewis in his wake, left the car and walked toward where the old man was busily sifting through the contents of a trash can.

"Morning," Dear said in a friendly voice. "What are you doing?"

The man neither looked up from the trash can nor returned the greeting. "Working," he said. "What the hell does it look like?"

"Make a pretty good living this way?" Dear continued.

"Shit no, mister," the man said as he looked at the expensive suit Dear was wearing. "You don't see me in no suit and tie, do you?"

Dear laughed. "Listen, I've got twenty dollars for you if you'll do me a little favor, no questions asked."

"Whatcha got in mind?"

Pointing in the direction of Terry Lea King's apartment, he asked the man if he would wait for her to put her garbage out by the curb, then bring it to him.

"You got a deal," the man said, folding the twenty into the bib pocket of his overalls and walking away. It was a minute before Dear and Lewis, who had hurried back to their car, realized the man was headed toward the King house, hobbling across the small lawn and up onto the porch to retrieve the garbage bags.

As he approached his benefactors, dragging the bags alongside him, Dear and Lewis slumped low in the front seat and frantically tried to wave him off. The old man continued their way until he stood at the window on the driver's side. "Where you want these bags?" he asked.

As he was placing them in the back seat as Dear instructed, Terry Lea and her husband, Denny, appeared on their front porch their eyes shielded against the morning sun, watching the bizarre transaction. Dear hurriedly started the car and sped away. "Remind me never to hire that guy again," he said as Bill Lewis broke into laughter.

Despite its comic overtones, the escapade yielded some small treasures of information. Amidst the fast food wrappers, discarded milk cartons, and rotting produce, Dear found several wadded messages addressed to Terry Lea, asking her to call Barry Boyd, and some used hypodermic needles. There was nothing damaging enough to prompt an arrest, but the contents produced new links between Terry Lea King and Boyd. A laboratory examination of the needles would no doubt also reinforce the suspicions of Terry Lea's drug use.

"Jack Anderson would be damn proud," Lewis said as he watched Dear finish his search.

"Not really," Dear replied. "Remember, he had an assistant do this."

The fact that members of the Akron media had begun applying pressure at the courthouse, demanding updates on the progress of the investigation, had triggered yet another meeting in Chief Duvall's office.

It was agreed that things had stalled. Dear's assistants had continued to come up with interesting stories of personal habits and background material on the members of the Milo family but had nothing that would provide a new direction to the investigation. Lewis and Munsey, having covered much the same ground as Villanueva and Riddle, admitted they were stymied and getting bored with what was beginning to look like a hopeless task.

"We've got to bust something loose ourselves," Dear said.

He was tired of hiding in car trunks and pilfering garbage, and he felt it was time to roll the dice. "I say we arrest Terry Lea King."

"… and watch a two-ton false arrest suit fall down around our heads," added Munsey.

"We've got more probable cause than we need," Dear argued. "We pick her drugged-out ass up and get her in here and she'll fall to pieces. Give her a few hours away from a needle and she'll jump through hoops for us."

Lewis took Munsey's side. "I don't see it. Even if we do arrest her, there's not enough hard evidence for a conviction. We make big news one day, then get our butts scalded by the press when we have to turn her loose."

"I'm telling you," Dear yelled, "we bust her and all the other players are going to come out of the woodwork. Dammit to hell, I know what I'm talking about."

"What you're forgetting," Munsey said, "is it's our tails on the line on this thing. You don't have anything to lose."

"I've got my reputation," Dear roared back. "That means just as much to me as your ass does to you."

Momchilov had sat quietly throughout the conversation. Only when it heated to the point where the voices could be heard far down the hall did he stand up and speak. He was, he pointed out, the man officially in charge of the investigation. "I think we ought to pop her."

Lewis and Munsey stopped arguing. They could see that Duvall, by his silence, supported the move.

"What we'll do," Momchilov explained, "is get arrest and search warrants for both places Terry Lea stays. We arrest her, bring her down here and see if she'll roll over on Barry Boyd. We've got Lemon's statement for probable cause. There comes a time when you have to gamble."

"When?" Dear asked.

"Tomorrow, as soon as the paperwork's ready and we can get our people together." Momchilov added that he planned to use at least six officers at each address.

It was shortly after noon on October 21 when a parade of cars left the courthouse parking lot. Dear rode with Momchilov in one of the cars headed toward Medina, where they expected to find Terry Lea King.

Upon arrival, Momchilov and two deputies approached the front door while Dear hurried to the back of the house in the company of three other deputies.

There was no answer to Momchilov's first knock. Then, after pounding the door even harder, he heard a male voice call out from inside. "Who is it?"

"Summit County sheriff's office," the detective yelled. "We have a warrant for the arrest of Terry Lea King."

A lengthy silence followed, then Momchilov began pounding on the door again. Another minute passed before the door opened just a few inches. Momchilov wasted no time pushing his way inside, his gun trained on Cal Loomis, the man Terry Lea King had supposedly fallen in love with. Loomis stood against the living room wall, barefoot and shirtless.

The minute Dear was aware that Momchilov was in the house, he unlocked the back door with a credit card and led the other deputies inside. In the front room they could see Momchilov showing Loomis two folded documents. "This," he said, "is the arrest warrant for Terry Lea King. And this is a warrant to search your premises."

"What the hell are you looking for?" the frightened Loomis asked.

"Read the warrant," Momchilov said. "It speaks for itself."

In the back bedroom, two deputies found Terry Lea King, naked and standing in a corner with a blank look on her face. Momchilov called for a woman deputy, who stood watch as

Terry Lea pulled on a pair of jeans and a long-sleeved purple blouse.

The female officer then escorted her to the living room. "I have a warrant for your arrest for the murder of Constantine R. (Dean) Milo," Momchilov said. He then read her rights as she was being handcuffed.

Terry Lea said nothing, staring directly into Momchilov's eyes throughout the procedure.

The search of the house produced an arsenal. Over forty firearms—pistols, rifles, and shotguns—were found hidden in various places. None, however, was a .32 automatic.

To the surprise of the arresting officers, no drugs were found.

Leaving the search chores to the deputies, Momchilov, Dear, the woman deputy, and Terry Lea King left for Akron, where a search was already under way at Terry Lea's house.

They arrived to find the place ringed by television cameramen and by radio and newspaper reporters, all of them eager to get a look at the person who had finally been arrested in connection with the Milo murder. Momchilov looked at Dear. He said nothing, but it was clear what he was thinking. Munsey and Lewis were right. If this didn't work out, there would be hell to pay.

Terry Lea King made no attempt to hide from the cameras as she walked up the front steps of her home, hands cuffed behind her.

While the search of the house was going on, Dear sought out Terry Lea's husband. Denny King was a computer operator who, like Ray Lemon, still preferred the dress and lifestyle of a bygone hippie generation. Dear found him sitting in the living room, on the verge of tears as he watched the activity around him.

"I don't understand all this," he said. "What's our little girl going to think?" Eleven-year-old Lisa King was in school.

"Mr. King," Dear said, "I've heard good things about you. People have told me how dedicated you are to your little girl. I'm sorry you've become involved in all this. But I'm afraid I can't understand—"

Denny King seemed to know what the investigator was going to say and he interrupted. "I know it doesn't make much sense, but I love Terry. She may not be the perfect mother and all that. And I know she's got that guy out in Medina she stays with. But I think she loves me, loves us. I'm not her judge, just her husband."

Dear felt a genuine sympathy for him, at the same time wondering how any husband could be so permissive. "Denny," he said, "your wife's in serious trouble, you know. Are you involved in any way with the death of Dean Milo?"

"No sir, I'm not."

"Do you know Barry Boyd?"

"Yeah, he comes by now and then."

"Were you aware that he was involved with Terry in putting the murder scheme together?"

"I don't believe Terry put together any murder. Maybe she knew something about it, but she wasn't part of it. All I know is, one night she came home—she'd been out with Barry—and asked if I'd believe someone was willing to pay ten thousand dollars to have somebody killed. I didn't think much about it. It was just bar talk she'd heard. Hell, she was always coming up with something crazy like that. That's just Terry.

"I didn't even answer her, just let it go in one ear and out the other. She never brought it up again. Like I say, that's just Terry."

Then he began to cry.

At the Summit County sheriff's office, Dear stood against the tile wall across from the booking desk, watching as Terry Lea King was being processed. Perhaps at one time she had been a pretty girl, but no more. Her hair was tangled and her eyes were ringed with shadows and had no sparkle. Even makeup could not have hidden the fact that her complexion had long ago lost the battle to too many drugs and fast foods. If her figure was anything special, the fact was well hidden by the way she dressed. Dear caught himself wondering how she could ever have been one of the highest-paid go-go dancers in town.

She nervously pulled at the sleeves of her blouse as the booking clerk filled out the forms. Dear walked over to her. "Let me take a look," he said, reaching toward one of her sleeves.

Terry Lea flashed a look of pure hatred in his direction, then extended her arm. Rolling up the sleeve, Dear saw that the arm was black and blue, swollen to twice normal size. Needle tracks crisscrossed the veins like some madman's tic-tac-toe game. The other arm was no better.

She looked exhausted and sweat had matted her hair against her forehead. Her jaundiced color and the dullness of her eyes told Dear that she was suffering from hepatitis.

For a moment, he felt a twinge of pity for Terry Lea King.

Those who interrogated her in relays through the afternoon and into the night didn't. She fixed an icy stare on each officer as he entered the room to question her, rarely even blinking, maintaining total silence as the same questions were hurled at her time and time again.

"That," said one of the department's most experienced interrogators as he stepped out to get a cup of coffee, "is one cold bitch. She's got more nuts than half the men I know." Aware that any good defense lawyer would make an issue of any statement given by a prisoner pushed to the brink of exhaustion, Momchilov ordered an end to the questioning and had Terry Lea sent to a cell. Maybe she would be more willing to talk after a few hours' rest—and no needles to stick in her arm to stop the shaking and nausea he knew would soon be visiting her.

It was near midnight when Dear and Momchilov walked into the clear, chilling air, headed toward the parking lot. The detective lit a cigarette and inhaled deeply.

"You always smoke this much?" Dear asked.

"Yeah," Momchilov said. "And if things don't get a helluva lot better soon, I'm gonna get more serious about my drinking."

Dear knew that the detective was bone-weary of the tedious case, tired of the stop-and-go nature of the investigation. "Look," he said, "I want you to know that I admire the way you handled this thing. It took some nerve to make the decision to go ahead and arrest her."

"That whore isn't going to make it easy for us, you know," Momchilov said. "She was tough as hell back there."

"She'll give it up."

"If she doesn't, I might be looking for another job pretty soon," Momchilov said.

"You got one working for me anytime you're ready," Dear said.

Momchilov didn't respond. Pitching his cigarette into the street, he headed toward the parking lot. He was at his car, the door open, when he yelled back in Dear's direction. "Hey," he said, "I forgot to tell you something."

"What's that?"

"Barry Boyd's lawyer has agreed to let him be polygraphed in the morning."

Dear was stunned. Momchilov was in his car and backing away before Dear could ask what had caused the sudden change of heart. Pulling the collar of his coat to his ears, he watched the red taillights disappear into the cold darkness.

"I'll be damned," he said as he began walking toward his rented car.

11

The parade of interrogators hoping to convince Terry Lea King to confess were going through an exercise in frustration. If she chafed at being held in the county jail, she refused to let it show. She would sit for hours, taking long drags on her Marlboros as she matched stares with each officer who had her called from her cell to the interview room. On the rare occasions when she did answer a question, it was only with a terse word or two.

Yes, she acknowledged, she had been arrested before. But it was left to a clerk in the records section to learn that it had been for marijuana possession in 1972. She had been out of work for the past three months. She admitted that she owned two guns, a .38 Colt revolver and a .22 caliber rifle, both gifts from boyfriends. No, she did not have a license for the revolver.

And no, she knew nothing of any plot to murder Dean Milo.

Dear and Momchilov, both among those who spent time talking with Terry Lea, were surprised that drug withdrawal had not weakened her.

"She's tough," Dear observed.

"Know what I think?" Momchilov said. "I think she doesn't give a shit one way or another. And those are the hardest nuts to crack."

To add to the frustration, Barry Boyd's polygraph examination was judged inconclusive. There had been some evidence of deception, but not enough to prove Boyd was lying about participating in Milo's murder.

Dear was standing in the crowded detective bureau when Boyd walked from the polygraph room, making no attempt to disguise his elation. Smiling, he looked at the investigator. "If you people would spend more time looking in the right areas instead of harassing me," he said, "maybe you could solve this case."

As Dear glared at him, Boyd turned and began to walk away.

"Boyd," Dear said, then followed the attorney, "I don't give a damn if you did pass that test. It doesn't matter one iota to me. You're guilty," he whispered in the attorney's ear. "You know it and I know it. And I'm going to prove it."

"You're nuts," Boyd said. "If you know what's good for you, you'll leave me alone."

If it was meant to be a threat, Dear thought, it was weakly delivered. He remained convinced that just below the polished, poised exterior, Boyd was a frightened man very near the breaking point.

But then, he had felt much the same way about Terry Lea King. And now he was beginning to wonder.

During the first week of November the Summit County Court of Common Pleas ruled that control of Milo Barber and Beauty Supply should revert back to the Milo family. Immediately following Milo's death, the court had taken control of the company, establishing a temporary trusteeship that would oversee operations during the litigation, with company comptroller Paul Vaughn serving as acting president. The court's ruling was to be put into effect on November 10.

It was on that day that Bill Dear received a call requesting his attendance at a meeting in the office of one of the Milo company's new vice presidents, Lonnie Curtis.

No time had been wasted following the court's ruling. Dean Milo's entire hand-picked management team had been terminated and a new board of directors elected. Fred Milo assumed the title of president with Lonnie and Sophie Curtis serving as vice presidents. Maggie Milo was given no decision-making powers in the new corporate structure.

Curtis, tanned and well dressed, remained seated behind his desk as Dear was shown into his office. Without pleasantries he introduced the investigator to George Pappas, a highly regarded Akron attorney, then went directly to the purpose of the meeting.

"Mr. Dear," the new vice president said, "so far this company has paid you a total of thirty-five thousand dollars. We would like to know what you have to show for it."

"I have a good deal to show for it."

"Then let's hear about it," Curtis challenged. "I want to know what we've gotten for the money we've paid you."

Dear stiffened and let several seconds pass before he answered. "Mr. Curtis, I have no intentions of discussing this investigation with you."

"You're telling me that even though we're paying the bills we don't have the right to know what we're buying," Curtis said, his voice taking on an indignant tone.

"When I took this case, my agreement with the company was that all information I gathered would be strictly confidential and would be available only to the police. I plan to live up to that agreement."

"You're talking about the former Milo B&B management. In case you haven't noticed, the company now has a new set of executives. We are now the Milo Company and we are the ones paying you. Therefore, we are entitled to a full report of your findings thus far."

Dear held his ground. "This is an ongoing investigation," he said, "and I don't intend to discuss it with you or any other members of your organization."

Pappas shifted forward in his oversized leather chair and turned to face the investigator. "Mr. Dear," he said, "am I to understand that you feel even if the Milo Company continues to pay your bills it will not be privileged to any of the information you gather?"

"That's right."

Pappas shook his head and folded his hands together before continuing. "Then, even if I recommend that the organization continue its financing of your investigation into Dean Milo's death, you refuse to tell us anything you have learned or might learn?"

Dear nodded.

"Are you investigating the Milo family?"

"I'm investigating everyone who had any connection with Dean Milo."

Pappas cleared his throat, appearing to enjoy this kind of cross-examination. "More specifically, Mr. Dear, are you investigating Lonnie and his wife? Or Fred Milo?"

Dear smiled for the first time since he had entered the room. "Yes."

"I think you would agree that this is highly unusual," Pappas continued. "Do I understand you to say that you feel Mr. Curtis here should pay you to conduct an investigation of him? What kind of a businessman do you think he would be if he agreed to such an outlandish arrangement?"

Dear rose from his chair, straightening his jacket, then pointed a finger in the direction of Curtis. "What kind of man is he if he doesn't agree? And what about Fred and Sophie? They've lost a brother, dammit. Don't they want to know who did it?"

Weary of the game that was being played and now convinced he had been called to the meeting to be told his services were no longer needed, Dear let his rage build. "If these people you represent really care, why haven't they ever agreed to talk with me? Why are they so afraid to answer my questions? You tell me just what the hell is going on here. I'm sick of it."

Dear turned to Curtis. "You're talking about money, but I don't see a nickel's worth of concern about Dean Milo ... or justice." Curtis said nothing.

Pappas watched as the two men glared at each other, then broke the chilled silence. "Mr. Dear," he said, "it is going to be very difficult for me to recommend to my clients that they continue to pay you under the conditions that you have set forth."

"Are you saying I'm fired?"

"I'll have to discuss the matter with the board of directors," the attorney said. "You'll have their decision this afternoon."

Dear began walking toward the door. "I can hardly wait," he said.

As soon as he left company headquarters, he called George Tsarnas and asked if he and Maggie Milo could meet with him right away. "They're going to give me the ax," he said.

"It figures," Tsarnas replied.

Maggie Milo was in the Tsarnas den, staring out the window as Dear related the conversation that had taken place in Lonnie Curtis's office. She seemed lost in thought.

Only after he finished did she turn and look at him. "That," she said, "proves what I've been saying all along. The family is involved in the murder of my husband." Her chin quivered slightly as she fought back tears.

Tsarnas said gently, "You're tired."

"I'm beyond tired," she said. "I'm exhausted. And sick of all this. I want it to be over." Folding her hands in her lap, she began to cry. "I want my husband back."

The two men sat silently until Maggie had composed herself. "I'm sorry," she said. "It's just been so hard."

She rose and approached Dear. "You're my only hope of finding out who killed Dean. Please say you will stay on the case. I'll see that you are paid."

Even before she made her offer Dear had made up his mind to continue the investigation even without payment. He had come too far to quit. Late that afternoon Dear received a telephone call from George Pappas at the Holiday Inn. "The board has reached its decision," the attorney said. "They've decided not to continue with your services."

With her bond set at $500,000, Terry Lea King had remained in custody, passing the time she was not being interrogated with long stretches of sleep. Though she continued her refusal to answer any questions about the crimes she was charged with, she was, in all other respects, a model prisoner.

Until the afternoon of November 13.

She had requested that a jail matron allow her to make a telephone call and was escorted from her cell to a holding area. There, she persuaded the matron to loosen the hand-cuffs she was required to wear each time she left her cell, complaining that their pressure hurt her needle-infected arms.

After doing so, the matron left her prisoner alone to make her call. When she returned, Terry Lea King had disappeared. Word spread quickly through the jail that the prime suspect in the Milo murder had escaped.

The frantic search did not last long, however. Terry Lea had not even made it out of the building. A deputy found her hiding behind a door in one of the downstairs locker rooms.

Dear, who had rushed to the jail as soon as Momchilov called to report this latest turn of events, was relieved that Terry Lea had been found so quickly and, on the other hand, pleased that she had attempted to escape. "Innocent people don't try to break out of jail," he observed.

Momchilov agreed. "What she and her attorney should be doing," he said, "is pushing like hell for a speedy trial. The truth of the matter is, we haven't got shit on her. As things stand right now, it's her word against that goof ball Lemon's. An attorney with any snap at all would tear him apart on the stand."

Fred Zuch, the Summit County prosecutor assigned to the case, agreed. He, in fact, had been the only prosecutor willing to take the case. A former Akron police officer who had earned his law degree in night school, Zuch believed that Terry Lea King was guilty, in light of the circumstantial evidence, but he had strong doubts about a conviction. He was pressuring the investigators for more evidence.

"You're going to have to tie Barry Boyd into this thing," he said.

Dear and Momchilov agreed. But that hope dimmed dramatically when Joe Villanueva called. "Boyd's run," Villanueva said. "I tried to pick him up at his office but he hasn't been there in days. I've been by his house a dozen times with no luck. He hasn't been to any of his hangouts. I've even checked the hospitals. It's like the sonuvabitch just went up in a puff of smoke."

Dear had his associate check with Ed Pierce, Boyd's attorney, and with a Shaker Heights doctor he knew Boyd had been seeing. Neither had any idea of his whereabouts. Villanueva secretly placed matchsticks in the door of Boyd's house one night, then checked back regularly to see if they had been dislodged by anyone coming or going. For days the matches remained in place. In time, Villanueva began knocking at Boyd's front door, but he got no answer.

"I'm going to drive up to Cleveland," Dear said. Weeks earlier Villanueva had reported that Boyd was seeing a woman named Sally Reeves, described as a pretty registered nurse who lived in a Cleveland apartment near the hospital where she worked. "Maybe he's hiding behind her petticoat."

It was late in the evening when Bill Dear found the address Villanueva had given him. He already had his card in hand when Sally Reeves opened the door. "I'm a private investigator," he said. "I'd like to ask you some questions."

"What about?" the nurse asked. Dear was relieved that her tone showed no hostility.

"I'm investigating the murder of Dean Milo in Akron," he said.

Sally Reeves looked puzzled, then invited him in. "I'm afraid I don't know anyone named Milo," she said. "And I certainly don't know anything about any murder."

As she spoke Dear surveyed the small living room area of her apartment. On one wall hung photographs of two smiling boys. "My sons," Sally said. "They've already gone to bed."

"I apologize for stopping by so late," Dear said, "but it's important. Do you have any idea where I might find Barry Boyd?"

A look of sudden concern crossed the woman's face. "Has something happened to him?"

"Not that I know of. We've just been unable to locate him for the past several days."

Sally Reeves motioned for the investigator to sit on the sofa. "I'm worried about him, too," she said. "I haven't seen or heard from him in five days. Is he in some kind of trouble?"

"I'm afraid he's gotten himself into a situation he can't get out of," Dear replied. "I've met him and I have the impression he's in over his head and needs some help. If I can find him …"

"Does it have something to do with the murder you mentioned?"

Dear nodded.

Her face twisted into a pained expression and she began nervously wringing her hands. "Barry's a sweet, gentle man. Whatever you think he's done, you're wrong. There's no way he could be involved in something like that."

"How's he been acting lately?"

The question seemed to surprise her. She looked at Dear for several seconds, as if wondering how much he knew about her relationship with Boyd. "Something is bothering him," she admitted. "He's been drinking more and more. I'm afraid it's going to kill him if he doesn't get some help. If I didn't love him so much, I'd have sent him away long ago."

She began to talk about her troubled first marriage. Her husband hadn't been a heavy drinker when they first married, she said, but the problems that come from a low income and the quick arrival of two children had helped make him an alcoholic. By the time they divorced, he had beaten her and the children on more occasions than she could remember. Barry had never raised a violent hand to her or the boys, she said, but the drinking frightened her. "I can really pick them," she added."

"Sally," Dear said gently, "I want you to think carefully about what I'm going to ask. It's important. Has Barry made any calls from here to a person named Lonnie Curtis ... or Fred Milo? Or have they called for him here?"

She shook her head. "The names don't ring a bell. Barry's gotten calls here, though. Several times I've noticed that he would talk in a very low voice. Sometimes he would go into the bedroom to take the call. I just assumed it was business with some client and didn't try to listen."

"Do you have any idea where he might be?"

"I wish I did," she said. "I'm worried to death. Lately, when he gets drunk, he talks really crazy."

"About what?"

"Committing suicide," she said, beginning to cry.

"Do you think he was serious?"

"He would just ramble, saying crazy things. Like he was ruining my life and didn't deserve me or the boys. He said one day I would find out what a terrible person he really was. But then he would sober up and everything would be okay."

She seemed to search Dear's face for some reassurance that Barry Boyd was not in danger. "Sally," he said, "I'm sorry to worry you with all this. I know you don't know me, but let me assure you I want to help Barry if I can. He needs help. And if you need me, please call."

As he left the apartment and walked toward his car, he felt a twinge of guilt. The suggestion that he wanted to help Barry Boyd had not been rehearsed. Nor had it completely been a lie. Boyd, he was convinced, was the key to unlocking the mystery of Dean Milo's murder. But he could not bring himself to believe the scared lawyer had pulled the trigger. He was some sort of go-between, playing far out of his league. The only thing that stood between him and admission of his involvement was fear of the consequences.

Dear sat in his car for several minutes before starting the engine. There, in the parking lot of a Cleveland apartment complex, it finally occurred to him that the nearly overwhelming motivation that had driven him to the point of obsession in pursuit of Dean Milo's murderer had a name. He had seen it all around him since his arrival in Ohio, on the faces of many of those he had interviewed. It was the reason he had gone to such lengths, working around the clock, hiding in the trunks of cars, sacrificing his own marriage. It was fear—in his case, fear of failure, fear that he might not be able to solve what he now judged one of the most important investigations of his career.

The discovery that he and Barry Boyd had something in common troubled him as he made the drive back to Akron.

It was three days later when Sally Reeves reached Dear at his motel room. "I heard from Barry," she said.

"Is he okay?"

"I can't tell," she said. "He sounded more depressed than ever. He didn't say much; just that he wanted me to know he's okay and not to worry about him."

"Did he say where he was?"

Sally Reeves's answer staggered the investigator. "He's at

his house. He says he's been there all the time."

How, Dear wondered, had he managed to hole up in his own house for over a week without anyone knowing? Where was his car? Why would he want to live in a darkened house, never turning on a light or answering the telephone, not checking the mail or picking up the newspaper? Had he gone on a marathon binge, drinking himself into a stupor and waking only to do it again?

Whatever the answers, it was clear that Barry Boyd had signaled his resurrection with his call to Sally Reeves. It was time to step up the pressure.

Dear called Villanueva to relate the news of Boyd's whereabouts. "Stick to him like you're his Siamese twin," he ordered. "I want him to know—beyond a shadow of a doubt—that you're a step behind him everywhere he goes. It's time to make him crack."

"I'm on my way to his house now," Villanueva said.

Barry Boyd emerged from his self-imposed exile pale and disoriented. He walked with the shuffle of an old man, his head down and his hands always buried deep in his pockets. A look of physical pain seemed frozen to his face.

Villanueva had made little attempt to hide the fact he was shadowing Boyd. "The guy's walking around on another planet," Villanueva told Dear. "Unless I go up and introduce myself, he's not going to ever know I'm around. I've never seen anything like it."

That remark suggested the next move. "Go up to him," Dear said, "give him your card, and tell him you've been assigned to follow him. Be polite, but make sure he understands you're serious. Let's see how he reacts."

Villanueva gave his boss a stunned look. He'd long since lost track of the number of people he'd been assigned to trail during his career, but never had he been asked to walk up to the subject of a surveillance and introduce himself.

"What have we got to lose?" Dear asked.

The following day Villanueva did as instructed when he encountered Boyd on the street in front of his office. Boyd stared at the card through bloodshot, watery eyes as Villanueva explained his mission. The lawyer continued looking at the card, as if searching for some message he might have missed in it, then without even entering his office building began walking back toward the parking lot. He got into his car and drove directly home with Villanueva close behind.

The house remained dark. The rabbit had retreated back to his hole.

Dear was in the office of the county prosecutor when Villanueva telephoned to report this most recent development, and when Dear relayed the message, Zuch said, "If he's going to play Howard Hughes on us, we're in big trouble."

Terry Lea King's attorney had finally filed a motion demanding a speedy trial. Appearing before Judge Frank Bayer, he had insisted that there was not sufficient evidence to continue holding his client in custody. "Judge," he said, "they're trampling all over the Constitution on this thing. It's not right."

The judge consulted his calendar and found a cancellation on November 26, less than a week away. "I'll hear the case then," he said.

"Either of you believe in miracles?" Zuch asked after summoning Momchilov and Dear to his office to tell them of the judge's decision. "We need one now."

He had played his last card, he explained, by asking that Terry Lea King be tried for first-degree murder; conviction on that charge would result in a life sentence. In turn, Zuch had told defense attorney Jerry Montgomery that he would be willing to accept a guilty plea to the lesser charge of complicity if Terry Lea would disclose everything she knew about the Milo murder. Conviction on the lesser charge carried a prison term of between seven and twenty-five years.

Montgomery, no newcomer to the judicial bargaining table, quickly refused the offer. The best Zuch was able to do was persuade the judge to grant a two-week continuance on a promise that new evidence would be forthcoming in a matter of days

From where, he had no idea.

A weighty depression settled over the investigative team as the trial date neared. Dear and his associates cut their sleeping time to just a few hours nightly and they gathered regularly in his motel room to review the growing mound of paperwork that had accumulated. The reports produced no new strategy, offered no overlooked clue.

When not with his staff, Dear was at the sheriff's office with Momchilov, in hopes they might find something in the official files that would produce some undiscovered lead. Dear watched the detective closely as he read, then reread reports, smoking one cigarette after another and commenting profanely as he discarded each file and reached for another.

Though Momchilov had not mentioned it, Dear knew that the courageous decision to arrest Terry Lea King, against the advice of Munsey and Lewis, now promised to result in a black mark against the detective.

While Dear felt empathy with Momchilov, he knew also that his own reputation was at stake. If Terry Lea King went free, the case would very likely fall apart. He did not look forward to the possibility of telling Maggie Milo that the thirty-thousand-dollar fee she had agreed to pay him to continue with the investigation had resulted in nothing but frustrating disappointment.

"There's not one damn thing left to do," Momchilov said as he wearily closed the last file and pitched it on his desk. Dear reluctantly agreed.

The only hope was the miracle that Zuch had said they needed.

12

On the morning of November 29, Dick Riddle sat alone in Bill Dear's motel room, idly reading through reports he had all but memorized. Like his boss, he had become despondent over the case and was privately hoping for word to return to Texas and some new assignment.

The phone rang several times before he reached to answer it.
"You Bill Dear?" a gruff voice demanded.
"Bill's not here right now. I'm his assistant."
"I don't want to talk to his fucking assistant. I want to talk with Bill Dear."

Riddle asked the caller his name and received only baritone laughter in response. "I'd be glad to take a message and get it to Bill." he offered.

"This is just between Bill Dear and me."
"Can you give me some idea what it is about?" Riddle asked in an attempt to keep the caller on the line.
"You taping this call?"
Riddle lied. "No."
"Tell your man that I know who killed Dean Milo. Tell him I've got the information he needs if he's got the money to pay for it. I'll get back with him." Then Riddle heard a sharp click signaling that the caller had hung up.

Riddle replaced the receiver and did not even take time to disengage the recorder before calling Dear at Momchilov's office.

After listening to the recording of the brief conversation over the phone, Dear told Riddle he was on his way to the motel. "Stay off the phone," he instructed Riddle. "If he's serious he'll probably call back soon. If I don't get there before he does, tell him we've talked and I'm tired of being jerked around by crank calls. Tell him he's got to meet with you first so you can check him out. Give him the impression I'm not really interested until he can convince us he's got something worth listening to."

Even before Dear could make the short drive from the courthouse to the motel, the phone in his room rang again.

"I'm going to make this short and sweet," the caller said. "First, I want you to know I've moved to another phone, so don't get any ideas about tracing this call. All I want to know is when I can see Dear."

"I just talked with him," Riddle replied. "He's not convinced you're legit. In fact, he told me he's about had it with calls from people saying they know something about the case."

"They didn't know what I do," the caller growled.

"He told me to tell you to meet with me first. You convince me you've got something, then he'll talk with you."

"Fuck it," the caller answered.

"Then I take it you really don't have the information you say you do," Riddle answered in as casual a tone of voice as he could muster.

The caller was silent for a moment, as if considering his options. "Okay," he finally said, "but I'm naming the meeting place."

"Just tell me when and where."

"Jack Horner's on Market Street... in an hour. And don't try any funny shit. If you guys want to solve this case you're going to have to do it my way." The caller had Riddle describe himself so that he might recognize him.

Dear arrived just minutes after Riddle had hung up and immediately gathered his team. Terry Hurley, Carl Lilly, and Villanueva were assigned to the surveillance van that had been driven from Dallas. Riddle would be wired and they would record whatever conversation took place with the informant.

If the caller arrived in an automobile, Dear told Villanueva, he was to get the license plate number as soon as it was safe to do so and call him at Momchilov's office immediately from the van phone.

Trying to hide a new surge of optimism, Dear gave out his instructions in a matter-of-fact way. There had already been too many disappointments during the course of the investigation; this time he would be careful not to raise hopes too soon.

"If all goes smoothly," Dear said, "tail the guy after he leaves. If something goes wrong and he tries to run, grab him if possible. This could be just another wild-goose chase," he concluded. Privately, he didn't think so. He had a feeling—that most electric enthusiasm gamblers with a hot hand occasionally experience—that something good was going to happen.

He paced nervously in Momchilov's small office until the phone rang and the detective handed him the receiver. Dear wrote down the license number Villanueva was calling in and handed it to Momchilov, who immediately disappeared to another part of the building.

In a matter of minutes, he was back with a computer printout. The informant now had a name and a description. Dear quickly read the information:

NAME: Shear, William Earl
DATE OF BIRTH: 12—6-47
SEX: Male
RACE: White
HEIGHT: 5'5"
WEIGHT: 168
EYES: Blue
HAIR: Brown
FLAG: AO

It was the last notation that most interested the men reading the information. Flag indicated there was more information to follow. The initials AO told what that information would be: arrests and offense of the man named William Shear.

"This one doesn't look like he's going to be a country clubber," Momchilov said as they walked down the hall to the computer room.

"With any luck," Dear said, "he'll be a real bad-ass."

William Shear did not disappoint. He had spent most of

his teenage years in and out of reform school. By the time he was an adult he had graduated to more serious offenses. Since 1973 he had been charged with bank robbery on six different occasions, once pistol-whipping a woman clerk when she failed to move fast enough to please him. He had been paroled from the Chillicothe, Ohio, correctional facility in December of 1977.

"Not the kind of guy you invite home to dinner," Momchilov said.

It was less than a half hour before a second call to Momchilov's office came from the van. This time it was Riddle, making no attempt to hide his enthusiasm. "Bill," he said, "this sleazeball wouldn't give me much and I didn't press it too hard, but what he said sounds damn good to me."

Dear was getting impatient with Riddle's breathless preliminaries. "What the hell did he say?"

"That your girl contacted him about a hit. He says he turned it down but knows who ultimately agreed to do it. He says he'll give us the name of the killer if he gets an ironclad promise that he gets the reward money.

I told him you would meet him in your hotel room in three hours."

Dear was delighted that Riddle had allowed ample time to make the necessary preparations before his meeting with the man he was now even more convinced could breathe new life into the investigation.

While Dear, Momchilov, and Riddle wired the motel room for sound, Carl Lilly went to the reservations desk and rented the room adjacent to the one in which Dear and Shear would be talking. From there, Momchilov and members of Dear's staff would monitor the conversation.

There was still over an hour to kill once everything had been put in place.

When a knock finally came at the door, Dear opened it to a face that looked as if it had served as a punching bag. Shear's nose had obviously been broken a number of times, and tiny scars rimmed eyebrows set high above cold eyes. Though he was almost thirty-three years old, Shear walked like a cocky teenager.

He said nothing as Dear waved him into the room. He went directly to the bathroom door and opened it. Dear had already pulled the shower curtain back to speed up the search he felt sure his visitor would conduct. For the next several minutes Shear remained silent as he checked the room for bugs. Finally satisfied, he sat on the end of the bed and looked up into the investigator's eyes.

"How do I know I'll get my fifty thousand if I tell you what you need to know?" he asked.

"If your information leads to the arrest of the person or persons who killed Dean Milo," Dear replied, "you've got my guarantee you'll be paid. I'll even put it in writing if you like."

"I've got what you need," Shear said.

"Then let's hear it.

Suddenly the arrogant front Shear had shown up to now disappeared. Rising from the bed, he began to pace. "What the fuck am I doing here?" he said. "This is bullshit. I don't need it. I'm getting the fuck out."

Dear was faced with a split-second decision. Either he tried to persuade Shear to stay, or he adopted a casual pose that indicated the visitor's decision was of no real importance to him.

He gambled. "The door's not locked," he said.

"I'm no fucking snitch," Shear said. "That's not my style. None of this business is my problem, see? It's just that I've got some serious money problems right now."

"And you think the reward can solve them, huh?"

"Yeah, something like that."

Dear sat in a chair near the window and looked out at the people walking on the sidewalk below. "It's your decision," he said.

Shear returned to his place on the end of the bed. "You're on the right track with Terry Lea King," he began.

He explained that he had known Terry Lea for years. They had done a lot of drugs together and had become friends in the process. It had been during the first week of June, he said, that she had called to ask him to stop by the apartment on Gordon Avenue.

"When I got to the house she took me up to her room in the attic," he said. "She told me, 'I've got a job for you that's worth big bucks.' She wanted me to waste some guy, some businessman."

In the next room, Momchilov glanced over at Dick Riddle and gave a thumbs-up sign. Things were finally working out.

"Did she mention Dean Milo's name?" the detective heard Dear ask.

"Not by name," Shear said. "She just told me she would get a picture of the guy, a description of his car, and a list of places where he could be found, shit like that. She said the job would pay ten thousand dollars and asked if I was interested. She said if I wasn't she was going to call Tom Mitchell."

"Who's Tom Mitchell?" Dear asked.

"He's another dude who ran with us, did some dope at Terry Lea's place. He and Terry Lea were real tight. Anyway, I told her to get all the details together and I'd get back in touch."

"And?"

"Hell, man, I was just buying a little time. What she was talking about knocked me on my ass. I just stalled her because I didn't want her to know how I really felt about what she was laying out. See, smoking people's not my thing. I've never killed anybody in my life."

"Then why didn't you just tell her that?"

"Look, you won't understand, but the people I hang around with would think I was a real chicken shit if I started getting all moralistic over a deal like this. And when people think you're a chicken shit, they start trying to fuck you over. I never had any intentions of taking her up on her offer for a minute, but I didn't want her—or anybody else—to know that."

It was not the first time Dear had been made aware of the perverted code that seemed to run through the criminal world. "I've been in this business a long time," he said to Shear. "I think I understand what you're saying."

"I had no beef with this businessman dude she was talking about," Shear continued. "No way I'm going to blow away some guy I don't even know."

"Did Terry Lea talk to you about it again?"

"She called twice and left messages for me to come see her

but ignored them. After a while I just forgot about the whole thing—until I read about the Milo dude getting rubbed out. Then everything clicked. I figured out what had gone down."

"How?"

"Tom Mitchell left town right after the murder took place."

"You know where he went?"

"Texas."

"What makes you so sure that Terry Lea talked him into killing Dean Milo?"

"Fuck, man, she told me. That's why I'm here—to tell you that Tom Mitchell's who you're looking for. See, I was at this place called Night People, a bar, and ran into Terry Lea one night. She had pumped so much shit into her arms that she was crawling on the ceiling. She was really crazy.

"We talked for a while and she finally brought it up. She asked if I knew who she got to do the killing we talked about. I said, 'Tom Mitchell?' and she just laughed her ass off and said, 'Yeah.' I asked if the Milo dude was the one he snuffed, and she said he was."

"When did this conversation take place?"

"Sometime in August, I think. Shit, I don't keep a diary."

Dear studied the man sitting on his bed. What he was saying was believable. If nothing else, he would enable them to make a stronger case against Terry Lea King if his story checked out. On the other hand, he had thrown a new name into the scenario, one Dear had not heard mentioned in all his lengthy search for people Terry Lea knew.

"Do you know Barry Boyd?" Dear asked.

"Known him for years," Shear said. "I've been to his house with Terry Lea a bunch of times. We'd do a little coke and just sit around, shooting the shit—"

Dear interrupted, anxious to ask his next question. "Is Boyd involved in the murder?"

"I'm just guessing," Shear said, "but I'd guess he is. Somebody had to give Terry Lea that ten grand, and I figure it had to be Boyd. From what I read in the papers, he represented the Milo family in his law practice. It fits, if you ask me."

With that, Shear walked to the bathroom and closed the

door behind him. He emerged moments later, zipping his jeans. "Okay," he said, "that's it. That's all I know. I figure it should be plenty to let you take care of your business. It—"

"—is not enough," Dear said, finishing the sentence for him.

"What the fuck are you talking about?"

"I like what you've told me. But if I'm going to pay you the reward, you're going to have to convince me that Tom Mitchell killed Dean Milo."

"How am I supposed to do that?"

"You get him to admit it," Dear said.

13

Bill Dear sat quietly pondering life's ironic twists as he looked from the window of the American Airlines jet beginning its descent. Below him the sprawling Texas countryside, with its ribbonlike highways and turnpikes converging on downtown Dallas, was coming into view. Toward the southern horizon he could faintly see the patchwork rows of rooftops that formed the suburbs of Lancaster, Cedar Hill, Duncanville, and DeSoto. Soon he would be able to catch a glimpse of his own home with its swimming pool and tennis court surface sparkling in the clear winter sun. If he were to look out the opposite window, he knew, he would be able to see his destination.

The investigation that had kept him thousands of miles from home for three months had now led him back to familiar surroundings. With luck, he was going to find the man who killed Dean Milo just a few short miles from where his journey had begun.

Seated next to him was William Shear. Across the aisle, following a flight attendant's orders to fasten their seat belts, were Momchilov and Lieutenant Bob Scalise of the Summit County sheriff's office.

The night before, Shear had called several friends in an attempt to find where in Texas Thomas Mitchell was now living, but none had an address or telephone number. Mitchell, it seemed, had severed all relationships by his hasty departure. Only after Dear had suggested a visit to Mitchell's former Akron residence was the question answered. Mitchell's former landlord had been asked to forward any mail he received to an address in Farmers Branch, Texas, a suburb of Dallas.

Shear had been obviously nervous during the flight, saying little until Dear once more outlined the plan he and Momchilov had developed. "The bottom line," Dear had said, "is that you have to get Thomas Mitchell to talk about the murder, to admit he's the one who killed Dean Milo. The minute I hear that, the reward's yours. That's the deal."

Shear was no longer playing the tough-guy role he had acted out in Dear's motel. Now somber and nervous, he reminded the investigator that Mitchell was a violent man. "If he picks up on what I'm trying to do," Shear said, "he'll fucking kill me."

Dear leaned back in his seat and returned his gaze to the welcomed terrain that seemed to be rising to meet the plane. "Nobody's going to get killed," he said. "That's why we're here with you."

At the airport, Momchilov rented a car and the four men drove directly to Carrollton, a northwest Dallas suburb, where they checked into a Holiday Inn. The two Summit County Sheriff's Department officers took rooms on either side of the one assigned to Shear. Though Momchilov suggested to Dear that he spend the night at his own home with his wife, the investigator preferred to stay close to Shear. "I don't want that sonuvabitch out of my sight until we get this done," he said.

Entering the room, the somber Shear tossed his weathered suitcase on the bed and immediately began to unpack, pulling out a shiny .357 magnum, which he held up to the light of the open window for inspection.

Dear was momentarily stunned speechless. Shear looked at his roommate with no trace of a smile. "If Mitchell finds out what I've done, he'll kill me for sure," he said. "I figure the only chance I have is to make sure I get him first."

Dear's shock changed to anger. He hurried across the room and took the gun. "I don't want to hear any of that shit," he said. "The gun stays here. Hell, if one of those officers next door finds out you're carrying a weapon, you're already in deep trouble."

"I don't give a fuck about those cops. It's my life that's on the line here."

"And that's why we're going to protect you," Dear yelled. "You're here for only one purpose: to help us arrest Tom Mitchell.

Nice and quiet, everything by the book. Nobody's going to get hurt unless they do something stupid. If you screw this up, you'll never see a dime of the reward. I can promise you that."

"How are you guys going to protect me?"

"We're going to be right with you. I'm going to ride in the trunk of the car, listening to everything that goes down. Momchilov and Scalise will be just a few hundred yards away, monitoring everything that happens. It's not like we've never done this kind of thing before. Dammit, I'm telling you we know what we're doing."

Shear looked at the gun Dear was now holding, shrugged, and stretched out on one of the beds. The investigator leaned against a writing table, staring at the weapon. "How in the hell did you get this gun here?" he asked.

"Carried it in my suitcase. How else?"

The idea that a convicted felon could so easily get through airport security with one of the most powerful handguns manufactured made Dear shudder.

Dear had just placed the gun in his own suitcase when a knock came at the door. Momchilov, still in the suit he had worn on the plane, talked as if Shear were not in the room. "Bob's gonna babysit your pal for a while," he said. "Let's go get a cup of coffee."

Once in the motel coffee shop, Momchilov wasted no time getting to the point he had to make. "Look," he said, "we can keep an eye on this guy. If you don't believe that, I resent the hell out of it. He's not going anywhere, so you can just relax. I want you to go upstairs, get your bag, and go home. Kiss your wife, take her out to dinner, take the night off. Hell, if you're uneasy, send some of your people over here to sit outside Shear's door. But, Bill, there's no need for you to be here."

Dear looked into the glass of water on the table in front of him. Momchilov, he knew, was right.

"If you don't go home," the detective continued, "you're a bigger sonuvabitch than I thought."

Dear smiled. "Thanks," he said.

That evening Dear took his wife to dinner. Jan, clearly glad to see him, said little about the case, instead filling the evening with a warmth and affection her husband had sorely missed during his three-month exile in Ohio. There was no mention of their distressful telephone conversations of recent weeks. They talked late into the night, about everything but the future, then went to bed.

It wasn't until the following morning that reality interrupted the reunion. As Dear was dressing to return to the Holiday Inn, where final plans would be made for a visit to Thomas Mitchell's home, Jan asked the question he had been dreading. Standing near the Christmas tree she had decorated a few days earlier, she pulled her housecoat tight around her and smiled. "When is this going to be over?" she asked. Though she had tried to lend a casual tone to the inquiry, Dear recognized the strain in her voice. "Bill, I need to know when you're coming home."

"Soon," he said. "That's the best I can do."

The smile disappeared and Jan did not reply.

"I've worked too hard on this case to give it up now," he said.

She nodded, saying nothing, and walked toward the kitchen. Only after he left did she begin to cry.

For several days, members of Dear's staff had kept watch on Thomas Mitchell's house, which was just a five-minute drive from the Holiday Inn. The thirty-two-year-old Vietnam vet and ex-convict with a record for armed robbery and grand larceny, they reported, was living with two women in a white frame house at the base of a hill on Albemarle Street

In Momchilov's motel room, Dear and the surveillance team briefed officers from the Farmers Branch Police Department. The local officers promised whatever back-up help might be needed. "Sounds like you folks have a real bad-ass on your hands," one of the Texans said. "We'd be happy for you to get him out of here as soon as possible."

"That's what we have in mind," Momchilov said. He then turned to Dear. "You sure you want to go for a ride in a car trunk again?" he asked. He then entertained the Farmers Branch policemen with the tale of Dear's carbon-monoxide ride in the back of Lemon's car.

One of the policemen laughed as Momchilov told of lifting the nearly unconscious Dear from the trunk following the visit to Medina. "Like I said," he volunteered, "we're here to help you fellas in any way we can. But I think we'll leave the hiding in car trunks up to you. We don't have much training in that area. You're on your own there."

"To tell the truth," Dear said, "I'm getting a little weary of it." Already he had placed electronic bugs beneath the front seat of the rental car Shear would be driving and connected them to the trunk. Momchilov would be able to monitor the conversations from Dear's surveillance van. Scalise would keep an eye on things from a car driven by Boots Hinton, son of a former Dallas County sheriff, who worked as one of Dear's associates.

"You know, down here in Texas," the Farmers Branch officer said, "whatever you get on tape that way isn't generally worth a shit in court."

Dear nodded. "Same in Ohio," he acknowledged. "But anything I hear is admissible in a court of law, in Texas or just about anywhere else."

"Well, sir, I hope you get an earful."

It was midafternoon as Shear drove in the direction of Mitchell's house. He twisted the dial of the radio until he found a local station paying tribute to John Lennon, the Beatle, who had been killed the night before in New York.

Lying in the darkened trunk, Dear could hear the driver talking to himself as the music played. "He did it. He did it. I know fucking well he did. He did it." It was as if Shear was trying to psych himself up for the encounter to come.

Then Dear heard a familiar sound, a click, as if the hammer of, a gun was being cocked.

"What the hell are you doing?" Dear yelled through the partition separating him from the interior of the car. He knew immediately that Shear had carried a second gun in his suitcase.

"Dammit, man," Shear yelled over the music. "I know Thomas killed Dean Milo. If he even thinks he's being set up, he'll blow a hole through me without even thinking about it."

"Put the gun under the seat," Dear commanded.

"I'm putting it in my jacket pocket."

"I said put it under the seat."

"Fuck you, pal. You aren't in much of a position to be telling anybody what to do right now."

Dear was furious. "When I get out of this trunk I'm going to kick the shit out of you."

"*If* you get out of the trunk," Shear said, turning up the volume on the radio.

Dear felt a rush of fear surge through his cramped body. With Shear armed and obviously nervous, things could go crazy. The police files on Mitchell had indicated he would likely be in possession of a gun. When he was last arrested he had been carrying a .32 pistol. He had even carried a pistol into a courtroom during one of his appearances.

The investigator managed to turn slightly and fit his hand around the handle of the .380 German Mauser he carried in a shoulder holster, whispering a silent prayer that he would not have to use it.

Meanwhile, in the front seat Shear had resumed his chant: "He did it. I know he did it. I know the sonuvabitch did it."

He kept it up until he stopped in front of the Albemarle Street address.

The next sound Dear picked up was Shear's pounding on the door of the house. When there was no answer, he knocked even louder, all the while continuing to talk to himself. "He's here. I know the sonuvabitch is here," he kept saying. But there was no answer.

From the trunk Dear could hear Shear's footsteps as he walked back in the direction of the parked car, cursing to himself in a low voice. Wilted in disappointment, the investigator began to focus his thoughts on an early release from the blackened interior of the trunk when he heard another noise. Another car had arrived. Dear heard the engine noise die and a door slam. The next voice he heard was unfamiliar.

"Hey, Bill," Thomas Mitchell was saying, "what the hell are you doing here?"

"I just got in town and thought I'd drop by and see how

you're doing," Shear answered. There was a calmness in his voice that surprised Dear.

"Get yourself a new car?"

"Naw. Hell, no. I rented it at the airport."

"So, what brings you down to Texas?"

Shear wasted no more time with pleasantries. "Tom, we need to go someplace and talk. It's important. I'm in a little jam."

"Come on in the house. Nobody's home."

"Maybe it would be better if we just drove around for a few minutes."

"Hell, come on in. I'll get you a beer."

Dear was pleased that Shear had not pressed the issue of talking in the car, risking the chance of causing Mitchell to become suspicious. He heard them enter the house.

"Nice Christmas tree," he heard Shear say.

The two sat in what Dear assumed was the living room, sipping beer as they talked briefly of mutual acquaintances back in Akron. Several minutes passed before Shear explained the purpose of his visit.

"Tom, I got to have some money, quick. I need it bad."

Mitchell laughed. "I hope you didn't make a trip all the way down here to ask me for a loan. I'm so fucking broke I can't pay attention. This construction job I've got isn't worth a shit. Bad weather keeps us off the job half the time these days."

"Don't jerk me around, man," Shear replied. "The cops are saying I killed Dean Milo. I got to disappear."

He waited for a moment for Mitchell to acknowledge but got no response. "Hell, I'm no hit man. We both know that."

Still Mitchell said nothing.

"I know you did it," Shear continued.

"I don't know what you're talking about."

"Don't bullshit me, man. We both know you did the guy. I didn't invest every penny I have to fly down here for nothing."

Mitchell's voice indicated disbelief. "Man, this is crazy. I'm sorry you're getting heat, but I can't do much for you. Maybe I can scratch up enough to get you a plane ticket back home, but that's the best I can do."

Shear remained firm. "I want part of the ten thousand you

got for doing the hit."

"What the hell gave you the idea I've got ten grand?"

"Terry Lea told me. Hell, man, she offered the deal to me first. I'm no dumbass. I know you left town the night Milo was killed. So don't try to shit me about this?"

Mitchell sighed. "Okay, she did offer me ten thousand. But that doesn't mean I killed the guy," he said.

"If you think I'm going to take the fall for you on this thing, you're crazy. I've got to disappear. I need two, three thousand. And that's cheap. If I wanted to hang your ass out to dry, I could make fifty."

"What are you talking about?"

"There's some private eye from Texas up in Akron, working the case. He's offering fifty thousand reward, no fucking questions asked, for anyone who can deliver the right information."

"I'm telling you, man, I didn't kill the guy. I didn't get any money." Tom Mitchell's voice mirrored his anger. "You're trying to blackmail me. Shit, I thought we were pals ..."

Shear ignored the accusation. "I talked to Terry Lea a week before she was arrested. She told me you killed the guy."

"She's lying. Hell yes, she offered me the deal. And I agreed to do it for the ten thousand. Just before I left town, this friend of hers—I think it was that lawyer—dropped off a package that had pictures of Milo and his house and cars, shit like that. There was a schedule of places he would be.

"I was strapped for cash at the time and I considered it. I thought maybe I'd come on down here to Texas first, then go back and do it. But when I got here I found out the job had already been done, so I forgot about it."

"That's bullshit."

"I don't give a shit what you believe," Mitchell fired back. "That's the way it went down."

Muffled sounds signaled that Shear had apparently risen and was walking toward the door. "I've tried to be fair with you," he said, "and you're sitting there fucking with me. Think about it. You've forced me up against the wall on this thing. You've got until morning. I'll be back in touch."

"You're crazy."

"No," Shear said, "just desperate."

Dear could hear the door slam and the sounds of Shear's hurried walk toward the car.

Back at the Holiday Inn, Shear paced in front of Dear and Momchilov, his movements dictated by bursts of nervous energy. "The sonuvabitch did it," he said repeatedly. "I told you he did it," pointing his finger at Dear.

"No, he didn't say he did it." The stern look on Dear's face showed less than total enthusiasm over the outcome of the mission. Behind the look, however, Dear was pleased with what his informant had come away with. Mitchell's admission that Terry Lea King had solicited him for murder would make their case against her. Too, Dear was sure the man who had delivered the package of information on Milo was Barry Boyd. And even if Mitchell said no more, they had enough to file charges against him for conspiracy to commit murder.

Momchilov placed a long distance call to Fred Zuch in the Summit County Prosecutor's Office to advise him of what had happened. Delighted with the news, Zuch said he would immediately send a warrant for Mitchell's arrest to the Farmers Branch Police Department. The charge, he said, would be aggravated murder.

"It's his bargaining tool," Momchilov said to Dear after the phone conversation ended. "Mitchell's smart enough to know that would put him away for a helluva long time. If he's willing to cooperate, Zuch says he'll reduce it to a lesser charge, something like conspiracy to commit murder. My bet is he'll go for it."

Dear nodded. "It's about time something good happened," he said.

As they sat in the motel room, planning their next move, the soft-spoken Scalise, who lay stretched on one of the beds, sat up and joined the conversation. "I don't like the idea of waiting until morning," he said. "The idea of sitting around, twiddling our thumbs while Mitchell's just a few blocks away, bothers me. We've got what we need. I say we should go get him as soon as the warrant arrives."

"I agree," said Momchilov.

Dear, who had sensed a ring of truth in Mitchell's story, had begun to think that they would have to look further for the man who killed Dean Milo. It was unlikely that Dear would get Mitchell to say anything more incriminating than what they already had on tape. Dear, for his own reasons, was anxious to have Mitchell in custody.

A phone call was placed to the Farmers Branch police, asking to be alerted the minute the arrest warrant arrived from Akron. In the meantime, Momchilov said, he was going to drive over and keep an eye on Mitchell's house. Dear told him to use the surveillance van, then instructed his associate Boots Hinton to back up Momchilov in one of the company cars.

"While we're waiting," Dear said, "I'm going to have Shear call and take one more shot."

On the telephone, Shear was even more aggressive than before as he told Mitchell that he had changed his mind and was planning to leave town in a matter of hours. "What about the money?" he asked.

"I don't have it."

"Then I go to the private investigator."

"Suits the shit out of me," Mitchell said and slammed the receiver down.

Dear, who had monitored the call on an extension phone, looked at Shear for several seconds. "What does he have on you?" the investigator finally asked.

"What do you mean?"

"Cut the bullshit, Bill. The guy's not worried about you turning snitch. What's the deal?"

"We did an armed robbery together a while back. Damn near got caught. I had to hit a cop over the head with the butt of a gun."

While Mitchell was on the phone with Shear, a neighbor had climbed over the back fence and knocked at the back door. "There's some dude in a van up the block," the neighbor said. "I think he's watching your house."

Mitchell stormed out the front door and stood on the porch,

shading his eyes with one hand as he looked in Momchilov's direction. The detective, surprised by the sudden appearance, slumped in the driver's seat as Mitchell began running toward him, pulling on a jacket as he hurried down the street.

Momchilov had rolled up the window and locked the doors by the time Mitchell arrived. "What the fuck are you doing here?" he demanded. "You a cop?"

Momchilov did not answer.

"I'm calling the police," Mitchell yelled, then turned and began running back toward his house. Momchilov quickly started the engine and drove away, not even glancing over at the stunned Boots Hinton, who had watched the entire sequence from less than a block away.

Dear, surprised to learn that the detective had been spotted during a surveillance, took a call from a Farmers Branch police officer shortly after Momchilov's return to the Holiday Inn. "Your boy just called in a complaint," the officer said. "Said somebody in a van was watching his house and wants us to check it out. You guys need to be a little more careful." There was an amused tone in his voice that Dear chose to ignore.

"Have you seen anything of the warrant yet?"

"It came in just a couple of minutes ago."

"Can you get your people over here so we can run through this thing? We're going to pick him up tonight."

"We're on our way."

A full Texas moon illuminated the area just after midnight as members of the Farmers Branch SWAT team surrounded the Mitchell house. Dear and Scalise crouched in a row of hedges near the front porch, watching as two uniformed officers walked toward the front door with a handcuffed Momchilov between them.

One of the officers knocked several times before a woman's voice answered.

"Is Tom Mitchell here, ma'am?"

"Yeah, he's here."

"We're the police. We need to talk to him."

The young woman opened the door slightly and looked

at the officers, then at the handcuffed man standing somberly between them. In a moment the door opened wider and Mitchell appeared.

"What can I do for you?" he asked.

"Sir, the officer said, shoving Momchilov a step forward, "is this the prowler you reported earlier in the day?"

"That's him."

With that, Momchilov let the handcuffs fall to the cement porch and quickly drew a .38 Police Special, which he aimed at Mitchell's head. "I have a warrant for your arrest," the detective said, "for the murder of Constantine R. (Dean) Milo. You have the right to …"

The color drained from Mitchell's face and he began to shake. Before Momchilov had completed reciting the Miranda warning, the uniformed officers had applied handcuffs.

Dear rode in the squad car with Mitchell as he was being transported to the Farmers Branch police headquarters, watching as the prisoner slowly regained his composure. By the time they pulled into the parking lot near the jail, Mitchell was playing the role of a man totally unfamiliar with the arrest process. "I think some attorney is going to be interested in knowing how my civil rights have been violated," he said. "You people have no right to just haul somebody out of his home in the middle of the night like this."

Dear just smiled. "It's going to get a helluva lot worse," he said.

It was then that a second car pulled into the lot. Mitchell caught a glimpse of William Shear sitting in the back seat.

In the small, sparse interview room, Mitchell looked first at Momchilov, then Dear. "I know what this is all about now," he said. "It's that fucking Shear, isn't it?"

Neither answered.

"I don't expect you guys to believe me," Mitchell continued, "but he's lying. That's the God's truth. I didn't have anything to do with killing that guy in Akron."

Momchilov placed a waiver of extradition in front of him. "I'm not signing anything," Mitchell said.

Dear, seated across from the prisoner, leaned over the table until his face was just inches away from Mitchell's. "Listen, pal," he said. "I live in this state, and if you stay around here I'm going to harass you until you'll be willing to walk back to Ohio. The smartest thing you can possibly do is sign that waiver and get the hell out of here."

Mitchell glared as Dear continued. "If your involvement was no more than what you told Shear, you've got something working for you. I've seen your rap sheet. You're smart enough to know that the charge you're looking at would put you away until you're too old to give a shit whether you ever get out or not. I suggest you think real hard about cooperating."

Momchilov placed a photograph of Terry Lea King on the table in front of Mitchell. "You know her?"

"That's Terry Lea."

The detective then flipped a second photograph onto the table. "Know him?"

"I don't know him," Mitchell said softly, "but I know who he is. It's Dean Milo." He then looked up at Dear. "What kind of deal are you offering?"

"It depends on your involvement," Dear said. "Right now we can build a pretty good case against you for aggravated murder."

"I told you I didn't kill the guy. I didn't have anything to do with it."

"Then why don't you just tell us the whole story?"

"I've got to think about it."

"We've got nothing but time," Momchilov said, standing up to leave. Dear even promised Mitchell he would guarantee him a plane ticket to wherever he wanted to go once he had served whatever sentence he received.

Mitchell was transferred to the Dallas County jail for the night and a local judge was called from a sound sleep to set bail at $300,000. The following morning he was flown to Akron, handcuffed to Momchilov, saying nothing during the trip.

Even as they were headed home, Lieutenant Bill Lewis was preparing to administer a polygraph examination to Terry Lea, whose trial was scheduled to begin in five days.

She was asked if she knew who had killed Dean Milo, if she'd given anyone money to carry out the murder, if she offered money to Thomas Mitchell to commit the crime, and if Barry Boyd had told her someone in the Milo family wanted Dean Milo killed. She answered no to each question.

And, as expected, she failed the test.

The arrival of Mitchell signaled a flurry of renewed media excitement. Though no details of his arrest had been made public, the *Akron Beacon Journal* ran a photograph of Mitchell being escorted to the booking desk beneath a banner headline story indicating a break had finally come in the Milo murder. One of the matrons in the county jail was instructed to be sure that Terry Lea King saw the paper.

Mitchell met immediately with a court-appointed attorney and, after again being made aware of the seriousness of the charges he was facing, asked to talk with Momchilov and Dear.

"You ready to help us out?" the detective asked.

"I'll tell you what I know. That's all I can do."

"Did you kill Dean Milo?"

"No. I didn't kill him," Mitchell stated firmly. "Terry Lea made me the offer. She might even think I did it. But I didn't. I might be guilty of something, but it damn sure isn't murder. That's the God's honest truth."

"We're listening."

"I went to Terry Lea, see, and told her I was strapped and needed some way to make some quick money. That's when she told me she knew of a murder contract. She said it was worth ten grand."

"Did she say who was supposed to be killed?" Dear asked.

"No. Hell, I didn't even take her seriously. But I told her I'd think about it. Then a week or so later she came over to my place—sometime around the middle of June—and mentioned it again. But she was so strung out that I didn't think anything about it."

"She didn't give you any money?"

"She didn't give me anything."

"Then what?"

"It was when I was packing my shit up and getting ready to move to Texas," Mitchell continued. "I had just taken a shower when this dude knocks at the front door. I went downstairs and he asks if I'm Tom Mitchell. I said I was and he handed me this big brown envelope and said that Terry Lea had told him to give it to me."

"Did you know him?"

"No. He just handed me the envelope and turned and left. I didn't know what to think. I just had a towel wrapped around me, but I went outside to watch him get in his car, a white Ford. I went back in the house and wrote down the license plate number on the outside of the envelope he'd given me."

"What did the guy look like?"

"Maybe thirty years old. A white guy, clean-cut, light brown hair. Dressed like a businessman."

Anticipating the next question, Mitchell continued with his narrative. "I opened the envelope and found two pieces of legal-sized paper with writing on them and a couple of pictures of Dean Milo. There was a bunch of stuff about where he went, when he would probably be there; something about when he was going to be out of town, what kind of car he would be driving; shit like that.

"All that information was written on one piece of paper. On the other was instructions about the payoff. It said he would meet me at the airport or wherever I wanted. I was supposed to carry a folded newspaper and lay it down and walk away for a few minutes. When I came back it would have ten thousand dollars in it."

"Did it say anything else?"

"Yeah, that I was supposed to burn everything after I finished reading it."

"Did you?"

"Not right away. I took the envelope with me to Texas. Then one night my former landlord called and told me that Terry Lea had been busted for murder. I asked him if he knew who she was supposed to have killed, and he said he couldn't remember. I told him to hang on a minute and went and found the envelope. When I asked him if the guy's name was Dean

Milo, he said yeah, that was the guy.

"That's when I went out on the back porch and burned the stuff. That's all I know."

When the interrogation was completed, Mitchell agreed to take a polygraph test. The results indicated that he was not the killer of Dean Milo. In exchange for his cooperation and agreement to testify at the trial of Terry Lea King, charges against him were reduced to obstruction of justice.

"You mean if I hadn't burned the stuff the guy gave me I'd have walked on this thing?" he later asked Momchilov.

"I wouldn't have bet on it," the detective said.

As soon as Mitchell's statement was typed, Fred Zuch called Terry Lea King and her attorney, Jerry Montgomery, to his office. "We now have two witnesses who can implicate you in the murder of Dean Milo," the prosecutor told the frail-looking woman who sat in wrinkled jail-issue clothing, appearing much older than she had when he had first seen her. "The charge against you can mean life in prison. Or you can take the deal I'm authorized by the district attorney to offer and get out in no more than four years. It's a take-it-or-leave-it proposition. The choice is yours. I suggest you talk it over with your lawyer."

Terry Lea and Montgomery were escorted into another room by a jailer and returned in a matter of minutes. As they re-entered Zuch's office, Momchilov and Dear were seated in the corner of the room.

"What do you want to hear?" Terry Lea asked in a defeated voice.

"Just tell us the story—from the beginning," Momchilov said.

Terry Lea King took a deep breath and lit a cigarette. "One afternoon I was over at Barry Boyd's house. He started talking about this greedy guy who somebody wanted out of the way. He said that there would be a lot of happy people when the guy was dead and gone."

"Did he tell you he wanted him killed?"

"I never got the impression that he had anything against him. He just talked about how this guy was trying to move his family out of some business. But after a while he told me he could pay ten thousand dollars to someone who would help the family get rid of the guy."

The men in Zuch's office listened with fascination as Terry Lea King's monotone answered many of the questions they had wrestled with for so many months. Boyd, she said, had wanted the hit to take place as quickly as possible. At first, he had thought it should be done at either Milo's home or office, but then, after learning that Milo was planning a trip to Florida, he had said that it might be better to stage it down there.

Boyd had eventually supplied her with much of the same information on Dean Milo that he later passed on to Mitchell: photographs, telephone numbers, places he frequented, and license plate numbers of the cars he drove.

He had also given her a package that contained five thousand dollars in twenty-, fifty-, and one-hundred-dollar bills. It was, she said, to be the down payment to whomever she got to do the job.

"What is Thomas Mitchell's involvement?" Momchilov asked.

"He called one day to ask if I was interested in buying some airline coupons," she said. "He was moving somewhere and needed some money. I told him I didn't want to buy them. Right after I hung up, Barry called me. I told him about Tom needing money. That's when he suggested that I offer the deal to Tom. He asked me if I would give him the information on Dean Milo. I told him I wouldn't do it but I would give him Tom's address."

"So Barry delivered the package to Tom Mitchell's house?"

"I guess so. I know later on he was really upset with Tom."

"Do you know why?"

"He was afraid Tom hadn't burned the stuff like he told him to."

"Why was Boyd so upset about that?"

"Because the note in the envelope was in his handwriting."

Late into the evening Momchilov and Dear sat in the detective's office, playing and replaying the tape of Terry Lea King's confession. Weary from their trip to Texas and the pressured days that had followed, they were elated that there would be no trial immediately.

"You know she's not telling the whole story," Momchilov said.

"She told us enough," Dear said. "Now we can go pick up the guy who can fill in the blanks."

A warrant for the arrest of Barry Boyd, they had been assured, would be ready first thing in the morning.

14

Larry Momchilov was driving through the cold, crisp, darkened Ohio countryside, en route to Cleveland to issue the warrant for Barry Boyd's arrest. Dear sat beside him, studying the highway that stretched before their speeding car.

It was the detective who broke the silence. "I guess you'll be glad to get back to Dallas," he said.

Dear nodded but gave no indication he wanted to pursue the conversation, so Momchilov continued: "If someone had told me a few weeks ago that this was going to be wrapped up by Christmas, I'd have said they were crazy."

Like most members of the Akron law enforcement community, Momchilov felt sure that when Boyd was arrested, he would soon tell who had been hired to murder Dean Milo. Then it would be little more than a matter of getting another warrant, locating the suspect, and turning the rest over to the prosecutor's office. Dear's job—to find the person responsible for the crime—was nearing an end.

Momchilov was going to miss him.

The initial plan had been to arrest Boyd at his home, but a frantic call from Sally Reeves had caused a last-minute change in strategy.

Having found the card Dear had left her on his previous visit, she had tried first to reach him at his motel room, then called the number at the Summit County sheriff's office.

"I'm worried about Barry," she said, her voice a signal of hysteria. "He's been drinking and acting crazy, really crazy."

"Is he there now?"

"Yes. And he's talking about killing himself. He's like a maniac, saying all kinds of horrible things. I'm scared."

"Does he have a gun?" Dear asked.

"I think so."

"Can you keep him there for about an hour?"

The woman began to cry. "I don't know," she said. "I've never seen him acting like this before. I'm afraid he might hurt the children."

"We'll be there as quickly as we can," Dear said. "Just try to keep him as calm as possible."

There was a brief silence on the other end of the line as Sally Reeves composed herself. "You won't hurt him, will you?"

"Trust me," Dear said.

Thus the decision to arrest Barry Boyd in Cleveland had been hastily made. Momchilov called Bill Lewis and Dick Munsey and alerted them to what was taking place. Their work on the case, he felt, should be rewarded by being in on the arrest. He gave them the address and told them to meet him and Dear there as quickly as possible.

Minutes later, the detective, warrant in his jacket pocket, was speeding along Interstate 271 at eighty-five miles per hour.

Lewis and Munsey were parked down the block from the Reeves apartment when Momchilov and Dear arrived. A dozen Cleveland police officers, advised of the situation by the sheriff's dispatcher in Akron, began arriving just minutes later.

While the uniformed officers stationed themselves strategically, the four men who had arrived from Akron approached the door. Pausing to make certain all the back-up personnel were in place, Momchilov knocked.

When Sally Reeves answered, the detective identified himself, displaying his shield. "We need to see Barry Boyd," he said.

Even as he spoke he could see the attorney standing unsteadily at the top of the staircase. Without a word, Lewis and Munsey hurried past Momchilov and the frightened woman to where the dazed Boyd stood, dressed in jeans, knit shirt, and tennis shoes. They handcuffed him as Momchilov again recited the Miranda warning.

The arrest took no more than thirty seconds. Boyd and the officers were gone without Sally Reeves's children even knowing what had taken place.

On the way back to Akron, the drunken Boyd attempted to explain to Munsey that his attorney had tried to make a deal with former Summit County prosecutor Stephan Gabalac. "He was going to give me immunity ... complete immunity," Boyd said in a slurred voice, "but when he lost the election the deal fell through. Screwed everything up ..."

Munsey made no response. Immediately following the arrest, Momchilov had insisted that no one talk with the prisoner on the way back to Akron. Any statement given by a suspect while intoxicated is unusable in court. "Don't even comment on the weather to the asshole," Momchilov said. "If he tries to confess, just tell him to shut up. We've come too far to blow this thing now. He'll tell us what we want to know soon enough."

An hour later Barry Boyd was placed in a third-floor cell in the Summit County jail. "We'll let him sleep it off," Momchilov said, "then we start making his life miserable."

"I think," Bill Dear replied, "that it already is."

Later that night, before returning to his motel, Dear took the elevator up to the third floor to check on Boyd. Instead of sleeping, the attorney sat on the edge of his cell bunk, his hands covering his face. His body jerked convulsively as he sobbed, unaware that Dear was watching.

Dear marveled at the sight. The man sitting in the cell barely resembled the one he had first confronted in his downtown law office. Boyd had lost a great deal of weight and looked as if he had aged twenty years. For a moment, the investigator felt pity for the man he had been pursuing with a vengeance for so long.

As Dear was turning to leave, Boyd looked up and saw him. Wiping his face, he hurriedly staggered to the front of the cell and extended his hand through the bars. "Dear," he said, "I want to talk to you. I'll tell you all about it, the whole deal."

Having waited so long to hear what the man was now so eager to tell, Dear had to shake his head. "Not now," he said.

"You need to get some rest, then talk to an attorney."

"I'm a goddamn attorney. I know my rights. And I know what I need to do. Dammit, I want to tell you about it. I've been wanting to tell somebody about it for a long time." He then started to cry again.

Concerned that Boyd might attempt suicide after he left, Dear summoned a captain and told him that the prisoner wanted to talk. After being read his rights, Barry said, "I can give you everything you want. The family is involved. I want to tell you about it… I have to tell you."

Dear felt a rush of adrenaline. He had heard enough. The rest, he decided, would have to wait.

"Barry, just relax. Before we go any further, you need to talk to your attorney. I'll be back in the morning."

While Momchilov and Dear waited for the much-anticipated chance to question Boyd, a search warrant was obtained for the lawyer's house. There, investigators found a map of Bath with the street on which Dean Milo's house was located circled in red. In a Ziploc bag they found several photographs of Dean Milo, along with some money wrappers dated August and September. Documents found on his study desk indicated Boyd had apparently also been studying two court cases—one on the Miranda ruling, the other on a murder of passion.

On the morning of December 13, 1980, Barry Boyd met briefly with attorney Ed Pierce and was told that if he admitted what he knew about the murder and agreed to cooperate with the prosecution, Fred Zuch would allow him to plead guilty to a lesser count of conspiracy to commit aggravated murder.

An hour later he was escorted into Larry Momchilov's office, where the four men who had arrested him sat waiting.

Boyd slumped in the chair directly across from Dear. He focused on the private investigator with eyes sunk deep into their hollow sockets. "What do you want to know?" he asked.

Momchilov had turned the tape recorder on as soon as Boyd entered the room.

Dear wasted no time. "Who instigated the death of Dean Milo?"

Boyd showed no expression as he delivered the answer. "It was Fred Milo, his brother."

For the next hour the three officers and Dear listened to the most bizarre story of cold-blooded murder they had ever heard.

On the evening of January 19, 1980, Fred Milo had made an unannounced visit to the home of Barry Boyd. He appeared nervous and talked angrily about the way in which his brother had assumed control of Milo Barber and Beauty Supply. Fred paced and railed, the tone of his voice more bitter and harsh than Boyd had ever heard.

"He was acting really weird," Boyd told the gathering in Momchilov's office. "He seemed to be at the end of his rope with Dean running roughshod over him and kept talking about how the business had to return to being a family operation.

"Finally, he got around to it. He told me he wanted Dean killed and wanted me to find someone to do it."

"Why did he come to you?" Dear asked.

Boyd shrugged. "I was his friend, someone he trusted. And, I suppose, since I'm a lawyer he figured that I came in contact with the kind of people who might do what he wanted done."

Initially, Boyd insisted, he thought Fred Milo was joking, or, at the worst, just venting an anger that would soon be replaced by better judgment. Instead, Milo's obsession with the idea of having his brother murdered grew.

Milo continued to press the issue. He wanted the job done as soon as possible and for it to appear to be an accident.

"What were you to get out of all this?" Momchilov asked.

Boyd shifted in his chair, crossing his legs as he stared at the floor. "I'm not very good at turning people down," he said softly. "Especially someone with a lot of money. What did I expect to get out of it? Some legal work, I suppose. That's all. See, I was fed up with being broke. My type practice doesn't pay that much. Fred did mention something about my living in Bermuda and managing a resort hotel for him. But that was later on."

Fred began calling the attorney almost daily, asking for progress reports, each time insisting that the plan should be put into motion very soon. For several weeks Boyd played a game of his own, telling Milo that he was having difficulty finding someone. In truth, he had not even mentioned the matter to anyone else, hoping that Milo would realize the dangers of his idea and drop it.

"It was sometime in March," Boyd continued, "that I talked with a man I'd once represented. He was involved in organized crime and I met with him and asked what something like Fred was talking about would cost. He told me that it shouldn't be too hard to get the job done for something like five thousand dollars.

"At the same time, he told me I shouldn't get my hopes up about getting someone in his organization to do it. He didn't like the fact that this was a deal where a family member was involved. He said the whole deal would be like a field of land mines. There was too much of a chance that people wouldn't keep their mouths shut.

"I thought that by telling Fred how dangerous something of this nature was, he might forget the whole thing," Boyd continued. "Instead of being discouraged, he seemed encouraged. A few days later I received five thousand dollars in cash and a couple of photographs of Dean, which I was supposed to give to the individual I retained to do the job."

It was shortly thereafter that Boyd approached Terry Lea King. Hearing the proposal, she had told him that she might know someone who would be interested. "That's when she offered the deal to William Shear," Boyd said. "But he didn't want any part of it. I was back to square one.

"Fred got upset and decided to handle things himself."

The investigators, unprepared for the turn Boyd's story was apparently about to take, straightened in their chairs. Momchilov stole a glance at Dear in an attempt to read his reaction.

Boyd continued in a soft, steady voice. "He came over to the house during the Memorial Day weekend," he said, "and told me my services were no longer needed. He said he had made a contact with someone in Columbus, Ohio, and that the guy there had put him in touch with somebody out in Phoenix, Arizona. He said he had talked with someone in Phoenix and they were going to arrange the hit through Philadelphia. I didn't really know what to think. It all sounded crazy to me—like a plot from a bad gangster movie or something."

The man whom Milo had contacted in Columbus, Boyd said, was Ray Sesic, the former Milo B&B employee Dean Milo had fired for being a corporate spy. The Phoenix connection, he had later learned, was Tony Ridle, another former Milo B&B employee who had left because of differences with Dean Milo.

Bill Dear shook his head as he heard the names. He felt a new rush of anger as he realized that the cast of characters was growing. The case, which moments earlier had seemed so near to being resolved, had again become a maze of complications. Momchilov was wrong, he thought. There would be no way to wrap things up by Christmas.

"Is that when your role in the matter ended?" he asked.

Boyd shook his head. "No. Terry Lea called me sometime in July and said she had another guy who might be interested. His name was Tom Mitchell.

"I got in touch with Fred and asked if he wanted me to follow through on it, and he said yes. He told me he was becoming disillusioned with the lack of progress being made by the people he had been in touch with."

"That surprised me, because in early June Fred had come to my house and showed me six thousand dollars in cash he had with him. He needed the five thousand he had given me, so he could deliver money to Tony Ridle, who was flying into Cleveland to pick it up. It was my understanding that the eleven thousand dollars was to be the down payment to the people who were going to kill Dean.

"But after I talked with him about my conversation with Terry Lea King, Fred said to go ahead with it. So, I went to Mitchell's house and delivered the package."

At Momchilov's request, Boyd gave a description of the man he had delivered the package to. "I didn't know him," the attorney said. "And I just saw him briefly when he answered the door. All I said to him was, 'Terry Lea wanted me to give this to you.'"

"Do you know if Fred Milo actually delivered the money to Tony Ridle?" Momchilov asked.

"I heard that it was paid. See, Dean Milo was planning some kind of trip to Arizona. That's where the hit was going to take place. The story I got was that Ridle followed Dean around out there, looking for his chance, but he supposedly told Fred that Dean had been with some woman the entire time he was there and that there was no way the hit could be made to look like an accident.

"I think that's when Fred became convinced that his people weren't going to get the job done and came back to me."

Dear stood and began to pace in the small room, twisting at a ring on his index finger as he looked down at Boyd. "Let's stop here for just a minute," he said. "This story is getting crazy. Are you telling us that there were two plans working for the murder of Dean Milo?"

"That's right," Boyd said.

"And that this guy Ray Sesic was serving as a go-between for Fred Milo and Tony Ridle ... at the same time you were acting as the go-between with Terry Lea King and Tom Mitchell?"

"I imagine Sesic was getting the same kind of pressure I was from Fred."

Dear sighed and returned to his chair. "Then what?"

"Sometime in late June I took two thousand dollars to the Holiday Inn near the Cleveland airport and gave it to some guy who worked with Tony Ridle. I later learned that his name was Harry Knott and he was supposed to be the brains behind the hit team that Ridle had put together. He needed the money to buy a used car that he could drive to Florida. Evidently the plan had changed again and they were going to kill Dean in Florida, while he was there visiting his in-laws.

"For a while, I thought that's where it had happened. In fact, Ridle phoned Fred from down there and told him that Dean was dead."

"Ridle ran a scam on Milo," Ed Duvall observed.

"I don't really know," Boyd said. "The story I got later was that this guy Knott and whoever was with him had run over and killed somebody they thought was Dean Milo. But it turned out to be someone else. I know all this sounds crazy ..."

"More like a fairy tale," Momchilov replied.

Boyd ignored the detective's comment and continued. "Shortly after the Florida thing fell through, a couple of guys showed up at my house, saying they were from somewhere in West Virginia. They said Fred had hired them and that I was supposed to show them around. I took them by Dean's house, out to Milo B&B, and places where I knew Dean went from time to time.

"I don't know where Fred found them, or even if they were serious. They seemed scared to death the whole time I was driving them around. I never heard from them again."

Boyd's audience seemed nonplussed. Now he was indicating that there might have been as many as three hit teams working on the Dean Milo murder plot.

"You have to understand that Fred was getting really wild about this thing," Boyd said. "He was calling me daily, sometimes several times a day. He even suggested that I kill Dean. He said I could dress up like a jogger—there were always a lot of joggers in Dean's neighborhood—and just run over to the house, go in, and kill him. Once, in late July, he showed me a gun and said he might have to commit the murder himself, then try to get off on an insanity plea if he was caught.

"In the first week of August, just a few days before Dean was murdered, Fred had me send some more money out to Ridle in Arizona. I went to Western Union on August sixth and sent the money." That, Boyd insisted, was his final involvement in the plan to murder Dean Milo—except for Fred Milo's attempt to set him up as a potential alibi.

Fred had contacted him on August 7 or 8 about setting up a meeting between Fred and Dean Milo to try to work out some manner of settlement of the Milo B&B problems. Boyd had done so, arranging the meeting for August 10, unaware of the real purpose of Fred's request. If questioned about his brother's death, Fred would be able to point out innocently that even at the time of Dean's death he was attempting to meet with him in an effort to resolve the family problems. Barry Boyd could vouch for that.

On the evening of August 10, Boyd remembered, he was called to Fred Milo's house. He found Fred waiting for him outside by the mailbox. Through the car window, Milo handed him a slip of paper with a telephone number on it, saying, "Call this number tomorrow and ask for Tony. Ask him whether anything has happened." Fred then turned and went back into the house.

"What did he mean?" Momchilov asked.

"I'm just guessing, but he probably thought that Dean was dead and wanted me to contact Ridle to make sure. I really don't know. Fred wasn't making a lot of sense."

"You didn't know then that Dean was dead?" the detective asked.

"No I didn't know until the next day when Sheriff Troutman called me. I'd already called Ridle on Monday and he said he didn't know anything. I never called him back again."

Boyd had been telling his story for over an hour when Momchilov suggested they take a break. Leaving the attorney in the office, he and Dear stepped into the hall and exchanged looks of amazement.

"No way he could be inventing all this," the detective said.

Dear only nodded.

"How does a family get that fucked up?" Momchilov asked.

"Stupidity and greed," Dear said.

"So what do you think?"

Dear leaned against the wall, looking more tired than Momchilov had seen him in some time. "I think we've got a lot more work to do before this shitty mess is going to be over," he said.

Returning to the room, Momchilov handed a cup of coffee to Boyd and turned the tape recorder back on.

"Barry," he said, "do you know who killed Dean Milo?"

"Not really. I assume it was the people Ridle put together, but I don't know for sure. If it had been anyone I was involved with through Terry Lea, I'd have heard about it."

"What else can you tell us about Fred Milo?"

"He just kept acting more and more crazy. Back in October he came over to the house, acting strange. He led me upstairs to the bathroom and turned on the water, like he was afraid the place was bugged. He spoke in a whisper, telling me that we had to be careful about any future contact. He said he had heard that an arrest in the case was imminent.

"He told me he wanted nothing more to do with me. That we weren't to contact each other at all."

"You didn't see him after that?"

"Oh, yeah, I saw him. There was a meeting at the office of Dick Guster, the lawyer who was representing the family in the Milo B&B lawsuit, and I was asked to attend. Lonnie and Sophie Curtis were there. And Fred Milo.

"The purpose of the meeting was to determine what should be done about the lawsuit since Dean was dead and how to speed up the probation of his will. There was also some talk about whether the family members should take lie detector tests as the police who were investigating the murder were asking.

"At one point, Fred and I stepped out and went into another office. He had me call Tony Ridle in Arizona to find out what the final bill was. Can you imagine that? Calling Ridle from another lawyer's office? The guy had lost touch with reality."

"What did the final bill come to?" Dear asked.

"Thirty-nine thousand dollars. When I told Fred, his face turned red and he grabbed the phone out of my hand and started screaming at Ridle.

"The next day I went to the Western Union office and sent a partial payment. Hell, some of it was my own money."

Momchilov gave the attorney an incredulous look. "What do you mean, your money?"

Boyd shook his head as if apologizing. "See, Fred didn't want to raid his own bank account and raise suspicion. So I made the payments for him. I borrowed some money from Sally, some from my brother. It was crazy, I know. But I didn't have the nerve to tell him I wouldn't do it. See, he was so rich, I figured I would get it back with business he would have for me when he and the family took over the company ..." Tears were beginning to form in the corner of Barry Boyd's eyes as he tried to explain the unexplainable.

Clearing his throat, he continued. "I sent cash three more times," he said. "I'd take it to Cleveland to the airport and express mail it on American Airlines. Once I sent a diamond ring that way."

Dear jerked to attention at the mention of the ring. "Why a diamond ring?"

"It belonged to Fred's wife. He used it because he didn't want to make a big withdrawal from the bank."

If Boyd was telling the truth, as he believed he was, Dear knew that the paper trail would be easy to follow. Western Union and American Airlines kept excellent records. So did the telephone company. And the Holiday Inn in Cleveland where Boyd had delivered the two thousand dollars to Harry Knott would likely have a record of his stay.

The investigator was confident he would be able to verify the remarkable story Barry Boyd had told.

"Barry," Dear asked, "how in the hell did you pass that first polygraph test?"

For the first time during the grueling interrogation, Boyd smiled faintly. "I put a thumbtack in my shoe. I knew I couldn't beat the thing, so I figured the best I could get away with was an inconclusive reading. I just tried to screw up the whole process. Every time I answered a question truthfully, I jammed my big toe into the thumbtack so the machine would register an unusual reaction, even when I wasn't lying. Over the years, my clients have taught me quite a bit."

Dear had one more question. "What did you get out of all this?"

"Nothing," Boyd answered, again beginning to cry. "Not a goddamn thing."

The nearby tape recorder spun silently for several minutes as the law officers sat looking at the pitiful picture of a man who had been pressured into ruining his life.

It was Momchilov who finally reached across the desk and turned off the machine.

As soon as Boyd's confession had been taken, Munsey and Lewis drove him to Cleveland, where he showed them the Holiday Inn room where he had given Harry Knott the money to purchase a car for his trip to Florida, then the American Airlines counter from where he had sent payoffs to Tony Ridle and the Western Union office from which he had sent money to Arizona.

By the time they returned to Akron on the evening of December 13, the *Akron Beacon Journal* had already printed a story telling of the attorney's arrest in connection with the Milo murder. Though the story carried no information about his confession or the fact that he was cooperating with the authorities, it did state that Boyd's bail had been set at $200,000.

Though the newspaper was unaware, it was participating in a trap being set for Fred Milo. There was no intent of releasing Boyd until time for a hearing, even if he was able to raise the necessary $20,000 cash that would earn him his freedom.

"I want you to call Fred," Dear instructed, "and ask him to help you raise the bail money. See if you can get him to talk about Dean's murder."

On December 18, three days after Terry Lea King went to court to plead guilty to conspiracy to commit aggravated murder, Boyd placed a call to the headquarters of Milo Barber and Beauty Supply and asked to speak with Fred Milo.

"May I ask who's calling?" the receptionist said.

"Barry."

"Just a moment, please."

The voice that came on the phone was that of Lonnie Curtis.

"Lonnie, this is Barry. Where's Fred?"

There was a brief pause before Curtis answered. "We've been told not to talk," he said.

"By who? I need to talk to Fred. I helped him a month or so ago when he really needed it. Now I need some help from him."

"Barry, you'll have to talk to him," Curtis replied. Then the line went dead.

Several times during the day Boyd tried unsuccessfully to reach Fred Milo at his office. Each time he called, he was told that Fred was out. Finally he called Milo's home and spoke with Fred's wife, Kathy. She had read the newspaper account of his arrest and seen the television reports and seemed genuinely sympathetic. He explained that he was attempting to get money together for his bail. His parents, he told her, had promised half the necessary amount but he needed Fred's help on the rest.

"Hasn't he said anything about this to you?" Boyd asked. The question surprised Dear, who was listening to the recorded conversation on headphones. Boyd, now aware that he had been used by Fred Milo, was using Milo's wife in an attempt to have her incriminate her husband.

"Barry," she said, "he hasn't said anything about it. I expect him to be home no later than ten tonight. Maybe you can try back then. If not, I'll tell him you'll try to call him at the office in the morning, okay?"

Boyd thanked her, fully aware that he would be unable to make contact with Fred Milo, regardless of where he might call him.

He then volunteered to contact one of Fred's lawyers to see if pressure could be applied from another direction. Getting Sam Nukes on the phone, Boyd explained that Milo had refused to talk with him and pointed out that Fred and Lonnie Curtis owed him $6,700 for past legal work.

"Sam," Boyd pled, "that money would go a long way toward helping me make bond, so would you get the message to Fred as soon as you can? You might also remind him that he owes my brother money, too." Fred, he knew, would understand the message since he was aware that Boyd had borrowed money from his brother to make the payments to Ridle.

"I'll talk with him as soon as I can," Nukes said.

"So, should I call him later?" Boyd asked.

"No," Nukes said. "Let me handle it on this end and then get in touch with your attorney."

Boyd hung up and looked at Dear. "Let me keep calling him," he said. "I'd like to make him as nervous as I've been."

Dear smiled. "Sounds fair to me," he said.

The following day Boyd returned to his persistent calling of Milo B&B headquarters. Finally, to his surprise, he was connected with Fred Milo.

"This is Barry," he said immediately upon hearing Fred's voice.

"They told me not to talk to you," Milo said hurriedly. "I can't—"

"Dammit, you've got to help me," Boyd shouted. "I've got to get out of here."

Milo's voice was empty of emotion as he replied. "They told me not to talk with you," he said. "I've got to go."

"Fred—"

"God bless you, Barry," Fred Milo said, then hung up.

15

Downtown Akron sparkled and vibrated with the anticipation of the fast-approaching Christmas holidays as Ed Duvall stood at the window of his office, watching the traffic below. Passing station wagons carried freshly purchased cedars and firs; pedestrians, bundled against the December cold, hurried along the sidewalks, shopping bags bulging. Holiday decorations brightened the generally colorless Main Street.

Duvall, a man who still possessed a childlike enthusiasm for the Christmas season, had not even done any shopping. He, like the others gathered in his office, was feeling cheated.

It was Friday, December 19, and Sheriff Troutman had called the meeting in Duvall's office to plan the arrests of Fred Milo, Tony Ridle, and Ray Sesic. "You know," he said, "this is the kind of case the bleeding hearts who scream about prison overcrowding are talking about. At the rate we're going, this one is going to break the taxpayers. We're going to have a jail full of people all charged with one stinking murder."

Munsey and Lewis had, for several days, been in Columbus, keeping watch on Capital Beauty Supply, where Ray Sesic worked. They had also spent considerable time in nearby London, Ohio, where Sesic and his wife lived in a small, well-kept home in a neighborhood whose festive outdoor lighting signaled the anticipation of Christmas. Having watched Sesic go through his daily routine, they were satisfied he would be easy to locate once a warrant was issued.

Fred Milo, who had been watched carefully by Dear's associates, spent his days at Milo B&B headquarters and his evenings at home.

It had been decided that the ideal scenario would be to arrest all three suspects simultaneously, therefore eliminating the possibility of one alerting the others. Momchilov had requested the help of the Scottsdale, Arizona, police in locating Ridle, but they had not yet been able to find him.

"We'll wait through the weekend," Sheriff Troutman suggested. "If they haven't found Ridle by then, we arrest Milo and Sesic. Two out of three isn't bad."

Dear and Momchilov exchanged glances. Neither would be satisfied with anything less than the arrest of all three.

The uncertainty about Ridle ended that evening when Momchilov got a call from Scottsdale detective Richard Craven. He had found Ridle at his mother-in-law's home and had arrested him without incident. "We're booking him now," the detective said. "He'll be waiting here for you."

The long distance call triggered a flurry of activity. Pleased that there would not be a weekend of apprehensive waiting, Momchilov contacted Munsey and Lewis and told them to make the short drive to London and arrest Sesic. He and Dear would head the team that took Milo into custody.

It was just after midnight when they arrived in Bath, accompanied by sheriff's officers and Bath police. Waiting in an unmarked car just down the street from the Milo home, they saw Fred and his wife arriving home from a Christmas party.

Just seconds after entering the house, Milo returned to the lighted front porch, a young girl at his side pulling on her jacket.

"The baby sitter," Dear said. "He's going to take her home."

He and Momchilov waited in silence, each studying the now quiet neighborhood. A blanket of fresh snow glistened in the rainbow of holiday lights strung by residents. As they waited for Milo's return, a few snowflakes began falling.

"Looks like a picture from a Christmas card, doesn't it?" Momchilov observed.

Milo was back in a matter of minutes, pulling his car into the garage and turning off the lights as he re-entered the house. As soon as the garage door was shut, Momchilov, Duvall, and two other officers from the sheriff's department moved grimly toward the front door. Dear, in the company of another sheriff's deputy and a Bath police officer, went to the back of the house.

It was Kathy Milo who answered Momchilov's knock.

She was still wearing the dress she had worn to the party. She gave the detective a puzzled look. "Can I help you?" she asked.

"Is your husband here?" he asked, stepping inside.

"He's upstairs."

Momchilov walked to the foot of the staircase, followed by two of the accompanying officers. Another went to the back door and let Dear and the other two officers in. "Mr. Milo," Momchilov shouted.

Fred Milo appeared at the top of the stairs, a stunned expression on his face as he looked down on the gathering of law officers. His eyes moved quickly from face to face. "What are these people doing in my house?" he said with a forced indignation that fell woefully short. Then he saw Dear standing at the bottom of the stairs. "What is Bill Dear doing here?" There was a tremble in his voice.

Momchilov started up the stairs as Milo glared at the investigator. "Fred Milo," Momchilov said, "I have a warrant for your arrest for aggravated murder ..."

Kathy Milo's knees buckled and she placed her hands over her face. "Oh, my God," she screamed before Ed Duvall rushed to her side to prevent her fall.

Still standing at the top of the stairs, Fred Milo, his face now a portrait of terror, tried to steady himself against the banister. Trembling and near tears, he lost control of his bodily functions and a dark wet circle appeared on the front of his slacks.

"I'm not saying anything," he said in a voice that was reduced to a whisper. "I've got to go to the bathroom."

Momchilov waited until Milo had changed clothes before reading him his rights.

"Do you want to call your lawyer?" Dear asked as Milo was being handcuffed.

Apparently in shock, Milo did not answer.

"Do you want us to call him for you?"

"I can't answer that," the prisoner said.

"Were you at a party earlier this evening?"

"I can't answer that."

"Do you want to talk about Dean Milo's murder?"

"I can't answer that."

En route to the county jail, Duvall, a man who had spent a quarter century in law enforcement, first as a police officer, then with the sheriff's department, asked questions of Milo with little response.

Dear, seated in the front with Momchilov, watched Duvall, surprised at the intensity with which he was questioning Milo. The veteran officer was making no attempt to disguise his disgust for the prisoner.

"Why did you kill your brother?" Dear turned and asked.

Each time, Milo's answer was the same. "My lawyer has told me not to talk."

Meanwhile, in London, the arrest of Ray Sesic had been without incident. Munsey and Lewis, joined by the local authorities, had entered the Sesic home at almost the same time Momchilov had knocked on the Milo front door.

Sesic, wearing jeans and a pullover shirt, had answered the door. When told the purpose of the officer's visit, the thirty-year-old father of two asked only that he be allowed to get his jacket before he was taken away. "I'm glad it's over," he said as they prepared to leave for Akron.

As Munsey drove, Lewis questioned Sesic in a quiet but firm manner. "On a scale of one to ten," he said, "how involved were you in the death of Dean Milo?"

"If I tell you that," Sesic said, "I might as well tell you everything."

The snow had begun to fall more heavily as Munsey drove, listening to the conversation his partner and the prisoner were having. It had been sometime the previous May, Sesic said, when Fred Milo had visited him at Capital Beauty Supply and asked if he knew somebody who could do him a big favor. When Sesic asked what kind of favor, Fred had indicated he "needed to have someone permanently removed." Sesic was reasonably sure, even then, that he could guess the identity of that someone.

It was a month later when Milo had approached him again, asking if he had found anyone for the job. "I had forgotten about it," Sesic said, "and had assumed Fred had, too. But he brought it up again and admitted it was Dean he was talking about, I told him I would ask around."

That, he said, was when he contacted a friend, Tony Ridle, who owned a bar in Arizona. A couple of days later Ridle called Sesic to say he had found two men who would take the job and charge twenty-two thousand dollars. "I called Fred to tell him," Sesic said, "and after that I was pretty much out of it. Fred began dealing directly with Tony. The only other involvement I had was when one of them was trying to get in touch with the other. I was the go-between."

"Give me a 'for instance,'" Lewis said.

"Like the day before Dean was killed," Sesic said. "Fred called me and asked me to get in touch with Tony and let him know Dean was in Akron.

"Then on a Sunday night, August tenth, Ridle telephoned me to say the job had been done. I relayed the message to Fred."

"Did you have any conversations with Fred Milo after Dean's murder?" Lewis asked.

"Not much," Sesic said. "Fred came down to Columbus sometime in September and was bitching about the fact some private investigator had been brought into the investigation. He asked me if I thought there would be any trouble with Tony keeping his mouth shut. I told him I didn't think so."

Back in Akron, Sesic was given a polygraph test and passed. He then met with Fred Zuch and agreed to cooperate with the prosecutor's office in exchange for the opportunity to plead guilty to the reduced charge of conspiracy to commit aggravated murder.

Seated in Zuch's office, listening as Sesic retold his story, Dear wondered how someone with no criminal history would allow himself to become involved in such a cold-blooded scheme.

Just before a jailer arrived to escort Sesic back to his cell, Dear rose from his chair and walked across the room to where Ray sat, his cuffed hands folded in front of him. "Ray," the investigator said, "why did you get involved in this?"

"It's hard to say, really. I've asked myself that a thousand times. I guess it was just because I felt loyal to Fred. I considered him to be a good friend."

"Pretty expensive friendship," Dear replied. "It's going to cost you seven to twenty-five years."

Sesic made no reply.

In Arizona, the thirty-two-year-old Tony Ridle had made it clear to Scottsdale officers Rich Craven and Paul Arnold that he planned to fight extradition to Ohio. A short man with long brown hair, he, like Sesic, had no previous record of criminal activity.

Three days before Christmas, Dear, Munsey, and Zuch flew to Phoenix, where Ridle was being held. In his briefcase, Zuch carried a large stack of documents—subpoenaed telephone records establishing contact among Sesic, Fred Milo, and Ridle, and air express bills and Western Union records indicating that payments had been made for the murder—which he knew would be invaluable in court. He also knew they would serve as proof to Ridle that they were not arriving on a fishing expedition. Coupled with the statements of Boyd and Sesic, the documents pointed a guilty finger directly at the man the investigators planned to interrogate.

En route, Dear and Munsey decided on the age-old good cop-bad cop approach to the questioning of the man they felt could finally clear up the mysteries that remained about Dean Milo's murder.

Munsey agreed to be the "good cop." He was surprised at how quickly Tony Ridle began to tell his story.

"Why did you get involved?" Munsey asked.

"Hey, Dean Milo was an asshole, a terrible person," Ridle spat. I couldn't stand him. Nobody could, even his own fucking family."

"So you agreed to get involved in putting him away …"

Ridle glared at Munsey for a moment, then smiled. "You're going to have to talk to my lawyer about that. I didn't say I was involved. All I'm telling you is there weren't a lot of tears shed when Dean Milo died."

Munsey patiently prodded, attempting to approach the subject of Ridle's participation from a variety of angles with little success. After almost an hour it became evident that the good-cop approach wasn't going to work. The sergeant left the room and found Dear and Zuch waiting in the coffee room

Your turn," he said to the investigator. "We haven't exactly established a brotherly relationship. He says there's no way he's talking ... or going back to Ohio."

Dear was out of his chair quickly, headed for the hall that led to the small downstairs room where Ridle waited.

Privately, he hoped the prisoner would maintain the cocky, tough-guy pose they had seen upon their arrival.

The investigator wasted no time with small talk after entering the room. He looked down at Ridle, who sat with his legs crossed. "First of all," Dear began, "I want you to know I'm tired of this case. I've been chasing all over the country for the past couple of months and my patience is worn out. So, I'm not here to beat around the bush, understand?"

Ridle shrugged but said nothing as Dear continued, his voice growing louder with each sentence. "You can fight extradition all you and every attorney you can afford to hire want to," he said, "but you're going back to Ohio sooner or later. You're in a big mess, up to your skinny, worthless ass in alligators.

"The way I see it, you're nothing but a piece of shit. For a few lousy bucks you helped take a man's life. He's got a wife and kids back in Akron who won't ever be the same because of what you did. And that's why you're going to spend the rest of your crummy life in prison."

Dear was now raging, pointing his finger at Ridle as he paced and continued talking. "They'll like you in the pen. I hope to hell you get passed around like a piece of raw meat. Your ass will be so sore you'll never want to sit down."

Still, Ridle remained silent.

"If you've got any sense at all," Dear continued, "you'll get down on your knees and beg us to give you a break. See, we don't need you, really. But you damn sure need us. I'm going to level with you and tell you what we've got. Your buddy Ray Sesic has given us a signed confession which drops you right in the grease. He told us all about calling you to set up the hit. We've got dates, times, written records. We even know about the call you made to Sesic, telling him Dean Milo was dead—even before the body had been found. Barry Boyd has confessed and names you. All the pieces are there, pal. Just on the testimony of people we've already talked to, we can put you away for life.

"Think about it. You're never going to see your wife again. And one other thing: Whether you tell us about it or not, I'm going to make your life so fucking miserable you're going to wish it was you instead of Dean Milo who was killed." With the final declaration, Dear's face was just inches from Ridle's.

Saying nothing more, the investigator turned and began walking toward the door.

"What kind of deal can you make me?" Ridle asked.

"That's not my department," Dear said. "The assistant district attorney is outside. I'm not sure he's interested in making any deals."

"Talk to him, okay?"

Zuch had been waiting in the hall where he had been able to hear portions of Dear's tirade. He was smiling. "I get the impression you don't much care for the guy," he said.

"He's a slimy little bastard," Dear answered. "He wants a deal."

Zuch entered the room with Dear and Munsey. "I'm not here to negotiate," he said to Ridle. "This is a one-shot offer. Whether you take it or leave it doesn't really matter to me. But if you're willing to cooperate, I'll make you the same deal I've made with your friend Sesic."

"What are we talking about?" Ridle asked.

"Conspiracy to commit aggravated murder. Seven to twenty-five. That's it."

Ridle slumped in his chair, allowing his tangled legs to stretch in front of him. "What do I have to do?"

"Tell us what you know," Zuch said.

While Dear and Zuch listened, Munsey questioned Ridle in the same nonaggressive voice he had used earlier. "Let's start with when you were first contacted by Ray Sesic," he said.

"It was back in May of 1980."

"And what did he say?"

"He said he needed a big favor. That Fred Milo wanted his brother murdered. It was supposed to look like an accident. He wanted to know if I could help him arrange it."

"Did you?"

"I called this guy who is a partner with me in my club—Star System. His name's Harry Knott. I told him what the deal was and he said he would make a few calls and see if he could arrange something."

Munsey glanced over at Dear, as if waiting for him to ask the next question. When the investigator only nodded to indicate that he continue, Munsey returned his attention to Ridle. "Who is Harry Knott?"

"He's a dude who was handling the vending machines in my bar. You know, the pinball machines, cigarette machine, shit like that. He and his brother-in-law, a guy named Frank Piccirilli, had this company they called Action Amusement. When business started going downhill at my place, they came in as partners with me.

"Anyway, Harry got back to me and said he could arrange the hit. He said it would take three men and cost twelve thousand dollars, plus expenses. He said his people wanted half the money up front and the other half within three days after the killing took place."

"Did you relay the information to Sesic?"

"Yeah, I called him and told him what Harry had said. I told him the job could be done for twenty-two thousand."

"I thought you said this guy Knott had quoted a figure of twelve thousand."

Ridle smiled. "I added ten grand for myself," he said.

Thereafter, according to Ridle, Sesic relayed the information to Fred Milo. "Fred called me the next night," Ridle continued, "and said he would get the money together right away. I was supposed to fly to Cleveland and he would meet me at the airport with eleven thousand in cash."

"Did he meet you?"

"He was waiting for me when I got off the plane. He had

this black briefcase and gave it to me. Didn't say a word. I took the next flight back to Phoenix."

Harry Knott, a former Marine drill sergeant who had been forced to give up his service career because of bleeding ulcers, had met Ridle. When they opened the briefcase they found eleven thousand dollars in denominations ranging from fives to hundreds. There was also a photograph of Dean Milo.

"Harry gave me a thousand and told me I would get the rest of my share after he paid his people and took care of some expenses. That was fine with me. I knew he had some debts he needed to get cleared up in a hurry. I figured I'd get what was coming to me eventually, so I wasn't worried. Plus, I liked the idea of him handling all the financial transactions on the deal.

"He told me his people would be ready to do the job just as soon as they were told where the hit was to take place. He also said he planned to make a trip to Akron, just to look things over. He wanted to see where Dean Milo lived.

"While he was there, I got a call from Fred. He said that Dean was going to Clearwater, Florida, to visit some relatives or something and that he thought it might be a good idea if Dean was killed while he was out of town.

"When Knott called, I told him what Fred had said. He didn't seem too crazy about his people having to go all the way to Florida and said they would need more money. Another two thousand for expenses, he said. He talked like the three men who would kill Milo were there with him."

"So what did you do?" Munsey asked.

"I called Ray Sesic and told him what was coming down, that Harry said he had to have more money. Ray called back a few minutes later and said Fred was having someone deliver the money to a motel near the Cleveland airport where Harry was staying."

"When did you hear from Harry Knott again?"

"Four or five days—maybe a week—later. He came back to Phoenix and said things were too risky in Florida. He said his men were still there, just in case the opportunity arose, but he didn't sound too optimistic. He said Dean was always with somebody.

"But then, the very next night Harry called and said things had worked out. His men had done it. Dean was dead. So I called Ray to pass the message along."

"And ..."

"Just a few minutes later I got this call from Fred. He was screaming, really pissed, wanting to know what was going on. He said he had just seen Dean Milo pull into his goddamn driveway.

"Then Harry told me that his people had killed the wrong fucking guy. They'd run over somebody they thought was Milo. The whole thing was getting crazy as hell.

"So I called Fred back and told him what had happened, expecting him to throw another shit fit. He was mad at first, then, all of a sudden, he sounded real calm and proceeded to offer a ten-thousand-dollar bonus if the hit could be made in the next couple of days."

It had been on August 10 when Ridle received a second call from Harry Knott, insisting that Dean Milo was dead. "He told me he had been killed at his home, shot in the back of the head. Harry didn't seem too pleased with the way things had gone down, though. He said something about the guy who did it throwing the gun away in some woods near Milo's house. That really worried him.

"After I talked with Harry, I called Ray Sesic to pass along the information so he could give the news to Fred Milo and find out when we were going to get the rest of the money."

"How soon did you get it?" Munsey asked.

"It came in bits and pieces. Milo kept saying he was having trouble getting it all together. He was afraid to take it out of the bank because someone might get suspicious. Hell, he even gave us a diamond ring that belonged to his old lady. It was supposed to be worth something like forty grand."

"Okay," Munsey said, "so it was you and Harry Knott who were getting the money from Fred Milo."

"... and Frank Piccirilli, Harry's brother-in-law," Ridle added.

Dear, who had been leaning against the wall behind Ridle, lunged forward and spun the prisoner around in his chair. "You're making this thing sound like something you've taken out of the damn telephone book," he said. "Sesic, Harry Knott, three guys who he hired ... and Piccirilli. What's his connection?"

Ridle did not seem to grasp the degree of Dear's frustration as he looked up innocently. "Like I told you, he helped Harry get the hit team together. From what I understand, Piccirilli is tied into the mob in Philadelphia somehow. That's just what I've heard. Fuck, I don't really know."

Dear pondered the complicated picture Ridle was drawing. With each new discovery, it seemed, the final solution to the case seemed farther away. Ridle's story was beginning to resemble some desperation play designed by a maniacal football coach: Fred Milo to Ray Sesic; Sesic hands off to Tony Ridle; Ridle pitches to Harry Knott; Knott laterals to Frank Piccirilli. And, finally, it goes from Piccirilli to ... whom?

"I don't know for sure who all was actually involved in the killing," Ridle insisted. "The only name I ever heard was a dude named John Harris. He was one of Harry Knott's partners in the vending machine deal and also did some kind of work for Piccirilli."

"Do you think he might have been the triggerman?" Dear asked.

"I doubt it. From what I've heard, he's evidently a mean sonuvabitch, but I never got the impression he was the kind of guy who could kill somebody. That's one of the questions I can't give you the answer to ... because I honest-to-God don't know."

Hopefully, Dear thought, a warrant for the arrest of Harry Knot would furnish the final piece to the wearisome puzzle.

From Phoenix, Dear telephoned Momchilov to relate the bizarre story Ridle was telling. "It's like some kind of crazy riddle," he said. "Half the population of the United States was in on this. I'm beginning to wonder if it has an end." Momchilov agreed. "I called a friend of mine in Clearwater," he said, "and came up with another interesting little twist. I had him check to see if there was any unsolved hit-and-run death on the books down there. He ran it through the computer and, guess what."

"Nobody was killed," Dear said, as if adding the punch line to a bad joke.

"You got it," Momchilov said. "That whole deal was evidently just part of an attempt to get some more of old Fred's money before the jerk knew what was happening. Unfortunately, Dean showed up alive and well before they could get him to bite."

At least, Dear thought, there wasn't another unsolved murder to be tied into the case.

"Well, they got to him pretty good anyway," he told Momchilov. "If everything Sesic and Ridle are saying checks out—and I have a strong feeling it will—the figure of thirty-nine thousand that Boyd gave us is a damn low estimate.

"My math's not the greatest in the world, but the way I figure it—including the ring he threw into the deal—it cost Fred something over eighty thousand to get the job done."

Momchilov let out a low whistle. "Cost of crime's going up," he said.

For Fred Milo, the financial drain was far from ended. On the same day that Tony Ridle was confessing to his role in the murder, attorney George Pappas arrived at the sheriff's department booking desk with a receipt from the Akron Municipal Court, indicating he had just paid the $200,000 necessary to have his client released from custody.

And while Fred Milo was leaving the Summit County jail, a warrant was being prepared to send to Phoenix authorities for the arrest of Harry Knott.

Hoping to put the case aside for a few days, the exhausted Dear flew home on Christmas Eve, promising Momchilov he would meet him back in Phoenix on the morning of December 28 to begin what both hoped would be the final stages of the investigation.

When Dear stepped from the plane in Phoenix, Momchilov could tell the brief holiday had not been restful. "Have a nice Christmas?" the detective asked as they walked toward the parking lot.

"Jan wants a divorce," Dear replied.

16

Fascinated by the case he had been drawn into, Scottsdale detective Rich Craven was working long hours to help the Akron authorities and Dear. Not only had he located where Harry Knott lived, but he had managed to obtain documentation of $7,000 in payoffs and a canceled check for $3,600 from a Scottsdale jewelry store for the purchase of a diamond ring. The check had been made out to and endorsed by Harry J. Knott. A second endorsement had been made by a woman who signed on behalf of Star System, Tony Ridle's bar.

Calling Munsey with the news, he explained that the jeweler had removed the stones from the ring and sold them to another jeweler in New York for $11,600.

Munsey laughed at the news. "Sounds like Fred Milo pulled a fast one," he said.

"How's that?" Craven asked.

"He told Ridle that it was worth forty grand," Munsey said. While searching Fred Milo's house, authorities had found a receipt for the ring among Milo's personal business papers. He had purchased it in 1977 for $19,500.

"Did the jeweler there say what he did with the setting?"

"He's still got it," Craven replied. "I told him to hang on to it."

In less than an hour after they heard from Munsey, Momchilov and Dear were at the counter of Sandoval Marshall Jewelers. Dear purchased the setting of the ring, adding it to the trail of evidence that connected Fred Milo to the murder of his brother.

Additionally, Craven had gathered an impressive file of

information on John Harris. Talking with snitches he had developed over the years, Craven learned that Harris had a lengthy criminal record and a reputation as a ruthless and violent man. Since age sixteen he had been arrested no less than twenty-three times on crimes ranging from auto theft to grand larceny, hit-and-run to narcotics possession. He was described as being five-ten and weighing 275 pounds. Harris had worked as a loan shark, a numbers runner, and a pimp for a low-level mob family operating in the South Philadelphia area—the same family Ridle's brother-in-law Frank Piccirilli was associated with. A fast-talking, high-pressure salesman, Harris had reportedly also dealt drugs and firearms.

For a time, he and Harry Knott had been partners in a vending machine operation. Harris had also operated a chain of massage parlors.

"He was arrested back in August for receiving stolen property from some jewelry store," Craven told Munsey, "and never showed at his hearing. There's a warrant out for him right now."

When Dear and Momchilov visited Craven's office he recapped the information he had provided Munsey. "This guy," he said, "is apparently a real beauty. A bad-ass. Everyone calls him Big John and seems scared shitless of him."

He then suggested they might want to talk with a local massage parlor operator named Tom Mandy. "Supposedly, he knows Harris pretty well," Craven said. "But I'm not sure if he'll feel like talking much right now."

"Why's that?" Dear asked.

"Evidently he and one of the girls who work for him got into some kind of shitstorm last night. She shot at him five times and managed to connect once. Got him in the left arm. He's at Scottsdale Memorial Hospital right now."

"Maybe we should take him some flowers," Momchilov suggested.

In the hospital room, Craven questioned Mandy as Dear and Momchilov listened. Still in considerable pain from his gunshot wound, Mandy answered the detective's questions in a polite, straightforward manner. He admitted that he knew both Harry Knott and John Harris but had no business dealings with either.

"I let Harris charge a couple of hundred dollars' worth of long distance calls to my phone, that's all," Mandy said. "I figured he was good for it."

"When were these calls made?"

Mandy thought for a moment. "Back in July and August. Mostly he was calling me collect, from Philadelphia and Florida and Ohio, as I recall. The last one I remember was a collect call from the Cleveland airport. He called to ask me if I would pick him up when he got here. That was sometime early in August."

Dear looked at Momchilov as Mandy spoke. Both felt sure a check of Mandy's phone records would show that the call had come on August 10, the day Dean Milo was murdered. "Did you pick him up?" Craven continued.

"Yeah, me and a friend of mine named Joey Washington went out to Sky Harbor to get him. Harris had some other guy with him."

"What did the other guy look like?"

"Creepy-looking fella. Dirty blond hair, front teeth missing. Built like a weight lifter or maybe a boxer. I think his name was Dave, but John called him 'The Kid.' We dropped them off at the Caravan Motel."

"Did you see either of them after that?"

"The next day. We went out for a couple of drinks. I bought the first round and this guy Dave, he got really hot. He told Harris, 'Goddamn it, this is a horseshit deal. I should be buying the drinks. I blow a guy away for money and here I am without a fucking cent in my pocket to show for it.' Surprised the shit out of me."

"Did he say who he killed?"

"No. I figured it must have been somebody back in Cleveland."

"Was anything else said about a murder?" Mandy laughed. "Things got a little crazy right after that. This biker dude—a total fucking stranger—started really getting on Dave's case. Giving him a load of shit about not having any teeth, stuff like that. He had a bunch of his buddies with him and was mouthing off to impress them, I guess.

"Dave just sat there for a few minutes, taking it, saying nothing. Then, he got up very casually and walked over to the biker and beat the shit out of him. I mean, he laid the guy out cold. Then Dave came back over to the table and finished drinking his beer without a word. Strange guy."

An ambulance eventually arrived to take the injured biker to the emergency room, he recalled. The police came, asked a few questions, took some names, then left without making any arrests.

"Did you see either of them after that?"

"Harris called a couple of times. One time he said something about them knocking over a jewelry store because they were short of cash. He wanted to sell me a bunch of rings. I told him to fuck himself."

"Any idea where they are now?"

"No. You might check with Bennie Railey."

Railey, a small-time thief and dope peddler, had no idea of the whereabouts of Harris and his friend, but he added a significant detail to Mandy's story. Harris, he said, had told him that The Kid had killed some corporate executive in Akron, Ohio.

Learning from neighbors that Harry Knott had taken his family on a short vacation to California for a visit to Disneyland, Craven got a search warrant for his home. Among Knott's personal records was documentation of payoffs, telegrams advising him where to pick up money sent from Ohio, and telephone numbers linking Knott to Tony Ridle.

Coupled with Ridle's confession, these things justified the arrest of Harry Knott for murder.

"If we can find him," Momchilov said.

"I'll find him," Craven said. "When he gets back, I'll be camped on his doorstep."

Confident in the Scottsdale detective's ability, Dear and Momchilov decided to return to Akron and begin assembling the growing mass of evidence that Fred Zuch would need as he began preparing his case against Fred Milo. In addition to the damaging statement they had taken from Ridle, they now had the ring Milo had used as partial payment for the crime, the briefcase he had given to Ridle in the Cleveland airport and a winding, incriminating paper trail of crimes, dates, transactions, and phone calls.

The trick now was to put it all together in a simple order that would convince a jury of Fred Milo's involvement.

The trial had been tentatively set to begin in April. Fred Milo, back at work, was assuring friends and business associates that he would be found innocent.

While Dear and Momchilov were in Arizona, Munsey and Lewis had methodically put together a detailed time flow chart, putting each piece of evidence into sequence. The chart, which began with Fred Milo's visit to Barry Boyd's house when he mentioned that he needed "a favor," trailed the case through the murder and payoffs.

And, using information provided by Craven, they had been able to add another piece of physical evidence. Checking phone records supplied by Mandy, Craven found that several collect calls had come from motels where John Harris and his friend had stayed. According to the night clerk at the Lookout Motel in Fort Wright, Kentucky, two men answering their description had stayed there. According to the registration information they had provided, they were driving a 1971 Oldsmobile with Arizona license plates.

Munsey had checked with the Department of Motor Vehicles and was able to establish that John Harris had sold the car to a man named Juan Chavez in Cleveland for fifty dollars. The transaction, he learned, had taken place on the afternoon of August 10—the same day Dean Milo was murdered.

"The description Chavez gave of Harris matches," Munsey told Dear. "Hell, he signed his real name to the receipt. I don't think there's any question it's our man. And I'll bet you a steak dinner that's the car they were driving the night of the murder. A four-door Ninety-Eight, olive green with a black vinyl top."

The information delighted Dear. "Before I bet with you," he told Munsey, "I need to go talk to somebody." He immediately drove to Bath, back into the neighborhood where his investigation had begun months earlier.

Parking near the cul-de-sac leading to the Milo home, he walked across the street to the home of R. D. Hall, one of the many neighbors he had initially interviewed. Since the day they had spoken, with Hall expressing concern that there was underworld involvement in his neighbor's death, Dear had strongly felt he knew more than he indicated.

Hall answered the door and immediately recognized the investigator.

Dear went straight to the purpose of his visit. "When we talked initially," he said, "I know you were very concerned that the Mafia might somehow be involved in Dean Milo's death. I can now assure you that isn't the case."

Hall nodded but said nothing.

"I was wondering if maybe you might have remembered anything since we last spoke."

"Why don't you come on in out of the cold?" Hall said.

In the kitchen Hall poured coffee, focusing his attention on the steam rising from his cup for several seconds before speaking. "There is something," he finally said. "In the early morning hours of August ninth, I was awakened by what sounded like a loud car muffler. I got up and went to the bedroom window and saw an old model Oldsmobile—dirty green with a black top—pull up in front of the Milo house. A man got out of the passenger side and went to the door. He was there for maybe a minute, then returned to the car. Then they drove away."

Dear studied Hall's face, secretly hoping he had his dates wrong, since Dean Milo had been murdered on the tenth. "Are you certain that it was early on August ninth?"

"Positive," Hall said. "That's why I decided not to mention it. It didn't seem important. In fact, I saw Dean pull into his driveway later that day."

The question that now rolled around in Dear's mind was another, he knew, without an answer. Had the killers arrived at Milo's house a night early, only to find he was not at home?

Only the men who had been in the car could provide the answer.

Distraught over his personal problems and more anxious than ever to see the final pieces of the case fall into place, Dear left Momchilov, Munsey, and Lewis to help Zuch with preparations for the Milo trial and returned to Arizona in hopes of locating Harry Knott and Frank Piccirilli.

Knott's common-law wife insisted she had not seen her husband in days and had no idea where he might be.

Dear then turned his attention to Piccirilli, who had already insisted to Craven that he knew nothing about any murder plot. Aware that there was very little evidence to link Piccirilli to the plot, Dear decided to apply an unorthodox brand of pressure. His initial conversation with Piccirilli's wife had been fruitless but, after having learned that Piccirilli was having an affair with a friend of his wife, then watching him pay several visits to the trailer park where the woman lived, Dear placed a call to Piccirilli's home.

"You've told me that I've been lying to you about your husband's activities," Dear said. "But he's the one who is lying and he's going to pull you down into all this if you don't cooperate and tell us what you know."

"You're a damn liar," she screamed into the phone. "I want you to leave us alone or I'm going to call the police."

"Why don't you drive over to Joy Stephens's trailer right now?" Dear suggested. "What you'll find if you do is your poor, innocent husband in bed with her." Then he hung up.

Returning to the trailer park, Dear had been there only a few minutes when Piccirilli's wife drove up, parked in front of the trailer he had been watching, and rushed inside. The investigator smiled, started his car, and drove away.

Early that evening Piccirilli telephoned Craven, complaining about Dear's tactics and saying he was coming to the Scottsdale police station to talk things over. "I want to get this shit straightened out, once and for all," he told the detective, "but I don't want that asshole private eye there."

At the police station, the short, stocky Piccirilli, his black hair combed straight back in a style that had gone out with the fifties, sat glaring at Craven.

He answered the detective's questions with an economy of

words. Yes, he admitted, he was married to Harry Knott's sister, and he and Harry had been partners in the vending machine business. They had been boyhood friends back in Philadelphia. He knew Tony Ridle only as his brother-in-law's partner in the bar Star System.

"Where's Harry now?" Craven asked.

"I haven't seen him since before Christmas," Piccirilli said.

"What about John Harris?"

Piccirilli shrugged. "Haven't seen him, either."

Piccirilli denied having any mob family connections in Philadelphia and insisted he had heard nothing about any hit that was supposed to have taken place in Ohio.

The interview, Craven knew, was going nowhere.

"Listen," the detective said, "we've got a warrant out for Harry's arrest, so if you hear from him it would be in your best interest to let us know."

"I'll do it," Piccirilli said. "You just tell that goddamn Bill Dear to stay the fuck away from me."

Piccirilli quickly left, leaving Craven sitting alone in the small room where the interview had taken place. Staring at the door through which the man had gone, the detective folded his arms and said, "You lying bastard."

On February 2 Dear received an excited call from Craven. An anonymous tipster had informed him that Knott and Harris were being hidden by friends at an address on the outskirts of Oklahoma City. "Harris is supposedly using the name David Ross," Craven said.

Dear made no attempt to hide his own excitement. "Call the Oklahoma State Police and fill them in. I'm on my way to the airport," he said.

He missed them by forty-eight hours. But a man who had met the two during their brief stay in the trailer park said he had heard them talking about going to Miami. With the help of the Oklahoma authorities, a check of the airlines revealed that a passenger named David Ross had purchased a ticket from Eastern Airlines to Miami. From there he was to take Air Bahamas to Nassau.

From the airport Dear placed a call to an FBI friend in the Bahamas, asking that an all-points bulletin go out immediately for the two men, then caught the next flight out.

In the islands he missed Knott and Harris by less than an hour. Going directly to a bar near the Nassau airport where Knott and Harris had been seen, he showed the bartender photographs of the two men. He was told they had left to catch a mail boat.

"Where does it go?" Dear asked.

"It doesn't have a particular route," the bartender said. "It stops at hundreds of little islands, dropping off mail and picking up bananas. The captain's sort of a free spirit; he goes where he wants to and makes up his schedule as he goes. There are seven hundred islands out there, pal. Your guess is as good as mine."

Clearly, Knott and Harris, aware they were being pursued, planned to stay on the move.

Taking a long shot, Dear booked passage on a departing banana boat in hopes of catching up with the two fugitives. For his efforts he got nothing but five days of seasickness. He finally gave up the chase on a postage-stamp-sized island with a wobbly dock and two ramshackle buildings that housed all six of the people who lived there. To his relief, another boat lay in port, headed back to Nassau.

He returned to Akron, where all efforts were focused on preparing for the Fred Milo trial. Jury selection was just three weeks away. The feeling gnawed at Dear that the trial would get under way with the actual murderers still not in custody.

17

From the moment Rich Craven met Momchilov and Dear and first learned the details of the murder investigation, he had been caught up in the case. Since making the arrest of Tony Ridle, he had spent hours of his own off-duty time trying to get additional information from his Scottsdale connections.

On a Thursday afternoon, just a week before jury selection was to get under way for the murder trial of Fred Milo, Craven sat behind his desk reading through the sizable file he had accumulated. He had read and reread each of the statements he, Munsey, and Dear had taken but was reading them again in hopes that there might be something he might have overlooked.

As Craven was going through the statement of massage parlor operator Tom Mandy, in which he described the fight between the biker and the man known as The Kid, he sat up in his chair. Mandy had mentioned that when the police arrived, The Kid had given a fake name, although Mandy did not remember what it was. Craven knew the disturbance call at the bar had been answered by the Tempe police and immediately telephoned a friend in the department, asking if he would check the files and get him the name of the officer who was responsible for writing a report on the incident.

In a matter of minutes the officer was on the phone and had already pulled the file Craven was asking about. He had, he said, taken the names of two men at the scene. "One," he said, "was a guy named John Harris. A big, fat guy."

"What about the other one?" Craven asked. "The one with no front teeth."

"Bass," the Tempe officer said. "David Bass."

Craven immediately ran the name through the Arizona Central Police Index, a computer system that cross-references aliases with actual names. Initially, the computer information indicated that a warrant had been issued for the arrest of a David Bass in 1979 for the burglary of a mortuary. Then, cross-referencing the name, the computer indicated that David Bass was a name used by David Harden, whose last known residence was Covington, Kentucky. Harden, twenty-one years old, was five-ten, weighed 175 pounds, and had blond hair and green eyes. He had a variety of tattoos and several front teeth missing.

A wide grin broke across Craven's face as the last bit of information came up on the screen. "Damn," he said, then began searching for Larry Momchilov's telephone number.

"This may be a long shot," he said to the Akron detective, "but I think I might have the name of your killer."

The trial of Fred Milo began on April 27 in the Court of Common Pleas in Columbus after attorney George Pappas and three attorneys assisting him with the defense had argued successfully for a change of venue.

When he was told that there was a strong possibility that the man who had actually killed Dean Milo might soon be located, prosecutor Fred Zuch expressed little interest.

"To arrest him now," Zuch told Dear, "would throw a monkey wrench into the whole thing. I don't want things any more complicated than they are right now. We've got a good plan of attack and we're going to stick with it."

This attitude infuriated Dear. "Goddamn it, Fred," he yelled, "if this is the guy who pulled the trigger and we can bring him in, it wraps everything up in a nice, neat package."

"I don't want him right now," Zuch replied. "Pappas is planning an insanity defense so damned screwy that no one in the world is going to buy it. We've got what we need to win this thing without adding another character to the script."

"I hope to hell you're right," Dear said. Zuch's overconfidence worried him deeply.

Pappas, generally recognized as one of Ohio's premier defense attorneys, planned to attempt to convince the jury that the murder of Dean Milo had resulted as a bizarre stroke of bad luck, committed by persons unknown long after his client had given up on his own plot.

He readily admitted that Fred Milo had spoken with a number of people about having his brother murdered, but claimed that he was insane at the time. The actual murder had been done, no doubt, by some business enemy of Dean Milo.

To lend credibility to the insanity defense, Pappas showed a videotape of Fred Milo being interviewed by a renowned Detroit psychiatrist named Emmanuel Tanay. On the tape, jurors saw a distraught Milo insisting that his brother was, in fact, still alive, being held hostage somewhere. The man who had so aggressively negotiated the takeover of Milo Barber and Beauty Supply was, he said, a look-alike brought in by Akron lawyers George Tsarnas and Sam Goldman to run the company at their direction.

Tsarnas, in particular, had the ability to manage such "replacements," Milo had told the psychiatrist.

It had been after Sotir and Katina Milo were asked to leave the company Christmas party, Fred stated, that he was finally convinced that the man he thought was Dean Milo wasn't really his brother and began to plot ways to have the "double" killed.

"I had all kinds of unrealistic plans," Fred admitted. "One time I thought about tying him to the railroad tracks. Once I thought it might work if I tied him to the mouth of a cannon."

As bizarre as the "replacement" story was, Fred Milo's videotaped performance was impressive. If he wasn't crazy, he did an outstanding job of playing the role.

Since Pappas had decided not to allow Milo to take the stand, the jury would not have the opportunity to hear his version of the improbable story firsthand.

Tanay took the stand following the showing of the videotape and spoke to the stunned jury in a soft, sincere voice. "Any time a thirty-six-year-old man who has absolutely no past criminal record goes around asking dozens of people to kill his brother, there is something terribly wrong. I would have to say such a person could not be acting responsibly," he said. "Additionally, it has been my experience that in almost all homicides where the victim is a relative or friend, the killer has been insane and not accountable for his actions."

Though Dear was aware that Zuch would put a psychiatrist on the stand to testify that Fred Milo was sane, the possibility of the defendant being allowed to enter a mental hospital, there to stay only until doctors decided he was well and no longer a threat to society, angered him.

During a recess he again approached Zuch about the possibility of seeking out David Harden. This time he had Momchilov as an ally.

"I don't even want to talk about it," Zuch said. "I don't want anyone even talking with him about this case. If we brought him in at this late date, Pappas would explode and demand a mistrial or, at the very least, a postponement. I can just see him prancing around with all that righteous anger over our coming up with a surprise witness. You know that the defense is entitled to know who our witnesses will be. I'm not going to stand here and debate judicial policy with you. Just leave it alone, okay? I know what I'm doing."

Momchilov, who had remained silent, finally spoke up. "He's wanted in Arizona on a burglary charge."

"Okay," Zuch said, "arrest him on that if you can find him. Take him back to Phoenix and put him in jail there. But don't talk with him about this case. Not until the trial is over. Period."

Turning back to Dear, Zuch placed his hand on the investigator's shoulder. "We're going to win this thing. We've got Terry Lea King's testimony. We've got Barry Boyd and Ray Sesic and Tony Ridle and a paper trail a blind man could follow. There's the briefcase, the ring, canceled checks. Hell, you can't have much more evidence than what we're going to be able to put on."

"But you don't have the killer," Dear growled.

"I don't think we need him."

"Well, I damn sure do."

Following up on Craven's information about Harden, Munsey and Lewis had learned that he had received a traffic ticket eight months earlier in Covington, Kentucky, just across the state line from Ohio. The truck, a computer check revealed, was owned by a man named Bill Cousins, who lived in a tiny community in Kentucky.

Dear immediately dispatched Carl Lilly, Terry Hurley, and Dick Riddle to locate Cousins. They found him with no trouble and he readily admitted that he had lent Harden his truck.

"But I haven't seen him in a long time," he insisted. "Which is just fine with me. The sonuvabitch is scary. He was always running his mouth about being some kind of big-shot hit man. He's a mean motherfucker."

"Do you have any idea where he might be now?" Riddle asked.

"Last I heard he was living with his girlfriend in a trailer house over in Mentor."

The girlfriend insisted she had no idea where David Harden might be found. "But if anyone knows where he is," she offered, "it would be John Ritchie. He's David's best friend."

While Riddle stayed to watch the girl's trailer in the event Harden came or she left to warn him of their presence, Lilly and Hurley went to the only bar in town and found Ritchie playing pool and drinking beer.

"We're trying to locate David Harden," Lilly said.

"Who the hell are you?"

"Private investigators."

Ritchie sipped from his beer and smiled. "What do you need Harden for? The murder?"

Lilly was briefly taken aback. "What murder are you talking about?" he finally replied.

"The one over in Ohio."

"What can you tell us about it?"

"Not a fucking thing," Ritchie said. "I can't go around talking shit against a friend."

"Not even if there's a reward?" Hurley said.

"It would have to be a big one."

"How big?"

Ritchie did not bother with game-playing. "Pretty fucking big," he said. "Five, ten thousand dollars."

"We might be able to get that for you if you've got the kind of information we need," Lilly said.

Ritchie smiled as he put down his beer and laid his pool cue on the table. "Why don't we go over to my place and talk about this in private? The guy I live with isn't there right now," he said. What he did not bother to add was that his roommate was David Harden.

Lilly and Hurley had just settled on the couch when the phone rang. Glancing over at the investigators as he spoke, Ritchie told the caller, "Naw, I haven't heard anything like that. Nobody's looking for you around here. Everything's pretty quiet." Hanging up, he smiled. "That was David," he said.

"Why don't you just tell us where he is?" Terry Hurley asked.

"I probably should," Ritchie said, "just to help him out. He's all fucked up on drugs, killing himself. I hate to see it because he's my friend."

"So, tell us and we'll see that he gets some help."

"What about the reward?"

"You'll have to talk to the man we work for about that," Lilly said.

"I'm ready," Ritchie said.

The long-distance call between Ritchie and Dear lasted no more than five minutes. He found the tone of Ritchie's voice irritating. He felt certain that, given time, he and his associates could pressure the information from the arrogant-sounding huckster. That, however, would take more time than Dear was willing to risk. Harden, he was convinced, had the answers to his questions and he wanted to talk with him as soon as possible. He agreed to pay Ritchie five thousand dollars immediately after Harden was taken into custody.

"He's in Room 7004 at Cincinnati General Hospital," Ritchie said. "He's got a bad case of hepatitis. He's registered under another name."

"David Bass?" Dear asked.

"Yeah," the surprised Ritchie acknowledged.

Dear contacted Michael Wolff, the sheriff's department legal adviser, told him what had happened, and asked that he pick up the necessary five thousand dollars from George Tsarnas, then phone Rich Craven in Arizona and arrange for a copy of the arrest warrant to be sent to the Cincinnati Police Department.

While the burglary warrant was being teletyped, Dear and Bill Lewis were flying to southern Ohio.

They were met at a private airstrip by Lilly, Hurley, and a nervous John Ritchie.

Dear showed the informant the five thousand. "You get this when we've got Harden," he said.

Ritchie looked at the stack of bills in the investigator's hand. "I've got to tell you one more thing," he said, his voice having lost the toughness Dear had heard over the phone. "David's been saying he would never be taken alive."

It was just after 3:00 p.m. on the first Saturday in May when Dear positioned himself near the door of Room 7004. To his right was Lieutenant Lewis. Both were wearing white doctor's smocks with stethoscopes hanging from their necks. Nurses had cleared everything from the halls to make room for the dozen heavily armed Cincinnati police officers who had arrived to help with the arrest.

Harden was sharing a room with an elderly man who had just undergone surgery earlier in the day. It had been Dear's idea to pose as a doctor and, with the help of two of the hospital nurses, get him out of the room before arresting Harden.

Taking a deep breath and nodding to the nurses, Dear walked into Room 7004, ignoring Harden and focusing his attention on the surgery patient. "How are you feeling?" he asked the patient while giving the impression he was studying information on a clipboard he was carrying.

"I'm still a little drowsy," the patient answered.

"Well, you're doing fine," Dear said in his best bedside manner. "The surgeon wants us to take you downstairs for a couple of quick tests. Nothing painful and nothing to be concerned about."

The mention of additional tests obviously worried the patient. "They're just routine, postoperative tests," Dear assured him. "They won't take long. You're going to be just fine."

With the help of the silent nurses, Dear wheeled the patient's bed from the room and down the hall to the elevator. He would be taken to another floor for safety's sake until his roommate was in custody.

Dear waited a few minutes before he walked back down the hall, past the team of police officers, and nodded toward Lewis. This time he flashed a smile at Harden, who lay propped up in his bed, covered by a bedsheet.

"I'm sorry about the disturbance a while ago," Dear said. Taking the clipboard, which Lewis was now holding, the investigator studied it briefly, then placed his hand on Harden's wrist as if taking the patient's pulse. "Well, Mr. Bass, how are you feeling today?"

"Okay," Harden said with a toothless half-smile.

Dear pretended to fluff the patient's pillow, his fingers hurriedly feeling for a possible weapon, then he laid the clipboard on Harden's lap.

His next prearranged move came quickly. Dear put his right hand on Harden's throat and with his left tore away the bedsheet to expose any weapon Harden might be hiding.

Lewis stepped forward quickly, his police revolver drawn and pointed toward the patient. "Freeze," the lieutenant said. "You're under arrest." As soon as Lewis spoke, the room filled with a half-dozen officers, each pointing a gun at Harden. Lewis quickly handcuffed the prisoner to the bed and read him his rights, explaining he was being arrested on a burglary warrant issued by the Phoenix Police Department.

Dear, keeping in mind Zuch's insistence that Harden not be questioned about the Milo murder, could not help making clear that they were not from Phoenix. "We've come from Akron, Mr. Harden," he said.

Harden's eyes darted from Lewis to Dear. The look of surprise on his face changed to one of fear. A man with a great deal of experience with law enforcement agencies, he knew no sheriff's detective would travel from Akron, Ohio, to make an arrest on a burglary case in Arizona.

With great restraint, Dear managed to follow Zuch's order not to question Harden about the murder of Dean Milo. Instead, he walked to the window of Harden's room and slowly ran his fingers through his hair. It was the signal that would indicate to Lilly, who waited in the car in the parking lot with Ritchie, that the arrest had been made.

Carl Lilly began counting out the five thousand dollars to the nervous young man beside him in the front seat.

Back in Columbus, the trial of Fred Milo continued with neither the jury nor members of the media aware that the man who had, in all likelihood, fired the shots that ended Dean Milo's life was finally in custody.

After the technical testimony from the coroner, crime lab technicians, and officers who had been at the murder scene, Zuch called Barry Boyd to the stand.

At the prosecutor's insistence, Boyd appeared in the courtroom wearing orange jail coveralls, looking out on an overflow crowd. He made a concerted effort to avoid eye contact with Fred Milo, the man who had been his best friend through high school and college, the man with whom he had double-dated and shared boyhood dreams, the man from whom he had lived just two blocks apart for most of his adolescent life. When Fred had run for student council, it had been Boyd who handled his campaign, printing flyers, making phone calls, and organizing support rallies. He had never admitted it, but he had idolized Fred Milo, envied him his quick wit and his charming personality. He had viewed Fred as a doer. He, himself, had been only a dreamer.

Still, the irony of the moment escaped Boyd as he was sworn in. It did not occur to him that his testimony would, for the first time in his life, provide him the upper hand in their relationship.

Zuch, friendly but businesslike, steered Boyd through the labyrinth of events that had ultimately led to his own arrest. For six hours he relived the nightmare as Pappas repeatedly jumped from the defense chair and in animated fashion fired off flurries of objections, most of which were overruled.

On cross-examination Pappas immediately set about to impeach Boyd's credibility, suggesting that a long-standing dependence on drugs and alcohol had seriously reduced his ability to distinguish truth from wildly imagined fantasies.

Expertly, he crafted a portrait of a low-life alcoholic falsely accusing an old friend with nothing more than jealousy and revenge as motives.

"Didn't you grow up with Freddie in the same neighborhood?" Pappas asked.

"Yes, I did."

"When you knew him back in kindergarten, he was a normal person, wasn't he?"

"Yes."

"And when you knew him in grade school did he in any way resemble the macabre, murder-plotting person you've described to the jury?"

"No, he didn't."

Pappas continued the line of questioning through the years of high school and college. To each query, Boyd answered that the Fred Milo he had known in his younger days had, in every way, seemed a normal person. But, yes, there had come a time not long ago when Boyd had noticed a change.

The defense attorney had set up his closing argument masterfully. Even the prosecution's star witness, he would point out, had seen a change occur in the defendant.

Though not the showman Pappas was, Zuch argued a well-constructed case, mixing the testimony of witnesses with the physical evidence that linked Fred Milo to the crime. He scorned the "replacement" theory that the defense had presented.

Pappas, meanwhile, matched him disdainful look for disdainful look. He treated the testimony of prosecution witnesses and the introduction of evidence as if they mattered not at all. His client, he repeatedly stated, had been insane at the time the murder plot was carried out.

In fact, he insisted, Fred Milo himself had been a victim, paying out large sums of money to people who were, in effect, blackmailing him and conning him, with no intention of actually committing the crime he was paying for.

The actual murder of Dean Milo, he proposed, was carried out by someone not even connected with his client; a lover, perhaps, or a jealous husband, maybe a business enemy.

In the halls of the Columbus courthouse, speculation began

to spread that the prosecution's case, despite its obvious strength, might be lost to Pappas's theatrics and his theory of insanity. Of concern to many who had sat through the proceedings was the fact the prosecution had failed to produce the person who had actually committed the crime.

On May 25, Judge Frank Bayer announced that the jury was unable to reach a verdict and declared a mistrial. He immediately ordered a new trial to be held in July.

The vote of the jury had been ten to two in favor of an innocent-by-reason-of-insanity verdict. Pappas had come within two votes of seeing his client walk out of the courtroom a free man.

Hearing the breakdown of the jury's voting, Bill Dear first felt anger, then relief. At least there would be a second chance.

The next time, a jury would get to hear from the man who carried out Fred Milo's murder plot.

18

David Harden was a textbook example of a social misfit. The oldest of four children, he had lived an aimless life since his parents had divorced when he was five years old. By age fifteen he had dropped out of school and left home, supporting himself with petty thefts and small-time drug dealing. In time, he was using more drugs than he was selling.

His wanderings eventually led him to Phoenix, where he met a girl, fell in love, and found his first steady job, with a local construction company. When his girlfriend told him she would never marry a speed freak, he quit drugs cold turkey and for almost three years he worked steadily and managed to control his habit.

It was the girl's family who eventually blocked the marriage, constantly pressuring their daughter to avoid Harden and seek out a husband with a brighter future. The breakup sent Harden onto the downhill slope again. He quit his job, began mainlining crystal, and stole for a living. Adopting a cocky, bullying attitude, he went out of his way to look for fights, often visiting gay bars to pick up a stranger, take him home, and then beat and rob him.

Two years before his arrest in connection with the Milo murder, he had twice been admitted to the Phoenix City Hospital following suicide attempts.

He had, he told one psychiatrist, often fantasized about killing someone and then reading his name in the paper and seeing himself on television.

Now, however, he seemed genuinely remorseful. The fantasy had turned into a real-life nightmare and, when Fred Zuch visited Phoenix in early June and offered to allow him to plead guilty to a charge of aggravated murder, Harden immediately accepted.

In exchange for his confession and cooperation during the second Milo trial, Zuch explained, he would receive a life sentence—which translated to no more than fifteen years in prison.

Sitting in the Phoenix jail, David Harden finally told his chilling story to Rich Craven and the delegation of investigators from Akron.

It had been in July of 1980 when he had met John Harris in a bar in Covington, Kentucky. They drank and shot pool until the bar closed, then went to the motel where Harris was staying.

"That's when he told me he knew how I could make some quick money," Harden said. "He showed me a picture of this guy and said someone wanted him killed. He said it would be worth two thousand dollars if I would do it."

Detective Craven, delighted at being given the opportunity to take Harden's statement, asked if Harris had told him of a plan to carry out the crime.

"Yeah, he showed me a gun. He said we were going to shoot him."

"What kind of gun was it?"

"A .32 automatic, with a homemade silencer on it."

They remained in Covington for several days, Harden recalled, while Harris made numerous telephone calls. Finally, he said, Harris told him it was time to go to Ohio.

"What kind of car was Harris driving?" Craven asked.

"A green Oldsmobile," Harden said.

He told of arriving in Akron, where Harris stopped at a shopping center and purchased plastic gloves and some trash bags. "He never did say what they were for," Harden pointed out. "In fact, he got real secretive about everything. We hung around Akron for a while, drinking and getting something to eat, then we drove on to Cleveland and checked into a TraveLodge. We were there for three or four days while John waited for some money he was supposed to pick up at Western Union."

During their stay in Cleveland, Harden said, they had driven back to the Akron area on one occasion, going out to the Milo Barber and Beauty Supply headquarters. "He showed me where this guy we were supposed to hit parked his car. That's when he told me what his name was: Dean Milo.

"He said we could wait until he came out of the building and I could just walk up to him. I was to ask if he was Dean Milo and if he said yes, I was supposed to shoot him right there. I told him he was fucking crazy if he thought I was going to walk up to somebody in a parking lot in broad daylight and shoot him.

"That's when I started having doubts about the whole deal and started trying to figure a way to get out of it. But Harris said we'd do it another way, so I decided to stay in.

"John made some phone calls and then said we were supposed to go back to Cleveland and wait. Milo was out of town and wouldn't be back for a few days. We checked out of the TraveLodge and moved into a place called the Valley View Motel on the outskirts of Cleveland."

Finally, after three days of waiting, Harris received a telephone call informing him that Dean Milo was back in town.

It was, Harden recalled, on a Friday night that he and Harris drove to Bath. Throughout the trip, Harris stressed the importance of making the hit quickly. "He's supposed to be home by himself," Harris said, "so we go in, pop him, and get the fuck out of there. Nice and quick."

The driver showed his companion a blank telegram he had taken during one of his visits to Western Union. "We tell the poor bastard that he's got a telegram," he said. "That gets the front door open. Not bad, huh?"

"We drove to the house that night," Harden continued. "It was sometime before midnight. Harris parked and all of a sudden starts telling me that I've got to do it by myself. He said it was more important for him to stay in the car so we could make a fast getaway. The bastard was getting cold feet.

"So, I went up to the front door and knocked. There was no answer, so I knocked again, louder. But no one came. Finally, I went back to the car.

"We drove over to a bowling alley and did some drinking, just killing time. Every ten minutes or so, John would go to a pay phone and call the Milo house to see if anybody answered. We stayed there until after two in the morning, but no one ever answered, so we drove back to Cleveland."

Later that day, Saturday, Harris received another telephone call. Following a brief conversation, he took the gun from the dresser in the motel room and smiled at his companion. "Tonight's the night," he said.

"He kept showing me how to use the fucking gun," Harden said. "Over and over, like I was a blithering idiot. He would put on those damn rubber gloves and load and unload it. He showed me how the safety worked and how to put the silencer—this homemade job—on the barrel.

"I could tell he was getting really nervous about the whole thing. He kept saying, 'You can do it, I know you can.'

"I knew I was in too deep to get out, so I spent most of the afternoon getting high. I just wanted to get it over with."

It was shortly after seven in the evening when Harris and Harden began yet another journey from Cleveland to the outskirts of Akron. Harden said nothing during the trip, occasionally reaching his right hand into the pocket of his jacket to feel the cool steel of the .32 he was carrying. With his left hand he squeezed on the neck of a bottle of whiskey from which he was sipping constantly.

"When we got there, John called the house again and got no answer. He came back to the car really pissed and nervous. Then he went back to the phone booth and called some dude in Arizona."

"He's out somewhere," Harris said, "but he's supposed to be home tonight. We won't have to wait much longer." He grabbed the whiskey bottle from Harden and drank deeply.

"You can do it," he said again, staring down at Harden with a crazed look. "You goddamn sure can. I know it."

An hour later he placed yet another call to the Milo home and heard a man's voice answer. Harris apologized for having dialed the wrong number.

"He's home," he said as he slid behind the steering wheel to begin the two-mile trip to 2694 Everest Circle.

As they pulled to a stop at the entrance to the cul-de-sac, Harris handed Harden the telegram. "Look," he said, "my man tells me there's big fucking money in the house—maybe twenty thousand—and a lot of expensive jewelry. After you take care of the guy, turn on the porch light when it's okay for me to come in."

Harden, feeling the effects of the drugs and whiskey he had been consuming since earlier in the day, looked at his partner's hands, which were gripping the steering wheel. For a brief second he wondered why Harris was wearing the rubber gloves when it was he who carried the gun, but he said nothing as he climbed from the car and began walking up the incline toward the Milo house.

For the first time it occurred to him that if he didn't carry out the plan, John Harris might well kill him.

As he slowly made his way to the front door, his legs felt rubbery and his mouth was dry. Finally reaching the porch, he rang the doorbell.

"Through the little window in the door," Harden said, "I could see this guy coming down the stairs, wearing nothing but his underwear. When he got to the door he asked who it was.

"I told him I was from Western Union and that I had a telegram for Mr. Dean Milo. He turned on a light there in the hall and started unlocking the door.

"As soon as he opened the door, I pushed my way in, kind of knocking him off balance. I pulled the gun from my back pocket and stuck it right in his face. I told him it was a robbery and to lay down on the floor."

Harden paused from his narrative and bent forward, burying his face in his hands. After a few seconds he looked up at Craven, tears sliding down his cheeks. "This is tougher than you think," he said.

"What happened next?" the detective replied.

"The guy was really scared," Harden continued. "He got down on the floor and started begging me not to hurt him. He said, 'Please... don't kill me.' I really started freaking out. I just wanted to get it over with and get the hell out of there."

He told of pulling the silencer from his pocket and placing it on the barrel of the gun. "I was standing over him," he said, "with the gun in my right hand. I had trouble with the silencer, so I decided to just kind of hold it to the barrel with my other hand.

"Then I put the gun to the back of his head and pulled the trigger. When the gun fired, this cotton inside the silencer exploded all over his head. It hurt like hell. For a second I thought maybe I'd shot myself in the hand."

"How many times did you shoot him?"

"See, I didn't see any blood and for some reason I thought maybe the gun hadn't fired. He wasn't moving but he was sort of mumbling. I was really scared. I told him not to move and ran over and got this pillow out of a chair. I figured it would muffle the sound. I put it over his head and pressed the barrel of the gun down on it and shot him again.

"After that he didn't move, so I knew he was dead."

Panic-stricken, Harden turned off the hallway light and, pulling the front door closed behind him, ran toward the car. Harris briefly argued that they should return and look for the money and jewels he had been told were in the house, but apparently recognizing the blind fear of his companion he dropped the idea and drove away.

Harden said he had a vague recollection of throwing the gun from a bridge somewhere between Akron and Cleveland.

Returning to the motel, Harden and Harris remained for the rest of the night, trying in vain to sleep. The following morning Harris sold the Oldsmobile and they caught a flight to Phoenix's Sky Harbor Airport.

The confession had finally answered many of the questions that had haunted Bill Dear from that first day he had stepped into the doorway of the Dean Milo home. The cotton found on Milo's body had been left there by the murderer, part of a makeshift silencer fashioned from a piece of lead pipe.

Dean's shorts were on backwards only because they had

been pulled on in his haste to answer the late-night ringing of the doorbell.

"What time was it when you killed him?" Dear asked Harden.

"It had to have been between one and two in the morning." The answer was important for several reasons, not the least of which was that it proved Dear, not Coroner Kyriakides, right about the time of death.

"One more question," Dear said. "How much did you actually get for killing Dean Milo?"

Harden did not answer immediately. "Harris finally gave me six hundred dollars," he said.

On July 29, David Harden took the stand at the second trial of Fred Milo and again told his gruesome story, destroying Pappas's theory that the murder had been carried out by someone not associated with his client. This time a jury of seven men and five women found Fred Milo guilty of aggravated murder and sentenced him to life in prison.

Seated in the Columbus courtroom directly behind the prosecution table, Bill Dear and Larry Momchilov shook hands as the verdict was read. "We finally won," Momchilov said.

Over the detective's shoulder, Dear saw Maggie Milo sitting alone, head bent, crying.

"Yeah, we did," Dear said, "but it wasn't any fun, was it?"

Outside, another sudden thunderstorm raged. Much as it had on the day Dean Milo's body had been found.

EPILOGUE

With Fred Milo sentenced to life imprisonment at Chillicothe State Prison, Bill Dear's job was officially ended. The investigations, however, continued.

Two weeks after Milo's conviction and a year to the day after the murder had been committed, Dear and Michael Wolff of the Summit County Sheriff's Department accompanied FBI agents to a Denver post office where John Harris was arrested.

Harris's mother, who lived in Tempe, Arizona, had telephoned Rich Craven to inform him that she had been contacted by her son, asking that she wire him fifty dollars.

Following a lengthy conversation with Dear, Harris agreed to waive extradition and was eventually returned to Akron, where he was tried and found guilty of aggravated murder and given a life sentence. And, while reluctant to discuss the murder, he readily volunteered to Dear that a ten-thousand-dollar contract for Dear's murder had been offered by Harry Knott and Frank Piccirilli.

Finally admitting his role in the murder after his conviction, Harris insisted that it had not been Knott who had approached him about the plot. Rather, it had been Piccirilli, Knott's brother-in-law. Piccirilli, in fact, had furnished him with the gun later used by Harden to murder Milo.

Harris then added yet another name to the incredible cast of characters. At one time a man named Bobby O'Brian, who lived in Miami, had been recruited by Piccirilli to kill Milo in Florida. He had been the one who called with the report of the mistaken-identity hit-and-run.

The FBI arrested Harry Knott on March 2, 1982, in Deming,

New Mexico, where he was operating a restaurant under the alias of Harry Martin. Knott's capture was the result of thousands of wanted posters bearing his picture, which had been distributed nationwide. Dear and Momchilov flew to New Mexico to confront the man they had so long been searching for. Upon their arrival, Knott raged at Dear, blaming him for his capture, and refused to talk until the investigator left the room. Dear, pleased to have finally seen the man he was after, readily obliged, leaving Momchilov to escort the prisoner back to Ohio. Knott stood trial and was found guilty of aggravated murder.

In Miami, O'Brian admitted to the federal authorities that he had been recruited by Frank Piccirilli to murder Dean Milo but insisted he had concocted the story of killing the wrong man only as a means of escaping from the plot. His purpose in telling of a nonexistent hit-and-run, he said, was motivated by fear that Piccirilli would have him murdered if he knew he had decided not to go through with the killing.

O'Brian pled guilty to obstruction of justice and was sentenced to a year in prison.

Piccirilli was apprehended at his home in Philadelphia and was returned to stand trial in Akron. With O'Brian serving as a key witness, he was found guilty of aggravated murder in June of 1983 and received life in prison. His sentencing came just two months shy of three years after the investigation of the murder had begun.

Piccirilli was the eleventh person convicted, earning prosecutor Fred Zuch and those who investigated the case a place in the Ohio judicial record books. No other single case in the state's history had resulted in as many convictions.

Most of the reward money that Dear had persuaded attorney George Tsarnas to offer went unpaid. Ray Lemon, who had led investigators to the Terry Lea King—Barry Boyd connection, received fifteen thousand dollars. William Shear, who led Dear to Tom Mitchell in Texas, received ten thousand, and John Ritchie, who provided the whereabouts of Harden, earned five thousand dollars.

In the spring of 1986, a civil trial was held in Akron to rule on a wrongful death suit that Maggie Milo had filed against her imprisoned brother-in-law. It was during the trial that Fred Milo finally admitted from the stand that he was responsible for Dean Milo's death. The court awarded Maggie $5.5 million in damages.

Recently, Bill Dear, still operating his private investigation agency in DeSoto, Texas, received a letter from Barry Boyd:

"I am writing to thank you," it began.

After meeting you in my office that day long ago, I was taken by your determination. You said that you were not going to leave Akron until the case was solved. And I believed you, even then.

It was precisely that determination which energized and gave direction to the Sheriff's investigators.

There is no question in my mind, based on my experience of practicing criminal law, that the Sheriff's investigators, fine as they are, would not have pursued the investigation with such vigor without your direction. I say this not because the Sheriff's Department does not contain capable people, but because of their limited frame of reference, the lack of support they receive from superiors, and the small amount of funds on which they have to operate. Couple that with the character of the person who first implicated Terry Lea King and the complexity of the case, [and] the county investigators were at a disadvantage from the start. The deciding factor in the case, I'm convinced, was your ability to react quickly along with your resources, creativity and nationwide frame of reference.

I am personally thankful for your experience and careful watch over me. In a nutshell, I think you saved my life.

Fred Milo applied unbearable pressure. He simply would not let me alone. He knew my soft spots and how to use me. And he did. Fred Milo, a long-time friend, was vicious to me. Because of the pressure I attempted suicide not once, but twice. I suppose had I been successful the crime would have been infinitely more difficult to solve. The investigation, you'll remember, was at a standstill until you talked to me.

If you hadn't been hired to work on the case, I don't think it would have been solved. Fred Milo would have won and escaped without any accounting. For not letting him accomplish that, I thank you ever so sincerely.

Prior to the trial, the protection you provided me was also indicative of your experience. It was absolutely essential because of the appalling ill will the Milo family feels toward me.

I owe you so much that it seems hollow to say only thank you.

Sincerely,
Barry Boyd

Bill Dear sat for a long time at his office desk, looking at the letter written in the shaky hand of a frightened man who had paid dearly for his weakness. The investigator found himself reflecting back on the demanding case, his satisfaction with its resolution still pricked by questions that would never be answered. That, he had long since realized, was one of the frustrations of his work. Real-life detective work bears little resemblance to that in fiction or on the movie screen, where everything is wrapped neatly in the final pages or last scene.

Many questions raised during the course of the Milo investigation would never be answered. And for Dear, a man who likes to complete a puzzle down to the last, smallest piece, they would forever be irritants, itches he would never be able to scratch away.

Why had Dean Milo kept those diamonds in his office desk? And what was it in the dead man's make-up which made him so fearful of the dark and being alone? Was the fact his shorts were on backwards when he answered the door that fateful night simply a matter of hurriedly pulling them on? The only man who could provide the answers was dead.

Why had Lonnie Curtis so adamantly refused to cooperate with him throughout the ordeal? And why, dammit, did no one in the neighborhood hear anything on the night Milo was shot? Why hadn't the dog barked?

They were questions, he knew, that he could expect to

surface at the least expected times, suddenly drawing him back to those long, demanding months spent in Ohio.

The most important thing, however, was known. The murder of Dean Milo had been generated by pure and evil greed. When all was said and done it was that simple, that tragic.

On the evening of May 14, 1988, in a ceremony in Fairlawn, Ohio, Bill Dear and Larry Momchilov were each presented the Grand Knights Medal of Michael the Archangel Police Legion for their work in solving the murder of Dean Milo. Each had been nominated for the prestigious citation by the awards committee of the American Police Hall of Fame.

Dear, divorced and still living in Texas, was the first private investigator ever to be so honored by the organization. In the years since his work on the Milo case he has continued to travel throughout the United States and Canada, making headlines with his investigations of crimes ranging from murder to the disappearance of children.

Larry Momchilov, despite repeated offers from Dear to join his investigative team, chose to remain with the Summit County Sheriff's Department. He and Dear are still close friends and stay in touch regularly.

Bill Lewis and Richard Munsey continue to work for the Summit County Sheriff's Department and Bath Township Police Department respectively. Richard Craven has left the Scottsdale, Arizona, Police Department and is now in private business. Fred Zuch remains with the Summit County Prosecutor's Office.

Maggie Milo sold her shares in the Milo Corporation and now resides in Florida. The company, which continues to grow and prosper, is being run by Lonnie and Sophie Curtis.

Fred Milo's applications for appeals on his conviction have all been denied and he remains in custody in the state prison in Chillicothe, Ohio. David Harden, Harry Knott, Frank Piccirilli, and John Harris are all still in prison. Harris recently applied for a new trial, stating in his request that Dr. A. H. Kyriakides of the Summit County Coronor's Office unlawfully withheld papers found in Dean Milo's briefcase from his attorney. Harris's petition suggests that information contained in those papers would have led investigators to some other suspect in the crime.

Barry Boyd is out of prison and now lives in Texas, where he recently earned his commercial pilot's license. Thomas Mitchell is out and also residing in Texas. Terry Lea King, Tony Ridle, Ray Sesic, and Bobby O'Brian have also been released from prison.

Dear kept his word to Mitchell, sending him a plane ticket to Dallas upon his release from prison.

William Shear, the man who was paid $10,000 for his help in the location and arrest of Thomas Mitchell, was recently murdered. The case remains unsolved.

PHOTOS

Dean Milo (*Chuck Innis, Milo Corporation*)

Sotir Milo, Dean's father
(*Akron Beacon Journal*)

Dean Milo's house in Bath, Ohio (*William Dear*)

Lieutenant Larry Momchilov (*left*) of the Summit Count Sheriff's Department and private detective William Dear check over subpoenas. (*Summit County Sheriff's Department*)

Thomas Mitchell (left) being taken into custody by Lieutenant Larry Momchilov (*Charles Pongracz III*)

Maggie Milo, widow of Dean Milo, as she testifies at the trial
(*Charles Rex Arbogast*)

Former Milo employee Ray Sesic on the witness stand (*Charles Rex Arbogast*)

William Dear (background) observes Fred Milo during his trial. (*Charles Rex Arbogast*)

Fred Milo confers with his attorney, George Pappas. (*Charles Rex Arbogast*)

Barry Boyd on the witness stand (*Charles Rex Arbogast*)

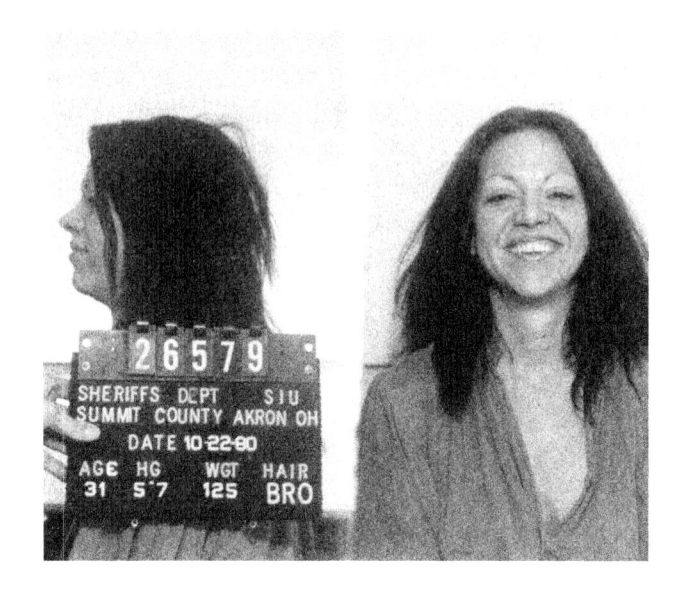

Terry Lea King

David Harden, alias The Kid

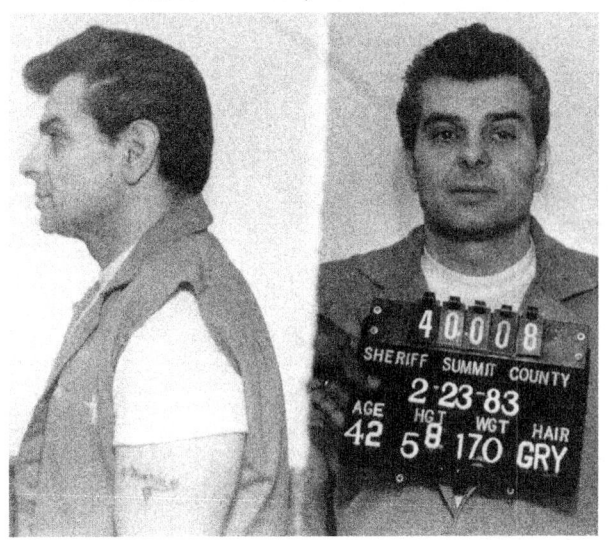

Frank Piccirilli

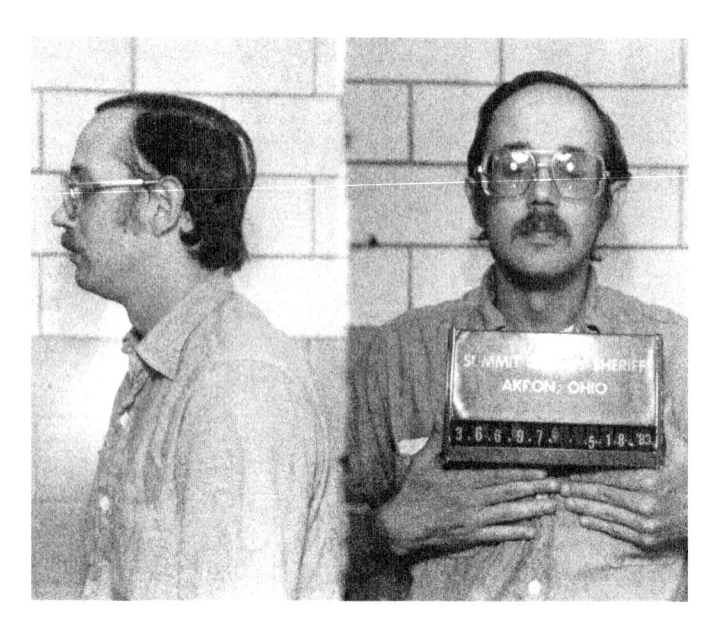

Tony Ridle

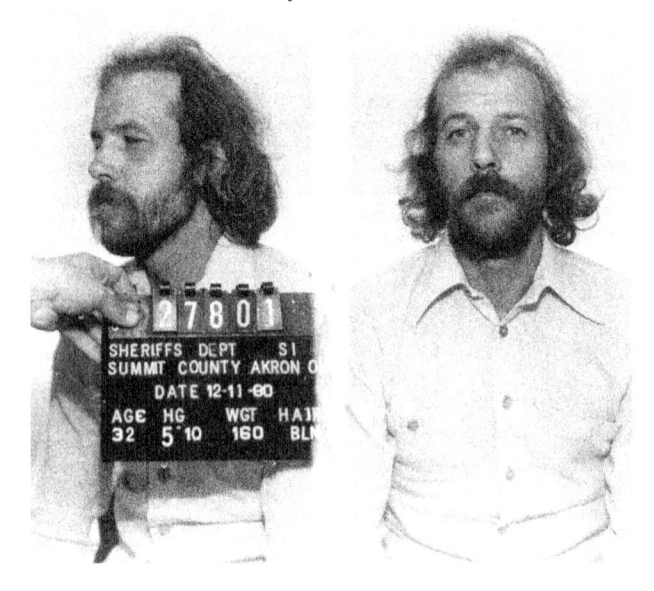

Thomas Mitchell

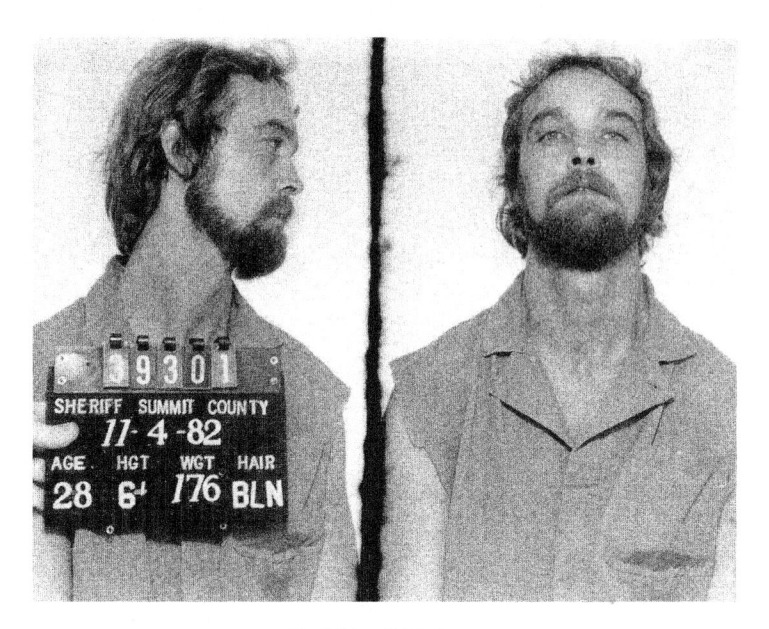

Bobby O'Brian

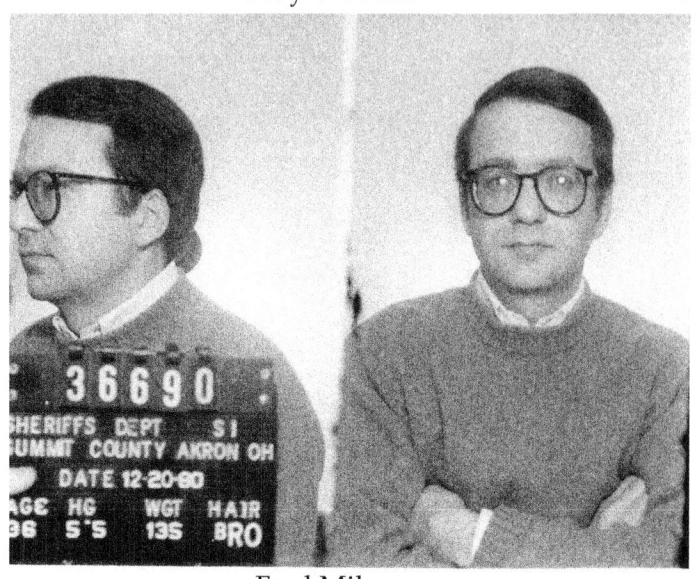

Fred Milo
All mug shots courtesy of Larry Momchilov

ABOUT THE AUTHORS

WILLIAM C. DEAR has worked all over the world, predominantly on homicide investigations. He began his career as a police officer in Miami, Florida, and in 1961, he opened his own investigation agency, William C. Dear and Associates, Inc., in Dallas, Texas. Dear is a renowned and entertaining speaker at conventions, training, workshops, and banquets. Dear has taught and lectured in the field of homicide to law enforcement around the world. He was also appointed by the court to the exhumation of Lee Harvey Oswald in 1981.

Dear has received national and international acclaim on cases that made worldwide news coverage, most notably for the Dean Milo murder in Akron, Ohio, which resulted in eleven arrests and convictions—the most ever in U.S. history for a single murder case. Dear was inducted into the American Police Hall of Fame in April 14, 1988, as a private investigator receiving the Archangel Award for the Milo murder case.

CARLTON STOWERS: Among the 40 books authored by Carlton Stowers are TO THE LAST BREATH and CARELESS WHISPERS, both winners of the Mystery Writers of America's Edgar Allen Poe Award as the Best Fact Crime Book of the Year, SCREAM AT THE SKY, INNOCENCE LOST, OPEN SECRETS and his autobiographical SINS OF THE SON.

Stowers' books have been selections of the Book of the Month Club, Literary Guild, Doubleday Book Club, Mystery Book Club, True Crime Book Club, Preferred Choice Book Club, Playboy Book Club, Military Book Club and Guideposts Book Club and five have been optioned by motion picture/TV production companies. CARELESS WHISPERS inspired the CBS Movie of the Week, "Sworn to Vengeance," and OPEN SECRETS was the basis for the ABC mini-series, "Telling Secrets." TO THE LAST BREATH was included in Readers' Digest's prestigious

TODAY'S BEST NON FICTION anthology and his writings have been translated into German, French, Japanese, Swedish, Dutch, Afrikaans and Spanish.

He has also authored or co-authored a number of books on sports, ranging from MARCUS, the autobiography of NFL standout Marcus Allen that spent six weeks on the Los Angeles Times bestseller list, to DALLAS COWBOYS: THE FIRST 25 YEARS, which reached No. 1 on the Dallas Morning News bestseller list. An article he wrote on football in a small Texas town was selected for inclusion in the 2004 BEST AMERICAN SPORTS WRITING anthology and evolved into his book, WHERE DREAMS DIE HARD, which Morning News columnist Judy Alter ranked as one of the Ten All-Time Best Books on Texas.

As a collaborator, he has written books with western movie icons Roy Rogers and Dale Evans (HAPPY TRAILS), Olympic pole vaulter Billy Olsen (REACHING HIGHER), former FBI Special Agent Larry Wansley (FBI UNDERCOVER), teacher Trent Jones (WHERE THE RAINBOWS WAIT) and private investigator William Dear (PLEASE … DON'T KILL ME). WITHIN THESE WALLS, written with former Texas prison chaplain Rev. Carroll Pickett, was the winner of the Texas Writers' League's 2002 Violet Crown Award as the year's Best Book of Texas Non-Fiction and a finalist for the PEN Southwest Literary Non-Fiction Book Award. Stowers' PARTNERS IN BLUE, a 100-year history of the Dallas Police Department, received a 1984 citation from the Dallas Police Association.

He has written non-fiction children's books, A HERO NAMED GEORGE and HARD LESSONS, which have been used by numerous elementary schools in their antidrug and antigang programs. His most recent children's book, STRENGTH OF THE HEART, was co-authored with Marcus Allen.

His COMANCHE TRAIL, was named a finalist for both the Western Fictioneers and Texas Institute of Letters Best First Novel awards in 2015.

Stowers' articles have appeared in such publications as Sports Illustrated, TV Guide, Time, People, Parade, Good Housekeeping, American Way, Boys' Life, the New York Times and Paris Match. DEATH IN A TEXAS DESERT, a collection of crime stories he wrote for the Dallas Observer was published in 2003.

ON TEXAS BACKROADS, a collection of essays written for American Way magazine, the New York Times, etc., was published in 2016.

Before turning to freelance writing, Stowers worked for several Texas newspapers, spending the last 12 years of his career with the Dallas Morning News.

He has earned numerous national and state awards for his journalism. A 17-time finalist in the annual five-state Dallas Press Club competition, he won eight Katie Awards. He is a four-time winner of the Stephen Philbin Award given by the Dallas Bar Association and has received a Texas Gavel Award from the State Bar of Texas for Outstanding Legal Reporting. He has earned a Community Action Network Media Award for Exceptional Merit, was a finalist for the Eugene Pullian Journalism Writing Award, has received seven Lone Star Awards from the Houston Press Club, and has been cited by the Texas Headliners Club, Associated Press Managing Editors Association, the UPI Editors Association, Texas Sportswriters Association, Western Media Publishing Association, the APEX Awards, North American Travel Journalists Association, Content Marketing Awards and the Dallas-Fort Worth Association of Black Communicators. CARELESS WHISPERS received the 1987 Best Book of the Year Oppie Award in the Reporting category.

In 1997 Stowers was honored as Author of the Year by the Friends of the Duncanville Library and in 2001 he was inducted into the Texas Institute of Letters. He is the recipient of the A.C. Greene Literary Award for Lifetime Achievement and the Best Southwest Bookfest Distinguished Author Award.

In 2010 he was inducted into the Texas Literary Hall of Fame and in 2011 was inducted into the Big Country Athletic Hall of Fame and named by the Press Club of Dallas as one of the Living Legends of North Texas Journalism.

Curious about other Crossroad Press books?
Stop by our site:
http://store.crossroadpress.com
We offer quality writing
in digital, audio, and print formats.

Enter the code FIRSTBOOK
to get 20% off your first order from our store!
Stop by today!

Printed in Great Britain
by Amazon

60909111R00147